PAUL SELIGSON
LEANNE GRAY
LUIZ OTÁVIO BARROS
TOM ABRAHAM
CRIS GONTOW

Level 3

English ID

Student's Book & Workbook Combo Edition
3B

Richmond

ID SB Language map

		Question syllabus	Vocabulary	Grammar	Speaking & Skills
6	6.1	What are you watching these days?	TV genres and expressions		Talk about TV habits
	6.2	What's your favorite TV show ever?		Restrictive relative clauses	Talk about first episodes of TV shows Write a quiz about movies / music
	6.3	What was the last movie you saw?		Non-restrictive relative clauses	Describe movies
	6.4	Where do you usually watch movies?	Movies		Create a story for a movie
	6.5	Who are the wildest celebrities you know?			Understand details
		When were you last surprised?			Express surprise
	Writing 6: A movie / book review p. 82		**ID Café 6:** Best in show p. 83		**Review 3** p. 84
7	7.1	Does technology rule your life?	Phrasal verbs		Talk about your habits
	7.2	What was the last little lie you told?		Reported speech (1)	Share stories about being deceived
	7.3	How much of your day is screen time?	Using touch screens	Indirect questions	Present an invention to make life easier
	7.4	Are machines with personality a good idea?		Reported speech (2)	Talk about machines with personality Write a questionnaire about tech habits
	7.5	How often do you use a pen?			Take notes while listening Talk about a book
		Do you enjoy a good argument?	Phrases for expressing your views		Debate a topic
	Writing 7: A complaint email p. 96		**ID Café 7:** The road NOT taken p. 97		
8	8.1	How important are looks?	Photography and photos		Talk about appearance and the effect of Photoshopping images
	8.2	Do you like watching illusions?		Modal perfects – *must have, can't have, might have / may have*	Describe how an illusion is done
	8.3	Have you ever cut your own hair?		Causative form	Talk about the things you do and the things you have / get done
	8.4	Do you have a lot of furniture in your room?	Furniture	Tag questions	Check information
	8.5	Is your listening improving?			Make predictions
		What's the hardest part of language learning?			Express preferences
	Writing 8: An opinion essay p. 108		**ID Café 8:** Small talk and smart phones p. 109		**Review 4** p. 110
9	9.1	Does crime worry you?	Crime and violence	Review of verb families	Talk about crime
	9.2	How could your city be improved?		Passive voice	Talk about a city's transformation
	9.3	Have you ever been to court?	Crime and punishment		Decide on the right punishment for crimes
	9.4	Where will you be living ten years from now?		Future perfect and continuous	Discuss ways to protect yourself from cyber crime
	9.5	Do you watch TV crime dramas?			Talk about stupid crimes Identify sarcasm
		Are you good at making excuses?	Phrases for giving excuses		Give excuses
	Writing 9: A formal letter p. 122		**ID Café 9:** A knight at the museum p. 123		
10	10.1	What drives you crazy?	Moods Binomials		Talk about temperament
	10.2	What do you love to hate?	Common expressions with *for* and *of*	Gerunds and infinitives	Talk about pet peeves Role-play an anger management session
	10.3	How assertive are you?		Verb + gerund or infinitive	Test your assertiveness
	10.4	How similar are you to your friends?	Phrasal verbs	Separable and inseparable phrasal verbs	Talk about toxic people Take a friendship test
	10.5	What do you find hardest about English?			Practice proofreading Talk about your mistakes in English
		Are you going to take an English exam?	Phrases for making recommendations		Make recommendations
	Writing 10: A forum post p. 134		**ID Café 10:** Mad men p. 135		**Review 5** p. 136

Grammar p. 148   Verbs p. 158   Sounds and usual spellings p. 160   Audioscript p. 168

ID WB Language map

		Question syllabus	Vocabulary	Grammar	Speaking & Skills
6	6.1	What are you watching these days?	TV genres & expressions / Compound nouns	Prepositions	Talk about TV preferences
	6.2	What's your favorite TV show ever?		Relative Clauses 1 / *a / an / the*	Ask & answer about TV preferences
	6.3	What was the last movie you saw?		Relative Clauses 2	
	6.4	Where do you usually watch movies?	Movies		Talk about surprising personal information
	6.5	Who are the wildest celebrities you know?			Talk about celebrities
7	7.1	Does technology rule your life?	Technology phrases		
	7.2	What was the last little lie you told?	*say* vs. *tell*	Reported Speech 1	Talk about the worst lie you've told
	7.3	How much of your day is screen time?		Indirect questions	
	7.4	Are machines with personality a good idea?		Reported Speech 2	Report requests & commands
	7.5	How often do you use a pen?	Activities		Talk about time spent on social media
8	8.1	How important are looks?			Talk about fake video technology
	8.2	Do you like watching illusions?		Modal perfects – *must have, can't have, may / might have*	Talk about street performances
	8.3	Have you ever cut your own hair?	*have* vs. *get*	Causative form	Talk about the things you do & the things you get done
	8.4	Do you have a lot of furniture in your room?	Furniture	Tag questions	Record a description of your house or apartment
	8.5	What's the hardest part of language learning?	Word formation		Write a comment about your listening skills
9	9.1	Does crime worry you?	Crime & violence	Review of verb families	Talk about famous crimes in your country
	9.2	How could your city be improved?		Passive voice	Talk about what makes you proud of your city
	9.3	Have you ever been to court?	Crime & punishment	Prepositions	Talk about yourself
	9.4	Where will you be living ten years from now?	Staying safe online / *by*	Future perfect / continuous	Talk about how you stay safe on social media
	9.5	Do you watch TV crime dramas?	Excuse phrases		
10	10.1	What drives you crazy?		Binomials	Share your favorite love, hate, or anger quote
	10.2	What do you love to hate?	Pet hates	Gerunds	Talk about a pet hate
	10.3	How assertive are you?		Verb + gerund or infinitive / Tense review	
	10.4	How similar are you to your friends?	Phrasal verbs	Separable & inseparable phrasal verbs / Reflexive pronouns	
	10.5	What do you find hardest about English?			Talk about your strengths & weaknesses in English

Audioscript p. 59   Answer key p. 66   Phrase Bank p. 73   Word List p. 76

English ID

Welcome to English ID!

Finally, an English course you can understand!

Famous **song lines** illustrate language from lessons.

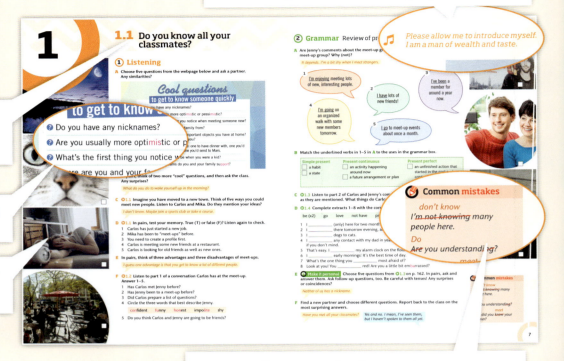

Lesson titles are questions to help you engage with the content.

Word stress in pink on new words.

Contextualized Picture Dictionary to present and review vocabulary.

Focus on **Common mistakes** accelerates accuracy.

ID Skills: extra reading and listening practice.

ID in Action: communication in common situations.

Authentic videos present topics in real contexts.

ID Café: sitcom videos to consolidate language.

Reviews systematically recycle language.

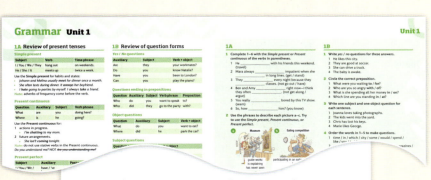

A complete **Grammar** reference with exercises.

Welcome

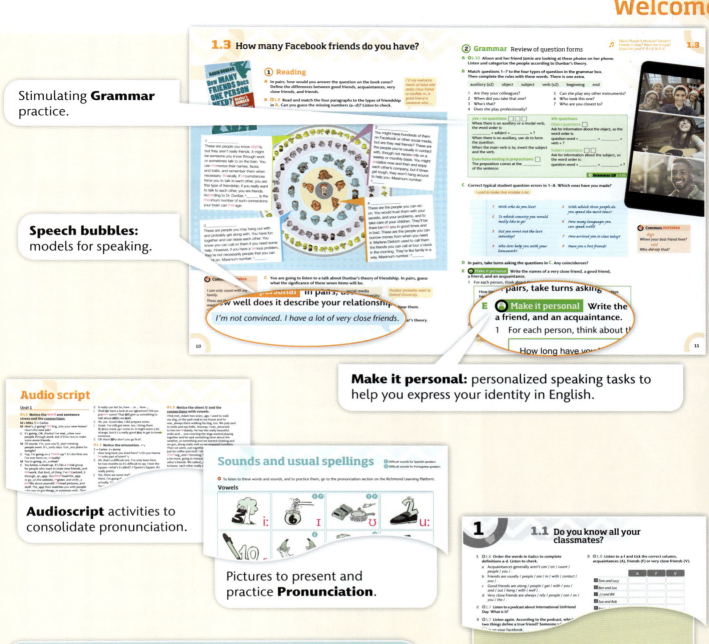

Stimulating **Grammar** practice.

Speech bubbles: models for speaking.

Make it personal: personalized speaking tasks to help you express your identity in English.

Audioscript activities to consolidate pronunciation.

Pictures to present and practice **Pronunciation**.

- **Richmond Learning Platform**
- Teachers and students can find all their resources in one place.
- **Richmond Test Manager** with interactive and printable tests.
- Activity types including pronunciation, common mistakes, and speaking.

Workbook to practice and consolidate lessons.

Phrase Bank to practice common expressions.

Learn to express your identity in English!

6

6.1 What are you watching these days?

1 Vocabulary TV genres and expressions

A ▶6.2 Match photos a–h to eight of the TV genres in question 1 of the survey. Listen to question 1 and repeat the genres. In your opinion, which are the best / worst shows on TV these days?

> ... isn't the worst show on TV, but it's not as good as it was.

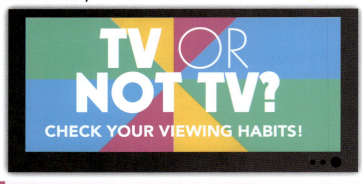

TV OR NOT TV?
CHECK YOUR VIEWING HABITS!

1 Which kinds of TV shows **are you into**?
- cartoons
- sports events
- stand-up comedy
- documentaries
- game shows
- music programs
- medical dramas
- *a* talk shows
- news programs
- reality TV
- sitcoms
- soap operas
- cooking programs
- wildlife programs

2 Are / Were you **addicted to** any show or genre?
- yes
- no   If so, which? _____

3 Is there any TV genre you can't stand?
- yes
- no   If so, which? _____

4 How do you prefer TV shows in other languages?
- dubbed
- with subtitles

5 Do you **subscribe to** any TV streaming services?
- yes
- no

6 When did you last watch an entire **season** of a show?
- never
- ages ago
- recently (specify _____)

7 What has the most influence on what you watch?
- favorable reviews
- friends' comments
- trailers
- other (specify _____)

8 How many of each of these devices do you have at home?
- computer
- tablet
- smart phone
- TV

Which do you use most to watch TV?

Common mistake

watch
I like to ~~see~~ TV at night.

72

There's nothing on the TV, nothing on the radio that means that much to me.

6.1

B ▶6.1 Match the **highlighted** words in **A** to their meanings. Listen to a talking dictionary to check.

1	_____ noun [C]	ads for a movie, showing extracts of it
2	_____ noun [C]	critics' opinions
3	_____ verb	pay regularly to receive something
4	*be into* verb	really like something
5	_____ noun [C]	all the episodes in one year of a series
6	_____ noun [C]	on-screen translation of speech
7	_____ verb	spoken in the viewer's native language
8	_____ adj.	unable to stop doing something

C Complete the comments with the items from **B**.

1 More than 100 million people worldwide *subscribe to* Netflix.
2 The latest *Star Wars* movie received great ___ from all the critics.
3 Sometimes, I can't read the ___ fast enough, and I miss some of the dialogue.
4 I used to love *Downton Abbey*, but I got bored after the third ___ and stopped watching.
5 I saw a ___ for the new series of *Stranger Things* yesterday. Exciting!
6 I don't like ___ TV shows. It's better to hear the original language.
7 I used to be ___ *The Simpsons* when I was younger. I could watch episode after episode.
8 Everyone ___ *Game of Thrones* these days, but I don't like it.

D ▶6.2 🗣 **Make it personal** Listen and do the survey in **A**. In pairs, compare answers. Any big differences? Who's the class TV addict?

> *I was totally addicted to* How I Met Your Mother *a few years ago.*

2 Listening

A ▶6.3 List five ways TV and viewing habits have changed since your parents' generation. Listen to a father and daughter and check any of your points that you hear. Are any other ideas mentioned?

> *People can watch TV anywhere and everywhere now.*

> *Yes, and my parents didn't use to have a remote control.*

B 🗣 **Make it personal** In groups, ask and answer 1–3. Any big differences?
1 Where do you watch TV? Who with? How much TV do you watch at home / somewhere else every week?
2 Would you prefer to watch TV the way the father did or the way the daughter does now? Why?
3 What's positive / negative about recent changes to TV programs and viewing habits? Is it similar for radio?
4 Does public TV have a future or will it all be private soon?

> *Well, these days you can subscribe to lots of different services, so we have a lot more options.*

> *True, but there are too many options sometimes.*

> *I sometimes watch English language programs with subtitles to practice my English.*

6.2 What's your favorite TV show ever?

1 Reading

A What do you know about *Stranger Things*? What genre is it?

> It looks like a sci-fi show.

B ▶6.4 *Stranger Things* is a TV show that almost didn't make it past the pilot episode. Listen to two friends talking about it and answer 1–3.
1 How many times was *Stranger Things* rejected by TV companies?
2 Why was it rejected?
3 How many seasons have there been so far?

C List five reasons why a show might get canceled.

> Maybe it's had really bad reviews.

D In groups of four, each read about a different show. Report back all you remember. Were any of your reasons in C there?

E ▶6.5 Listen, reread, and answer 1–6. Which show do you think sounds the best / worst? Why?
1 did the critics hate?
2 was a sci-fi program?
3 failed because the relationship between the actors wasn't realistic?
4 was a reality TV show?
5 involved three big Hollywood names?
6 managed to get one episode on TV?

> The *Secret Talents* show sounds awful! Who wants to know about celebrities' other talents?

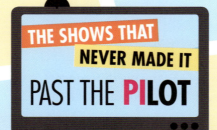

THE SHOWS THAT NEVER MADE IT PAST THE PILOT

Heat Vision and Jack

This pilot starred Jack Black and Owen Wilson and was directed by Ben Stiller. The plot centered around an astronaut who developed super powers. Black played the lead role and Owen Wilson was the voice of his talking motorbike! It sounds far-fetched and was not picked up by a TV station, but with such huge Hollywood actors, surely it deserved one series! Perhaps the superhero theme was ahead of its time.

Mr. & Mrs. Smith

After the success of the movie with Brad Pitt and Angelina Jolie, ABC planned a spin-off television series. The story was set six months later and followed assassins John and Jane Smith's "normal" life in the suburbs with some spy action thrown in. Martin Henderson, who starred in *Grey's Anatomy*, and Jordana Brewster from *The Fast and The Furious* were chosen for the lead roles. However, critics said there was no chemistry between the two actors, and the series was never made. It's too bad, as it seems like a show that would appeal to fans of the movie!

Secret Talents of the Stars

In this show, celebrities displayed talents we didn't know they had, and viewers would vote on the most talented celebrity. It sounds like a good idea, doesn't it? Unfortunately, in the pilot episode, the stars displayed talents that were similar to the ones they were already famous for. For example, ice skater Sasha Cohen showed off her acrobatic skills. Not entirely different from figure skating! The audience didn't see anything surprising or "secret," and the program was canceled after one episode because of low ratings.

The Osbournes: Reloaded

The Osbournes were huge on MTV. Ozzy Osbourne's career was reborn, and the family became famous. When the MTV series ended, the Osbournes tried making a variety show for Fox. The show consisted of comedy, celebrity interviews, and live music. The network spent a lot of money on making and promoting the series. However, it cut the first episode from one hour to thirty-five minutes, and it was very heavily criticized by critics and viewers. Five episodes were filmed, but the show was canceled after just one.

♪ Want you to make me feel
Like I'm the only girl in the world
Like I'm the only one that you'll ever love

6.2

F Match the underlined words and phrases in the article to the definitions.
1 based on something that already exists
2 difficult to believe because it is very unlikely
3 much more advanced / modern than most other things
4 to include something extra
5 the estimated audience size of a TV or radio show.

G ⬤ **Make it personal** In pairs, can you remember the pilot (or first) episode of your favorite TV show or movie series? What happened?

I loved the first episode of Mad Men. It was so stylish!

I'm old enough to remember going to the first Star Wars movie! We were amazed by the special effects.

2 Grammar Restrictive relative clauses

A Match the sentence halves, then do the grammar box. Circle the right answer in 1 and 2 (ignore rule 3 for the moment).
1 *Heat Vision and Jack* is about a man
2 *Mr. & Mrs. Smith* was a TV series
3 *Secret Talents of the Stars* starred celebrities
4 *The Osbournes: Reloaded* was a TV show
5 Winona Ryder plays a mother

a ☐ **that** was based on a movie.
b ☐ **whose** talents the audience had not seen.
c ☐ **who** develops superpowers.
d ☐ **whose** son has gone missing.
e ☐ **that** got canceled after one episode.

Common mistakes
~~who~~
She's the actor ~~that~~ was in those awful comedies.
They sent us an app that we found ~~it~~ very useful.

	whose	that	who
people			
things			

1 Use restrictive relative clauses like those in a–e to give **essential** / **extra** information about someone or something.
2 The clause usually comes **before** / **after** the noun it describes.
3 When the pronoun is the object, you _____ a relative pronoun.

➡ **Grammar 6A** p. 148

B Which sentence doesn't need a relative pronoun (*that, whose, who*)? Check in the article on p. 74. Then complete rule 3 in the grammar box.
1 It seems like a show that would appeal to fans of the movie!
2 In this show, celebrities displayed talents that we didn't know they had.

C Complete 1–5 with relative pronouns. Which two sentences don't need a relative pronoun?

1 *Glee* is a show _____ features high school students _____ can sing and dance.

2 Oprah Winfrey is a TV host _____ talent made her the most powerful woman on TV.

3 *Friends* is a sitcom _____ adults and kids still watch, even after 25 years.

4 Homer Simpson is a cartoon character _____ keeps saying "d'oh."

5 *The Tonight Show*, *The Late Show*, and *The Daily Show* are talk shows _____ millions of Americans watch.

D ⬤ **Make it personal** 📶 In small teams, write a 5-question quiz about TV, movies, or music. Search online to find and check information. Play against another team. Who can get more answers right? Try to use restrictive relative clauses.

1 _____ is the actor who starred in "24" and whose father is also a famous actor.
2 _____ is the TV show that was canceled by Fox and renewed by NBC the following day!
3 _____ is the musician who's married to Jay-Z and was in Destiny's Child.

I know the first one. It's Kiefer Sutherland, so that's one point to us.

And I have a feeling the answer to number two is "Brooklyn Nine-Nine."

And number 3 is definitely Beyoncé!

75

6.3 What was the last movie you saw?

1 Reading

A Which of the movies in the posters have you seen? Describe the plot for each in only four sentences, like this one for *Romeo and Juliet*.

"A boy and a girl fall in love and marry. They're forced to separate so she pretends to kill herself. Then he thinks she's dead so he kills himself. She finds him dead and really kills herself."

B ▶ 6.6 Insert phrases 1–4 in gaps a–d. Listen to check. Any pronunciation surprises? Do the gapped sentences in the article make sense without the phrases?

1 whose popularity was at its peak
2 who had been diagnosed with terminal cancer
3 who played Jake Sully
4 which became the fastest movie in history to reach a worldwide gross of $1 billion at the box office

 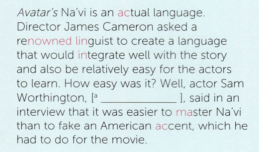

FOUR *curious* MOVIE FACTS

Avatar's Na'vi is an actual language. Director James Cameron asked a renowned linguist to create a language that would integrate well with the story and also be relatively easy for the actors to learn. How easy was it? Well, actor Sam Worthington, [a _____], said in an interview that it was easier to master Na'vi than to fake an American accent, which he had to do for the movie.

James Cameron, who also directed *Titanic*, initially didn't want the movie to have a theme song, even during the closing credits. Composer James Horner, however, secretly asked Celine Dion, [b _____], to record a demo of "My Heart Will Go On." Horner then played the song to James Cameron, who immediately changed his mind. The song won an Oscar and became one of the best-selling singles in history.

Actors Mark Hamill, who played the legendary Luke Skywalker, and John Boyega persuaded *Star Wars* director J.J. Abrams to allow *Star Wars* super-fan Daniel Fleetwood to see the movie before it was officially released. Fleetwood, [c _____], got to see the movie in a special screening at his home before he passed away.

Avengers: Infinity War, [d _____], was one of the best kept movie secrets ever! In order to keep the plot of the movie secret and avoid spoilers, Disney decided to give the cast* fake scripts**. The directors wanted to protect the movie, which eventually came out in 2018, because it had taken ten years to make. They wanted the audience to have the best experience possible when they went to see the movie.

*the group of actors in a movie or show
**the written story and instructions

2 Grammar Non-restrictive relative clauses

A Reread the movie facts article with the additions from **1B** and circle the correct alternatives in the grammar box.

1 Non-restrictive clauses give **essential** / **extra** information.
2 Non-restrictive relative clauses **use** / **don't use** commas.
3 You **can** / **can't** use *that* in a non-restrictive clause.
4 Non-restrictive clauses **always** / **don't always** need a relative pronoun.

→ Grammar 6C p. 148

Common mistake

My favorite Batman movie is The Dark Knight, *that* won four Oscars.   *which*

B Find and underline five more examples of clauses like this in the article.

C Connect sentences 1–4 with relative pronouns. Have you seen this movie?

🎵 *When the sharpest words wanna cut me down, I'm gonna send a flood, gonna drown them out, I am brave, I am bruised, I am who I'm meant to be, This is me.*

6.3

Did you know …?
1. *The Greatest Showman* was directed by Michael Gracey ~~He~~ , who had never directed a movie before.
2. This musical movie had a very popular soundtrack. It included hits like "This is Me" and "A Million Dreams".
3. The plot is based on the life of circus owner PT Barnum. He was born in 1810.
4. The main character is played by Hugh Jackman. His family is from Australia.

D Rewrite 1–4 using non-restrictive clauses. Write one more of your own.

1. Robert Downey Jr. was voted the best Marvel actor of all time by fans. He plays Iron Man.
2. The first *Iron Man* movie helped relaunch Downey Jnr.'s career. It was made in 2008.
3. Scarlett Johansson plays one of Marvel's first female superheroes in *Black Widow*. Her other movies include *Lost in Translation* and *Sing*.
4. *Avengers: Infinity War* is one of the highest grossing movies in history. It's the third *Avengers* film.
5. Stan Lee created many of the Marvel characters. He played cameo roles in many of the movies.

Robert Downey Jr., who plays Iron Man, was voted the best Marvel actor of all time by fans.

3 Pronunciation Pauses in speech

A ▶ 6.7 Listen to part of a radio quiz about movie director Ryan Coogler. Circle the correct answer for each question in the quiz.

1 *Infinity Wars*   *Black Panther*   *Guardians of the Galaxy*
2 Soccer   Motor racing   Boxing
3 Barack Obama   Steven Spielberg   Morgan Freeman

B ▶ 6.7 Pausing when you speak gives you time to think and helps the listener to follow you. Insert speech pauses (//) in 1–5 where necessary. Listen again to check. In pairs, practice imitating the speaker.
1. This week we've been talking about moviemakers who have changed American cinema.
2. The first question is about Ryan Coogler, who many people consider to be one of the finest new moviemakers around.
3. *Creed*, which also starred Sylvester Stallone, was a spin-off from a classic series of movies, *Rocky*.
4. Well, it's a kind of sport that involves two people and a ring.
5. The movie, which won Stallone a Golden Globe, was highly acclaimed by critics.

C **Make it personal** Write a short description of a movie you know. Then in groups, read it for the others to guess the movie. Use non-restrictive relative clauses.

_____, which was written in 1990, inspired one of the most successful movie franchises of all time. The stories are based on the science-fiction novels by Michael Crichton, who is an American author, screenwriter, movie director, and producer.

That's easy. I've seen all four of those movies. I do love dinosaurs. It's Jurassic Park.

6.4 Where do you usually watch movies?

1 Vocabulary Movies

A ▶6.8 In pairs, take our quiz and find out who knows more. Listen and choose the answer from the options given. Then listen to the correct answer to check.

Think you're an expert on movies and media? Try this quiz and prove it!

1. Which fantasy **prequel** to *The Lord of the Rings* did director Peter Jackson **shoot** in New Zealand between 2011 and 2013?

2. The video for which song by Luis Fonsi and Daddy Yankee became the most watched video in YouTube history, with over five billion views?

3. *Avengers: Infinity War* is an action movie about superheroes. The cast is like a "Who's Who" of Hollywood and includes many big names. Can you name three of them?

4. One of the biggest YouTube memes of 2013 was "Harlem Shake." There were over 33 hours of "Harlem Shake" **clips** uploaded every day. What did people do in the videos?

5. British actor Tom Holland **stars** as which wall-climbing superhero?

6. Andy Serkis, who was the gorilla in *King Kong*, had to learn to move like a chimpanzee in which famous **trilogy**?

7. What **role** does Liam Hemsworth play in the **block**buster *The Hunger Games*?

8. Which romance movie **set** in Indianapolis portrays two teenagers who are suffering from cancer?

9. Who wrote the script and directed the first *Star Wars* films?

B Match the highlighted words in the quiz to the definitions.

1	_____ noun [C]	a movie that is released after another, but tells the story before it
2	_____ verb	to take photos for a movie / to film
3	_____ verb	to put a story in a certain time and place
4	_____ noun [C]	an extract from a video; a short video
5	_____ noun [C]	the part, or character, that an actor plays in a movie
6	_____ verb	to be the main character in a movie

C ▶6.9 Listen to dialogues 1–3. Which three movies from **A** were they discussing?

D ▶6.9 Listen again. In which dialogues do they disagree? Who do you agree with?

E 🎤 Make it personal Have you seen 1–9 in **A**? What did you think of them? Compare opinions in groups. Any similarities? Who has seen the most?

> I've seen lots of "Harlem Shake" videos. My class made one and uploaded it.

> Really? I didn't like them to be honest. I thought they were weird.

⚠ Common mistakes

"Despacito" is a catchy ~~music~~.
        song / tune

music   is
The ~~musics~~ in that movie ~~are~~ great!

       like
Adele sings ~~as~~ a bird.

   as
She stars ~~like~~ Jay's second wife.

2 Listening

♪ *You still look like a movie.*
You still sound like a song.
My God, this reminds me
Of when we were young.

6.4

A In pairs, decide what is important to consider about the items below when making a video.

| filming | light | permission | sound | story |

You need a quality camera with a good lens and plenty of memory space.

B ▶6.10 Listen to / Watch the instructions on how to make a short video and see if your guesses are mentioned.

C ▶6.10 Read the summary notes on the video and try to remember the missing words. Then listen / watch again and fill in each blank with two words.

Tips and tricks to making a SHORT VIDEO

PLAN YOUR SHOOT
Think about: the topic. ¹_____ people? What do you want the video to ²_____ in the end?

USE THE TECHNOLOGY AVAILABLE TO YOU
You could use:
A ³_____, a camcorder, a webcam, or a ⁴_____.

CAPTURE YOUR CLIPS
Press the ⁵_____ a few seconds before you start. Use a tripod to stop the camera from moving. Extra shoots and ⁶_____ might be useful. Don't ⁷_____ the top of the subject's head.

BE CAREFUL WITH LIGHTING
Shoot in a well-lit area.
⁸_____ there is no bright light behind the subject.

PLAN THE LENGTH OF SHOOT
Plan ⁹_____ in advance.
Don't talk about one thing for ¹⁰_____.

D Read ▶6.10 on p. 169 to check. Compare the underlined items with those in **C**.

E Make five pieces of moviemaking advice and decide what elements in **A** they refer to.

1	Always	☐ you are allowed to film in public places.
2	Think about	☐ have a beginning, a middle, and an end.
3	Make sure	☐ moving shots, try attaching the camera to a skateboard or office chair.
4	Never	☐ continuity. If you have a shot from the middle of the day, the next scene shouldn't be at night.
5	If you want	☐ underestimate the emotional power of silence.

F 🔊 In groups, brainstorm and search online to find advice to include in a "how to" video on one of these topics. Use the underlined phrases from **E**.

How to get more views on YouTube   How to learn English faster   How to become a better dancer
How to live longer   How to study effectively   How to meet new people

G 🎬 **Make it personal** In groups of three, choose a title and decide your story. Tell the class and award an Oscar for the best idea. If you really like your idea, go out and film it—in English, of course!

One Wednesday evening

Rob and Rex

Thanks for everything

- *This retired couple fell in love a long time ago.*
- *But then they separated and married different people.*
- *Years later, they meet again and fall in love, and the movie is about how their children feel.*

6.5 Who are the wildest celebrities you know?

ID Skills Understanding details

A Complete the text about Sia with these words.

2014	Australia	broke	five
hits	musician	rising	single

¹_____ Sia Kate Isobelle Furler was born in ²_____ on December 18, 1975. Before ³_____, she'd made ⁴_____ unsuccessful solo albums, but written huge ⁵_____ for other artists, including "Titanium" with David Guetta, "Diamonds" with Rihanna, and "Wild Ones" with Flo Rida. Sia finally ⁶_____ through as a solo artist with her sixth studio album, "1000 Forms of Fear" and the hit ⁷_____ "Chandelier." Since then, Sia's star hasn't stopped ⁸_____.

B In pairs, share what you know about Ellen DeGeneres and her TV show. Imagine three questions Ellen asked Sia. What would you like to ask Sia?

> Ellen's an American TV host who interviews famous people.

> I think she asked Sia why she wears a wig like that.

> She must have done. It's the most obvious question.

C ▶6.11 Listen to Sue telling Joe about Ellen's interview with Sia. Where did Sue watch the show?

☐ on TV   ☐ live in the studio   ☐ on YouTube

D ▶6.12 Listen to the second part of the dialogue and check the picture that best represents what happened.

E ▶6.13 Listen to the full dialogue. True (T) or false (F)? Correct the false ones. Did you understand most of it this time? Read ▶6.12 and ▶6.13 to check. Compare in pairs. If you missed anything, try to figure out why.
1 Both Sue and Joe like Ellen.
2 Joe knows more about Sia than Sue.
3 Ellen asked a surprising question.
4 Sia doesn't like going to the grocery store.
5 Joe didn't know Sue was in the audience.
6 Sia did not reveal her face.

> I love James Corden's Carpool Karaoke, where he sings with musicians. Have you seen any of them? He actually did a great one with Sia!

F 🗣 **Make it personal** In pairs, answer 1–2. Any similarities?
1 Do you often watch / listen to / read celebrity interviews? If so, which shows / magazines / sites are you into?
2 Describe a funny / interesting / embarrassing celebrity interview you've seen.

⚠ Common mistake
It's not my thing.
~~It's doesn't go with me.~~ /
~~It's not the mine.~~

80

When were you last surprised? 6.5

ID in Action Expressing surprise

A ▶6.14 Use your intuition to complete 1–5. Listen to check. Say them as emphatically as you can.

1	What? Get _____ of here!	4	_____ you serious?
2	Really? You're _____, right?	5	_____ goodness!
3	_____ way!		

B ▶6.15 Listen to these extracts and underline the stressed syllables. Which are the most stressed?
1. She wrote those?
2. You were actually in the audience?
3. You mean they were just pretending?

Pronunciation Showing surprise

C ▶6.16 Read the information and listen to the mini-dialogue. In pairs, practice it, paying attention to stress and intonation. Who is the better mimic?

> - To show surprise, echo information using a questioning intonation.
> - Use word stress to highlight the really surprising information.
> - Notice the use of *actually* to show something is really true.

A Did you know Lady Gaga's real name is actually Ste**fa**ni Jo**anne** Angeli**na** Germa**not**ta?
B Huh? Her name's Stefani? No way! She doesn't look like a Stefani!
A Well, you didn't think it was really Lady Gaga, did you?!

D ▶6.17 Listen to the mini-dialogues. What is each speaker's question implying?

1. ☐ Not your sister?
   ☐ Not buying?
   ☐ Not pizza?

2. ☐ Not your wife?
   ☐ Not rent?
   ☐ Not bigger?

3. ☐ Not Paula?
   ☐ Not a cat?
   ☐ Not for Christmas?

4. ☐ Not five?
   ☐ Not months?
   ☐ Not vegetables?

E In pairs. A: read aloud questions from ▶6.17 on p. 169, stressing one of the underlined words. B: Listen and choose the correct option from **D**.

F 🧑 **Make it personal** In pairs, play **Surprise me!**
A: Tell B three surprising facts about yourself. One should be imaginary.
B: Express surprise. Say if you think they're true. Change roles.

> *Did I ever tell you that my sister once shared a cab with Emma Stone?*

> *No way! You mean your sister actually met Emma Stone?*

> *Yes, she offered to share her cab from the airport.*

> *That can't be true. I don't believe you.*

♪ *I'm gonna swing from the chandelier, from the chandelier*
I'm gonna live like tomorrow doesn't exist, like it doesn't exist

Writing 6 A movie / book review

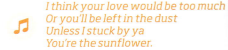
*I think your love would be too much
Or you'll be left in the dust
Unless I stuck by ya
You're the sunflower.*

A Read the review and circle the correct alternative in 1–4.
1. The movie is based on a **book** / **true story** and the reviewer liked it **more** / **less** than she had expected.
2. The main characters are four **teenagers** / **robots** trying to **win** / **lose** a game.
3. **Some** / **All** of the characters are interesting and original and develop **well** / **badly**.
4. It's **boring** / **funny** and follows on **badly** / **well** from the original movie.
5. The reviewer **was** / **wasn't** impressed and would give it **two** / **four** stars out of five.

REVIEW SECTION Jumanji: Welcome to the Jungle

1. If you like action and adventure, try *Jumanji: Welcome to the Jungle*. Based on a children's novel, and sequel to the much-loved 1995 film of the same name, this te**rrif**ic movie definitely ex**cee**ded my expectations.

2. The story is about four high school kids who discover an old video game console. They somehow end up in the game and become the avatars they chose. They have to beat the game or they will be stuck in Jumanji forever!

3. The movie **cap**tivates, not only because of the amazing special effects but also because of the int**rig**uing new characters we meet. Unfortunately, the male and female characters are a bit ste**re**otyped, but the story does focus on the way the characters change and think about themselves.

4. As well as the action-adventure element, this story has a lot of comedy and heart. Fans of the original movie will not be disappointed, as this version makes nos**tal**gic references to the first. Because of that, those who loved the hi**lar**ious Robin Williams will be deeply touched by the t**rib**ute this film makes to the wonderful actor.

5. In my opinion, this is a great version as it will keep the original fans happy and combines action, special effects, comedy, and nostalgia. I'd say it's a must-see and I'd certainly suggest you watch it.

B In which paragraph, 1–5, does the reviewer:
- [ ] recommend it or not?
- [ ] mention the positive points?
- [ ] describe the plot?
- [ ] mention any negative points?
- [ ] describe what's being reviewed?

C Read *Write it right!* Then find extreme adjectives meaning:
1. very good (x3)
2. very interesting
3. very funny
4. very popular

✓ Write it right!

In reviews, use a variety of adjectives, including extreme adjectives with appropriate adverbs (*really, absolutely, completely, not very*).
- names as adjectives
  Star Wars fans / X-Men movies / Twilight lovers

To give extra information, use non-restrictive clauses between commas:
- *Spider-Man: Into the Spider-Verse*, which is the seventh Spider-Man movie, is the first computer-animated version of Stan Lee's story.
- Spielberg, who is famous for action movies, directs *Ready Player One*, a sci-fi fantasy where technology offers an escape from overpopulation and climate change.

D Reread *Write it Right!* and punctuate this short review with three commas, two periods, and one question mark. Capitalize where necessary.

wonder woman which was released in 2017 tells the story of Diana, Princess of the Amazons when a pilot crashes on her remote island and tells her about the war in the world outside Diana leaves her home and sets off on a mission to save the world. israeli actor Gal Gadot plays Wonder Woman while stopping the war can Diana find out her true destiny

E *Your turn!* Choose a book / movie to review in 140–180 words.

Before	Make notes for five paragraphs as in **B**.
While	Write your review. Follow the tips in *Write it right!* and use a friendly, informal style.
After	Ask a partner to read and check it. Then send it to your teacher.

6 Best in show

1 Before watching

A Match the photos to descriptions 1–6.

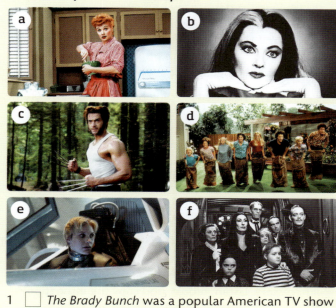

1. ☐ *The Brady Bunch* was a popular American TV show from the 1970s about a family.
2. ☐ A character from *X-Men* was called "Wolverine."
3. ☐ Starbuck was a fighter pilot on a popular science fiction TV show.
4. ☐ Lucille Ball was a famous redhead who had a show called *I Love Lucy*.
5. ☐ *The Addams Family* was a very creepy family that was on TV and on Broadway.
6. ☐ Lily Munster was a very nice "monster" who lived at 1313 Mockingbird Lane.

B 🎤 **Make it personal** Do you know any characters from **A**? Which are / were your favorite TV characters / sitcoms / series / theme tunes?

I think I've seen that Lucy show.

As a kid, I used to love the Addams Family *theme tune!*

2 While watching

A Watch to 3:12. Check all you hear.

1. ☐ Andrea looks like Lady Gaga and Morticia Addams.
2. ☐ Lucy doesn't know any 1960s TV shows.
3. ☐ The party will be full of nerds and geeks.
4. ☐ For the costume party, you dress as a character that you really like.
5. ☐ Andrea once won the "Best in Show" prize for her Superman costume.
6. ☐ Andrea thought dubbed TV shows were hilarious.
7. ☐ Diana Prince is Wonder Woman's alter ego.
8. ☐ Andrea says August is the family mutant.

B Order the story, 1–6. Then watch the rest to check.

☐ Andrea admires other costumes.
☐ Andrea confirms she isn't.
☐ August sees Paulo dressed as Superman.
☐ August thinks he'll win.
☐ Lucy says he did predict he'd lose to the perfect Superman.
☐ Lucy worries she's the only one from the 50s.

C Watch and check: August (A), Andrea (An), Lucy (L) or Paolo (P)?

	A	An	L	P
1 put on his wig first.				
2 tried on long and short wigs.				
3 repaired a costume.				
4 didn't really want to go.				
5 convinced her to go.				
6 forgot to check something.				
7 beat August last year.				
8 really expected to win.				
9 felt attracted to Paolo.				
10 felt defeated again.				

3 After watching

A Complete the extracts with *who* or *that*.

August She was the one [1]_____ kind of looked like a vampire.
August And the people [2]_____ will be there are cool people, not just nerds.
Lucy We watched so many American shows [3]_____ were dubbed in Spanish.
Lucy Am I the only one here [4]_____'s dressed as a character from the 1950s?
Lucy Well, didn't you say that the only person [5]_____ was going to beat you this year …

B *Play 20 questions!* **A:** Think of a famous person. **B:** Ask A *Yes / No* questions. How many questions did you have to ask before you guessed correctly?

Is this an actor who was on TV?   *Yes, it is.*

R3 Grammar and Vocabulary

A *Picture dictionary.* Cover the words or definitions on the pages below and remember.

pages	
60	5 money collocations
64	9 "product" words
67	the endings of 10 shopping phrases
72–73	8 TV genres
78	10 words from the quiz
161	2 words for each sound in lines 1 and 2 of the consonants chart (not the picture words)

B Order the **bold** words in 1–4 to make adjective phrases and cross out the word that doesn't fit.

1. These **boots / hiking / comfortable / strange** are perfect for the mountains.

2. *Set in Love* is a **romantic / short / novel / well-written** of over 800 pages.

3. Lose yourself in this **new / video game / tasty / exciting**.

4. Make your own TV show with our **old / equipment / digital / easy-to-use**.

C In pairs, think of two endings for 1–8. Compare with another pair. Who has the funniest endings?

1. If you hadn't posted that photo, …
2. My parents wouldn't have got married if …
3. I'd have sent you a text if …
4. If I'd been born in the U.S., …
5. We'd have watched the show if …
6. If my father hadn't studied law, …
7. If I'd gone to bed earlier, …
8. We wouldn't have missed the bus if …

D ▶R3.1 Match 1–5 to the correct response a–e. Listen to check.

1. Have you seen my keys anywhere?
2. Uh … my … dog ate my homework.
3. So there was this documentary about the UFOs in Roswell and …
4. Allan isn't answering his phone.
5. Hey, what language are they speaking?

a ☐ Have you tried Skyping him? He might be online.
b ☐ Oh, come on! You can't believe that, surely.
c ☐ I don't know. It can't be English because I don't understand a word.
d ☐ Not again! They could be anywhere!
e ☐ Oh really? You must think I'm stupid.

E In pairs, write a mini-dialogue to extend one of a–e in **C** by at least four lines. Role-play it for the class.

> *Well, I had them this morning. Can you help me look for them?*

F ▶R3.2 Add commas to these relative clause sentences if necessary. Listen, repeat, and copy the intonation.

1. I love my <u>MP3 player</u> which <u>has over 2,000 songs</u>.
2. I really like people <u>who laugh easily</u>.
3. <u>Javier Bardem</u> who starred in *No Country for Old Men* is one of my favorite actors.
4. <u>My son just graduated</u> which made me very proud.
5. It's difficult to find <u>people who you can count on</u>.
6. I'd like to get a phone that <u>takes better photos</u>.

G 🙂 **Make it personal** Change the underlined phrases in **F** to make 1–6 true for you.

H In pairs, add two more words with the same ending to each group. Mark the stress in the new words.

1. ac**tu**ally / **cur**rently
2. use**less** / care**less**
3. **ac**tion / **ques**tion
4. a**bi**lity / se**cu**rity
5. **com**fortable / re**cy**clable
6. **cel**ebrate / **grad**uate

I Correct the mistakes in each sentence. Check your answers in units 5 and 6.

> ⚠️ **Common mistakes**
>
> 1. If I knew you were here, I had have called. (2 mistakes)
> 2. Rob borrowed his phone for me. (2 mistakes)
> 3. That shirt look good. You should buy her. (2 mistakes)
> 4. It must to be difficult to be on debt. (2 mistakes)
> 5. When you pay with credit card online, you have to be carefull. (2 mistakes)
> 6. People which talk in theaters they annoy me. (2 mistakes)
> 7. That's the house in that they live. (2 mistakes)
> 8. Bruce Banner is a scientist who turn to the Hulk. (2 mistakes)
> 9. Panama, that is famous for the canal, is a city amazing. (2 mistakes)
> 10. If I had eat less lunch, I wouldn't been so sleepy in the afternoon. (2 mistakes)

Skills practice

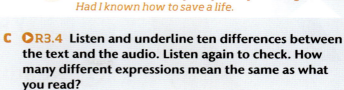

*Where did I go wrong?
I lost a friend somewhere along in the bitterness.
And I would have stayed up with you all night,
Had I known how to save a life.*

R3

A ▶ **R3.3** Listen to five sentences. What do they mean? Circle the correct alternative.
1. I'm **very sick / not joking**.
2. I think somebody **broke / will break** your machine.
3. He **likes / doesn't usually like** kids' movies.
4. They had **no money left / stolen money**.
5. They are **very popular / a waste of time**.

B Read the article and answer 1–6.
1. What do people receive from GoFundMe?
2. What does Peg want to do?
3. How did Peg learn about GoFundMe?
4. Who is Dan?
5. Do you pay to try GoFundMe?
6. Have you ever asked for sponsorship? If so, what happened?

I asked my friends and family. Only some of them gave me money though.

Help on the Internet

Why is everyone talking about GoFundMe? Because GoFundMe has helped thousands of people raise many millions of dollars online for amazing personal causes like school tuition, rock bands, medical bills, volunteer trips, business ideas, parties, travel expenses, even for animals and pets.

Let's take Peg, for example. Peg has a terrific opportunity to volunteer overseas but needs enough money for the flight and food. Luckily for Peg, her friends told her to check out GoFundMe, the easiest way to raise money online. Convinced by thousands of success stories, Peg decides to create her very own fundraising page on GoFundMe. Choosing a color, selecting a photo, and writing your information only takes a minute.

Now Peg's ready to tell the world about her cause. Inviting contacts and sharing with Facebook friends couldn't be easier. Peg's friend Dan notices her GoFundMe page on Facebook. Dan is happy to support his friend and gives her some money. He even helps tell other people for Peg. Peg gets an email each time a new donation is made. In just a few short days, she's nearly reached her goal. Once Peg's ready to get her money, she simply provides her banking information and receives the cash days later.

GoFundMe has helped Peg, and hundreds like her, raise lots of money online and can do the same for you. Click the "try it free" button and get started in less than a minute.

C ▶ **R3.4** Listen and underline ten differences between the text and the audio. Listen again to check. How many different expressions mean the same as what you read?

D *Feel 'n' Guess!* Play in groups.
A: Secretly put an object in a bag.
B, C, D: Feel it and speculate what it might be.

It's soft so it can't be a DVD.   *Yes, it might be a …*

E *Keep, Kill, Ignore.* Talk about the options in 1–6 and choose one to keep, one to kill, and one to ignore.

1	a	news programs	4	a	Horror
	b	soap operas		b	Romance
	c	sitcoms		c	Fantasy
2	a	cartoons	5	a	Dance music
	b	sports events		b	Rock music
	c	documentaries		c	Rap
3	a	YouTube	6	a	cell phones
	b	Facebook		b	laptops
	c	Twitter		c	vacations

I guess we could kill news programs. I get most of my news online anyway.

F *Shopping problems role-play.* In pairs, decide what kind of store you want to set your role-play in.
A: You're a customer. Buy something in the store, and then try to return it later.
B: You're the store assistant. Invent as many problems for the customer as you can.

Hi, do you have this in a bigger size?   *I'm sorry, we're all on our break now.*

On your break? Are you serious?

G ▶ **R3.5** 🎧 **Make it personal** *Question time!*
Listen to the 12 lesson titles from units 5 and 6 in random order. Pause after each one to ask and answer in pairs. Ask follow-up questions, too. Any surprises?

Would you ever lend money to anyone?   *Well, that would depend on who it was.*

7.1 Does technology rule your life?

1 Reading

A In pairs, what's the message in the cartoon? Did it make you smile? What complaints about technology have you heard (recently)?

> I heard something about a virus that made private social media information become public.

> Yes, I heard about that, too.

PROTESTING AGAINST NEW TECHNOLOGY – THE EARLY DAYS

B ▶ 7.1 In pairs, read only the introduction and first paragraph heading. Guess what the author will say. Then listen and read to check if you were right. Repeat with the other four paragraphs.

> I guess he or she will say we can check anything on our phones.

> And to be careful about fake news!

 Common mistake

~~Technology means communication without effort.~~ → effortless

MODERN TECHNOLOGY —The Bright Side!

Every day, we hear so much negativity about modern technology and its impact on society: There are no jobs. We have no social skills. It's killing our creativity. Beware of Identity Theft! World destruction! The list goes on … But let's just calm down. We know technology has a down side, but, for a moment, can we focus on the many benefits it brings to us?

Access to Information
Our parents used to have to go to a library and take out a book to find out the information they needed. Now, we access whatever we need to know instantly and anywhere. With the vast amount of data on the Internet, we can read the news, check the stock market, and buy tickets to a concert, all while we're on the train!

Innovation and Creativity
The possibilities seem limitless. It was difficult to start a business years ago, but now with online selling platforms, anyone can set up a business at home. Creative people can easily sell their work online. Another example is crowdfunding. This leads to the creation of new businesses, further creativity, and more technology!

Communication
Apparently, we are all zombies with our faces glued to our screens. Yes, we know we need to cut down on screen time and have more face-to-face time, but modern technology has made communication effortless! Before, it took weeks to get a letter to a relative in Australia. Now, we have email, cell phones, video conferencing, text messaging, and social media. You can reach anyone, anywhere, at any time.

Entertainment
Where would the entertainment industry be without technology? We can store and enjoy endless music and movies with streaming apps. Like that new song you just heard on the radio? Download it instantly! We can play games with people on the other side of the planet. It also makes it easier for artists to break into the entertainment industry. Ed Sheeran and Justin Bieber were both discovered on YouTube.

Education
Students can access courses remotely with distance learning. Of course, we also use technology in the classroom. Tablets and smartboards are commonplace, and lessons are much more engaging with visual information. But don't forget the countless educational apps you can download to help you pick up everything from French to ballroom dancing!

C In pairs, reread and find ...
1 two old-fashioned ways to access information.
2 three improvements to entertainment.
3 two ways technology increases innovation.
4 three improvements to education.
5 five ways dialogue has become easier.

♪ *They took the credit for your second symphony.
Rewritten by machine on new technology.*

7.1

D Complete 1–7 with the underlined items in the article. Which are true for you? Modify the others to make them true.

1 I know how to protect myself against _____.
2 Some people say that Millennials don't have good _____ because they spend too much time on their smart phones.
3 I find it really annoying when I'm _____ a movie and the Internet goes down!
4 Children should be limited to one or two hours of _____ a day.
5 I'd like to take a _____ course one day.
6 I think face-to-face meetings are much better than _____.
7 I like buying secondhand items from _____.

E 🗣 **Make it personal** *Technology – the dark side!* Imagine you're a member of an "I hate everything about technology" group. In threes, list all the negative aspects imaginable. Then share with the class. Which, if any, do you think are, or will be, serious problems?

There are too many choices now. It was easier to focus before.

Effortless? No way! It takes ages to learn to use technology well!

Yes, and people had better memories. You don't have to remember anything anymore. Your phone knows everything!

② Vocabulary Phrasal verbs

A Match the highlighted phrasal verbs in the article to the definitions. Any you didn't know?

1	_____	learn a new skill
2	_____	continue or persevere
3	_____	begin to feel more relaxed and less emotional
4	_____	start doing less of something
5	_____	get something officially from somewhere
6	_____	discover a fact or piece of information
7	_____	start something such as a business
8	_____	start to have success in your career

✏️ **Common mistakes**

My five-year-old needs to ~~reduce the~~ sugar. (cut down on)
I ~~take~~ a lot of English from subtitled movies. (pick up)
We've ~~asked~~ a loan to pay ⌄ our wedding. (taken out / for)

B ▶ 7.2 The phrasal verbs are in the wrong sentences. Put them into the correct places. Listen to check. In pairs, imagine the context 1–8 were said in.
1 I don't want to work for someone else. I'd rather cut down on my own company.
2 You'll break into Spanish quickly if you spend time in a Spanish-speaking country.
3 When did you go on these loans on your credit card? Now you've got a huge debt!
4 I don't know what time the train is, but I can easily calm down.
5 Please pick up with what you're doing, and don't let us interrupt you.
6 I'm trying to set up the amount of caffeine I drink.
7 She was angry at first, but we managed to take her out.
8 It must be difficult for artists to find out the U.S. music industry.

This sounds like a person who is fed up with their job.

C 🗣 **Make it personal** *Three of each!* Write down ...

- three things you should cut down on.
- three ways to pick up a new language.
- three things that help calm you down.
- three things you've found out so far during this course.

In groups, compare and ask questions. Any coincidences? Share one unusual response with the class.

Do you know any good apps that can help you pick up a language?

Yes, there are lots! Duolingo is a good one.

86

7.2 What was the last little lie you told?

1 Reading

A In your experience, do salespeople always tell the truth? What kinds of promises might they make or lies might they tell?

> They might say a color looks great on you when it really doesn't!

Common mistakes

~~tell~~
I try to not ~~say~~ lies.

They sometimes exaggerate the ~~true~~.
truth

B Read sales promises a–f and guess what device each one refers to.
a "Some of the keys are different, but it's basically the same thing."
b "Oh, yes, you can mount it on the wall yourself."
c "You'll be able to use it in any country, don't worry."
d "It works just as well as the famous brand, but at half the price."
e "There's lots of technical support online."
f "Look! It just arrived!"

> I think the first one could be a piano.

C Read the article and match promises a–f in **B** to tips 1–5. There's one extra promise.

But How Was I to Know?

Christmas is just around the corner and chances are you'll be buying someone you love a new digital device of some sort. Today we bring you five hot tips to guide your holiday shopping and avoid trouble down the road.

1 [_f_] Our first tip basically applies to any new gadget or household appliance. Companies race to launch new products before their competitors. This means the early versions of the new technology may contain all sorts of horrendous bugs and break down in a matter of weeks. Allow brand new products time on the market so the most serious defects can (hopefully!) be corrected.

2 [ ] Well, theoretically, yes, but if you miss a screw or two, the TV may come crashing down on you after a week. These things weigh more than 100 lbs, so either put it on a table or get a professional to do the job because the warranty doesn't cover stupidity.

3 [ ] The Rolex that your dad has been dreaming of is way too expensive, I know, but stay away from the cheap imitations you find on the streets. They might look good today, but what about next month? Not to mention that buying fake goods is illegal—Dad certainly won't thank you if the police catch him! Remember: If something looks too good to be true, it probably is.

4 [ ] Buying a cell phone abroad can save you a few bucks, but first you've got to check whether you can even use it back home. Make sure it's unlocked (that is, not tied to a particular carrier) and that the network is compatible. If you're scratching your head right now, get yourself a phone locally!

5 [ ] If you buy an imported computer, keep in mind that the keyboard layout may be a little different from what you're accustomed to. So what? Well, if you think you can learn to live without the "ç" or "ñ" keys, no big deal. Otherwise, think twice, or you may find yourself throwing the poor laptop out the window.

> I'd say tip 1 because it's the most general.

D ▶ 7.3 Listen, reread, and match photos a–e to the underlined words. Then match the highlighted words to definitions 1–5. What's the best tip, and which are irrelevant to you?

1	_____ noun [C]	a company that provides phone or Internet services
2	_____ noun [C]	the written promise to fix something for free
3	_____ verb	to put something on the market
4	_____ noun [C]	electronic problems in a device
5	_____ verb	to stop working

a

b

c

d

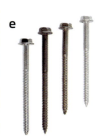
e

E 🗣 **Make it personal** In pairs, complete 1–3 with the correct form of words from **D**, and then answer them. Any big differences?

1 Have you ever had to use the _____ for a product that doesn't work?
2 On a scale of 0 to 10, how happy are you with your cell phone _____? Why?
3 Have you ever bought a product a few days after it was _____? Did you have any problems or inital _____? Would you recommend it to a friend?
4 Have you ever been in a vehicle which suddenly _____ mid-journey?

🎵 Well somebody told me you had a boyfriend
Who looked like a girlfriend
That I had in February of last year
It's not confidential, I've got potential.

> No, I guess I've just been lucky when I buy things.

2 Grammar Reported speech (1)

A ▶7.4 Listen and match the five dialogues to paragraphs 1–5 in **1C**.

B ▶7.5 Complete extracts 1–5 in pencil. Use your intuition! Listen to check.
1 The salesman said some of the keys _____ different.
2 He said that it _____ just as well as the famous brand.
3 The delivery guy told me I _____ mount it on the wall myself.
4 On the site, it said I _____ be able to use it in any country.
5 The store manager said it _____ just _____.

C Compare a–f in **1B** with 1–5 in **B** and circle the correct alternatives in the grammar box.

Reported statements
1 If the reporting verb is in the past (*said, told*), the main verb often **moves one tense back / remains the same**.
2 "That" is **necessary / optional**.
3 **Said / Told** requires an object (*me, her, John*).

➡ Grammar 7A p. 150

✏ **Common mistakes**
He said ~~me~~ he was sorry.
                                          would
She told ~~to~~ me that she ~~will~~ buy it.

D ▶7.6 Change the underlined words in 1–5 into reported speech. Listen to the end of the dialogues to check. All correct? Are any of the phrases or situations familiar to you?
1 "You will learn fast." He said …
2 "I'm here every week, and I can get you video games, too." He told me …
3 "It's easy, and it'll only take 10 minutes." He said …
4 "Lots of people have complained." They told …
5 "These tablets usually sell pretty quickly." She said that …

E ▶7.7 Report what each person said in cartoons 1–4. Listen to check. All correct? Are any of the phrases or situations familiar to you?

1 tell / do well   2 say / dog / be / friendly   3 tell / party / be / informal   4 say / you / not / arrive late

F 🗣 **Make it personal** Think of a time you were told something untrue or wrong. Prepare your answers to 1–3. In groups, share your stories. Any similarities?
1 What was the situation?
2 What did the person say? How did you react?
3 What happened in the end?

> When I was a kid, my parents convinced me that the tooth fairy really did exist. Well, …

> People often use the traffic as an excuse for being late. For example, …

7.3 How much of your day is screen time?

1 Vocabulary Using touch screens

Common mistake

This app was designed ~~for~~ a teenager. *(by)*

A Look at the photo. What do you think PleIQ might be? Who do you think it is designed for?

> PleIQ It looks like some type of ...

B Read the description to check. Were you right? How does PleIQ work? What are the benefits?

Worried about your child's **screen time**?

Tired of seeing them aimlessly swi**ping** left and right and scro**lling** through streams of pointless images? Look no further than PleIQ – a dy**na**mic new app which transforms tablets and smart phones into educational tools.

PleIQ combines physical and digital aspects. The set contains eight cubes with letters, numbers, and other symbols, and an app. With aug**men**ted reality (AR), the symbols shown on the blocks are transformed into interactive, 3D cartoons. Children show a block to the screen, they double-tap on the icon they want to play with, and they can zoom in to see more details.

This invention, by Venezuelan in**no**vator Edison Duran, attempts to improve screen time for children and reduce the educational divide by giving more children access to learning in their early years.

Parents have control. They can monitor their child's progress and add new items. Children can control how their app looks by dragging and dropping items into new locations.

With PleIQ, screen time is more con**struc**tive.

C ▶7.8 Cover **B** and match verbs 1–5 to the phrases. Listen and reread to check. Repeat the pink-stressed words. Then, in pairs, take turns miming 1–5 for the others to guess.

1 swipe   ☐ to see more details
2 scroll   ☐ through images
3 double-tap   ☐ left and right
4 zoom in   ☐ items into new locations
5 drag and drop   ☐ on an icon

D 😀 **Make it personal** In pairs, answer 1–3. Any good tips to share?
1 What are the best kids' apps you know? Why?
2 Each describe a favorite app, how it works, and why it's good.
3 How have apps improved your life? What's easier than it was before?

> I love Evernote Scannable! You just zoom into the document or card or whatever, and the app converts it into a scan. Then you can just scroll through all of your saved documents.

2 Listening

A ▶7.9 Neide Sellin is a young inventor from Brazil. What do you think her invention is? Listen to check.

> I'm not sure. It could be a vacuum cleaner.

B ▶7.9 Listen again. Number these 1–7 in the order you hear them. In pairs, explain their significance.

> That's the number of Brazilians who can't ...

☐ dog   ☐ 6.5 million   ☐ 100   ☐ 3,000
☐ airports   ☐ 2020   ☐ 253 million

C 😀 **Make it personal** 📶 In pairs, search online to find more inventions that have made the lives of people with disabilities easier.

> Stephen Hawking used a cheek-controlled communication system.

> And this meant he could speak through a computer.

3 Grammar Indirect questions

🎵 *The world I love, The tears I drop / To be part of the wave, can't stop / Ever wonder if it's all for you?*

7.3

A Find how questions 1–4 are asked in ▶ 7.9 on p. 170. Complete the chart.

Original question	Indirect question
1 What is her latest development?	_____
2 How many guide dogs are there in Brazil?	_____
3 Is this really a more affordable option?	_____
4 How much does it cost?	_____

B Compare the two types of questions in **A**. Then answer 1–4 in the grammar box.

1. Which sounds more polite, the original question or the indirect question?
2. What is the word order for the subject and verb in indirect questions?
3. What happens to the auxiliary *do* in an indirect question?
4. If the answer to the question is *yes / no*, which word do you need to add?

➔ **Grammar 7B** p. 150

⚠️ **Common mistakes**

Excuse me, could you tell me where (is) the station?

Do you know where did he go?
                                       went

C 🔊 Correct the questions about innovations. Then search online to find the answers.

1. Can you tell me when was Bluetooth first invented?
2. Do you know who did invent the first cordless vacuum cleaner?
3. I'd like to know how many years did it take to produce the first wireless earphones?
4. I wonder when will driverless cars come onto the market?
5. Could you tell me if will e-readers ever replace books?
6. Do you know when is the next iPhone coming out?

D ▶ 7.10 Read the review and complete indirect questions 1–5. Listen to check.

The Kenguru Car

" Tired of having to collapse your wheelchair?
Finally, a car designed with wheelchair users in mind!
Simply maneuver your chair straight into your car and off you go!
With a speed of 25 miles per hour and a range of 60 miles, you will be able to do your daily chores without any of the hassle.
The Kenguru currently costs $25,000, but with the incentive of clean, green energy, it's worth it! "

1	Who is it designed for?	Do you know _____ ?
2	How fast can it go?	I'd like to know _____ .
3	How will it be helpful?	Can you tell me _____ ?
4	How much does it cost?	Could you tell me _____ ?
5	Can it travel very far?	I wonder _____ .

E 👥 **Make it personal** *Time to innovate!* In threes, choose a category and invent something to make life quicker, easier, and more efficient. Present it for the class to ask questions. Vote for the best idea.

Driving and parking   Studying   Shopping   Communications   Housework   Food and cooking

Use these questions to help you plan your presentation.
- What is your invention and how does it work?
- How will it be helpful in everyday life?
- How much do you think it will cost to make?
- How difficult / easy do you think it will be to produce?
- Is there anything else like it already? How is yours better or different?

Could you tell us whether it could work in any type of car?

Do you know if people with disabilities would be able to use it?

7.4 Are machines with personality a good idea?

1 Listening

A In pairs, brainstorm how you (or people you know) use phone voice command features. Who uses it the most?

I use it a lot. I can tell it who to call. *I only use it to choose songs to play.*

> **Common mistake**
>
>   well
> It doesn't work very ~~good~~.

B 🔲 **Make it personal** In pairs, answer 1–3. Which of you likes voice recognition better?
1. Do you have any voice-activated devices at home / in your car? How well do they work?
2. What other devices / appliances should / could be voice-activated?
3. How "intelligent" do you think voice recognition will become in the future?

My GPS is voice-activated, but it's kind of stupid. *Oh yeah? How come?*

C ▶ 7.11 Listen to Bruce and Ann comparing their cell phones. Whose is better at voice recognition?

D ▶ 7.11 Listen again and answer 1–4 using one or two words. Are you more like Ann or Bruce?
1. Who gave Bruce his new phone?
2. What's his voice-recognition software called?
3. Did he expect the phone to be so smart?
4. What's Ann's voice-recognition software called?

I'm definitely more like ... because ...

E ▶ 7.11 Young people often use *like* in informal speech. Study examples 1–3. Then listen again. How many times do you hear the word *like*?
1. The party was, like, so cool. (filler speech)
2. I was like, "What are you doing?" and he was like, "Nothing." (quotative)
3. It took, like, forever to get here. (to signal exaggeration)

F ▶ 7.12 Listen to Ann asking Bruce's phone 1–5. Did it understand (U) or misunderstand (M)? Is it funny?
1. Where am I?
2. Will the weather get worse?
3. Do you love me?
4. Please call me an ambulance.
5. Make me a coffee.

G 🔲 **Make it personal** Machines with personality! Complete 1–4 with your opinion, then compare in groups.
1. In my opinion, this cartoon ...
2. My computer / tablet / phone thinks I'm ...
3. I think machines with personality ...
4. I'd like my ... to have a personality so ...

I'd love to be able to talk to my fridge. It could suggest recipes, count calories, and help me stay healthy!

2 Pronunciation *-ed* ending followed by /h/

A ▶ 7.13 Listen and repeat 1–3 from the dialogue in **1C**. Choose the correct alternatives in the box.
1. He asked if he bored me.
2. I asked him if he was hungry.
3. I asked her to text someone.

> When the final sound is /k/, *-ed* is pronounced: **/t/** / **/d/**
> The /k/ sound in *asked* is: **strong** / **weak**
> The /h/ sound in *him* and *her* is usually: **strong** / **weak**

B ▶ 7.14 *Dictation.* Listen and write Ann's five sentences. Then write them in direct speech.

3 Grammar Reported Speech (2)

*Cause she knew what was she was doin'
When she told me how to walk this way!
She told me to walk this way, talk this way.*

A Look at the examples in **1F** and **2B**. Are rules 1–6 true (T) or false (F)?

Reported questions, commands, and requests			
When reporting questions:		For commands and requests:	
1 use *do*, *does*, and *did*.	T / F	5 use *ask* for requests and *tell* for commands.	T / F
2 invert subject and auxiliary.	T / F		
3 move one tense back.	T / F	6 the main verb uses *(not)* + infinitive.	T / F
4 always use an object after *ask*.	T / F		

→ Grammar 7C p. 150

Common mistake

~~for~~
She asked me ∧ your contact details.

B Order the words to complete five "voice recognition disasters." Had any of your own?

Luke   I asked **my computer / read / to** my new email, and it started deleting messages instead!

Sue   I asked **it / rain / my phone / would / if** tonight and it said, "It's now 4 p.m."

Ron   The GPS told **to / turn / me** left, and I crashed into a tree.

Ian   The stereo asked **what / me / I / wanted** to listen to. I couldn't believe my ears!

Mitt   I asked **where / my GPS / I / was**, and he told **worry / me / to / not**. Can you believe that?

C Do you like autocorrect? Ever have problems with it? Last week it caused lots of problems for **Bruce** and **Ann**. Write their text conversations in reported speech.

I love autocorrect. That is, when it guesses correctly!

1
- Why are you late?
- I've just crashed my cat.
- What do you mean?
- No, no! Not my cat. The ___car___ !
- Hate autocorrect.

2
- Are you hungry?
- Yeah, I want vegetarian blood.
- What?
- OMG. What I meant to say was vegetarian _____!

3
- Are you coming to the party?
- Can't. I broke my uncle.
- What?
- I mean _____, but it's still serious.

D ▶7.15 In pairs, say what you think Ann and Bruce meant for 1–3 in **C**. Then listen to check.

You can crash into a cat, but you can't crash a cat, can you?

E **Make it personal**   **Tech questionnaire** In pairs, follow the instructions.
1 Write six questions to find out about your classmates. For example:

   *How many remote controls do you have and actually use?
   Do you ever think your phone knows what you're thinking?
   Do you think you need to cut down on your screen time?*

2 Ask as many of your classmates as you can. Make a note of their answers.
3 Report their answers back to your partner. Any unexpected answers?

Angelika said she hadn't changed her phone for three years!

Really? Paul told me that he'd changed his yesterday.

7.5 How often do you use a pen?

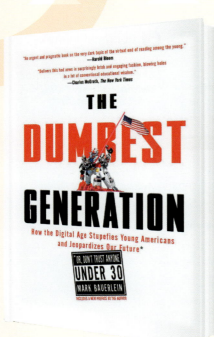

Skills Listening and note-taking

A Match words from the book cover to definitions 1–4. Who's the book about?

1	_____ verb	have confidence in
2	_____ adj.	most stupid
3	_____ verb	makes stupid
4	_____ verb	puts at risk

Common mistakes

It puts at risk ~~the~~ young people's futures.
People say~~s~~ this is true, but I disagree.

B ▶ 7.16 In pairs, answer 1–3. Listen to / Watch an interview to check. Would you consider reading a book like this?
1 How old do you think the author is? Why?
2 Which specific examples of digital culture do you think will be mentioned?
3 Which of these do you think American teens are becoming less interested in?

foreign a**f**fairs   **lei**sure reading   partying   politics
social networking   studying for class   visits to museums

Many are becoming less and less interested in foreign affairs.

C ▶ 7.16 Read about note-taking. Then listen / watch again and complete the notes. Do any of 1–6 surprise or worry you?

> Note-taking is a useful learning skill to develop. When taking notes you should write as fast and economically as possible. Here are three ways to do that:
> - Focus on the most important information (facts, dates, numbers) + ignore less relevant details.
> - Omit articles, auxiliary verbs + prepositions—not usually important information.
> - Use figures for numbers (7 out of 10 = 70%), symbols (> = more than) + abbreviations (sts = students).

1 Digital culture doesn't open teens to _____, artwork, _____, _____ + foreign affairs.

2 Most popular sites for teens: social networking = _____%

3 Time spent reading + studying: < _____ / week. (_____% of sts.)

4 Time spent social networking: _____ / week.

5 Dying habits: Leisure reading, visits to _____ + _____.

6 Technology in teenage bedroom: _____, _____, video game console, _____ → interesting than Antony, Cleopatra, and Caesar!

D **Make it personal** *Teens today. Are things changing?* In groups, decide what's
1) similar and
2) different in your country. Cover these points:
- Do you mainly agree?
- Do any of the facts in **C** surprise or worry you? Why (not)?
- Are teenagers becoming less engaged? More isolated? More adventurous?
- What are the top three priorities among teens where you liv**e**?

It seems to me that teenagers are a bit different.

Do you enjoy a good argument?

7.5

 **in Action** Expressing your views

A ▶7.17 A TV panel discussed *The Dumbest Generation*. Who do you think made the following points, and why? Listen to check. How many correct predictions?

A GOOD ARGUMENT
TV PANEL SHOW
HOST: female, 50 years old
GUESTS: Tom, 32 and Barbara, 19

YOUNG PEOPLE ARE ...

1 reading less and less.
2 using different media to read.
3 not reading less because of the Internet.
4 ignorant despite the Internet.
5 becoming more intelligent.
6 becoming less sociable.

B ▶7.17 Match points 1–6 in **A** to the supporting arguments below. Listen again to check. In your opinion, which are the weakest arguments?

☐ My son thought Rome was a country.
☐ People's IQs have increased in the last century.
☐ Bookstores are closing down.
☐ Teens spend too long locked up in their rooms.
☐ People started to read less at least 30 years ago.
☐ I've got hundreds of digital titles.

Common mistake
My parents had a terrible ~~discussion~~.
argument

I think the weakest arguments are the ones about Tom's son. I mean, who cares?

C Do you agree or disagree with the points in **A** 1–6? Why?

I think it's awful to say young people are ignorant. Of course we're not!

I know! We have access to so much information. How can we be ignorant?

I googled no 4, about ignorance. One site said 20% of Americans believe the sun revolves around the earth!

D 📶 Are you convinced by the supporting arguments in **B**? Choose a point from **A** to research online. Report your findings to the class.

E ▶7.18 Complete the chart with these words. Listen and check, and then repeat.

can't   hold   more   on   point   points   totally   true

No way! That's fake news!

Stating an opinion	We ¹_____ deny that …
Holding the floor	²_____ on a second, let me finish.
Clarifying	Well, it depends ³_____ what you mean by …
Partially agreeing	That may be ⁴_____, but don't you think …? Well, you may agree or disagree, but he makes some valid ⁵_____.
Strongly agreeing	Yeah, I couldn't agree ⁶_____. My ⁷_____ exactly!
Strongly disagreeing	I ⁸_____ disagree.

Welcome to "Hot Topic"! Our guests tonight are …

F 👤 **Make it personal** **A good argument** In threes (host and two guests), choose a discussion topic and role-play a three-minute TV panel. First, think of your main points and supporting arguments. Take notes. What's your conclusion?

Artificial intelligence will be used to replace teachers.
We won't need to learn other languages because we will have translation technology.
The Internet needs to be more strongly regulated.

♪ Yeah, we're just young, dumb and broke,
But we still got love to give

95

Writing 7   A complaint email

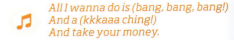

*All I wanna do is (bang, bang, bang!)
And a (kkkaaa ching!)
And take your money.*

A Julio Cruz recently bought an LED TV. Read his email. True (T) or false (F)?
1. He bought it at a shopping mall.
2. He's had problems with the TV since he bought it.
3. There are two problems with the TV itself.
4. He had two problems with the service.
5. He lost the receipt but still wants his money back.
6. He expects a fast solution.

To: customerservice@ledtv10.com
From: Julio Cruz
Subject: Refund

October 10, 2013.

(a) _____ ,

1   I am writing to express total dissatisfaction with my purchase of a 42-inch-LED TV from your online store nearly a month ago. Unfortunately, your product has not performed at all well, and your service has been completely inadequate, to say the least.

2   Firstly, when I turned it on there were several spots on the screen, so I immediately called your service department, who told me the spots would soon go away. However, the problem has gradually been getting worse, and now it is almost impossible to watch any program comfortably.

3   Secondly, I am very disappointed because I've contacted your online support countless times, but they always seemed uninterested and unwilling to help. For instance, I was informed that they would send a technician to solve the problem, but this never happened.

4   Although you advertise top quality, both your product and your service are well below the standards I expected. As you can imagine, I am not satisfied. Therefore, to resolve the problem, (b) _____ .
I attach a scanned copy of the receipt and must insist on receiving a full refund immediately or (c) _____ .

(d) _____ .
(e) _____ ,
Julio Cruz

B Match each paragraph to its purpose.
- [ ] action he wants to be taken
- [ ] reason for writing
- [ ] what happened when he used the product
- [ ] what happened when he complained

C Read *Write it right!* Then match 1–6 to gaps a–e in the email. There's one extra phrase.
1. Dear Sir / Madam
2. Yours sincerely
3. I would appreciate an immediate solution
4. Yours faithfully
5. I will be forced to take legal action
6. I look forward to hearing from you

✓ **Write it right!**

Start and end formal letters using:
- *Dear Mr. / Ms.* (+ last name) or *Dear Sir / Madam,* ...
- a closing sentence:
  I would appreciate a rapid response / I look forward to receiving your urgent reply.
- *Yours sincerely,* (if you know the recipient's name) or *Yours faithfully,* (if you don't).

To express dissatisfaction and demand action use **firm but polite phrases**:
- *I am writing to complain about ...*
- *I feel I am entitled to (compensation for all the inconvenience I have suffered).*

Avoid contractions or informal language.

D Underline the formal sentences in the email that correspond to 1–5.
1. Your service was horrible.
2. I've gotten in touch with you on the Internet.
3. Nobody wanted to help me.
4. You say your product's the best.
5. I want my money back.

E *Your turn!* Write a complaint email in 120–180 words.

Before	Choose a problem below and make notes for paragraphs 1–4 in **B**.
While	Follow the tips in *Write it right!* Use formal language.
After	Email it to a classmate to check before sending it to your teacher.

- You had a meal in a restaurant where the food and service was bad.
- You ordered an item of clothing online, but it is not as advertised on the website.
- You booked a holiday with a travel agency, but the hotel was not as advertised in the brochure.
- You took a long distance bus to a party. The bus left one hour late, arrived four hours late, and you missed the party.

7 The road NOT taken

 Café

1 Before watching

A Complete 1–5 with these words, and then match three of them to the photos.

| commuter | express | shocks | tow truck |
| transmission | | | |

1. ☐ A fast train that doesn't stop at every station is an _____.
2. ☐ A _____ moves a car that is broken down.
3. ☐ The _____ is the part of a vehicle that transmits the engine power to the wheels.
4. ☐ A _____ travels a long distance to work.
5. ☐ The _____ are the parts of a vehicle that absorb the energy from bumps in the road so the wheels run smoothly.

 a  b  c

B 🔘 Make it personal Has your vehicle ever broken down? If so, what did you do? Was it easy to repair?

Once I was on a bus that ran out of gas. The drivers behind us were furious.

2 While watching

A Watch the video and check the correct answer in 1–3.
1. What did August ask Rory and Daniel?
   ☐ He asked if they needed help.
   ☐ He asked if they needed him to pick up anything else.
2. What did Rory tell Daniel that Genevieve said?
   ☐ Her car had broken down.
   ☐ She decided not to have dinner with them.
3. What did Paolo tell Andrea and Zoey about the trains?
   ☐ He said they'd have to cross back over and go back the other way.
   ☐ He warned them their train was going express.

B Watch again. Who said each line?
1. Her car broke down on the expressway.
2. Dinner's going to get cold.
3. It'll just be a party for five.
4. They were expecting us twenty minutes ago.
5. But don't expect me for dinner.
6. This isn't our stop. We've missed it.
7. It passes our stop so we had to get off here.
8. You'll have to cross over to the other side.
9. We're not gonna make dinner.
10. That's so nice of you.

3 After watching

A Complete 1–5 with these verbs. There's one extra.

| asked | offered | complained |
| called | told | wondered |

1. August _____ if Rory needed anything else.
2. Genevieve _____ Rory to tell him that she wouldn't make dinner.
3. August _____ where they were and why they were late.
4. Genevieve _____ Andrea and Zoey that her car needed repairs.
5. Paolo _____ to wait for the train with Andrea and Zoey.

B Complete 1–4 with these times.

| 20 mins | 45 mins | 2 hours | a bit |

1. Genevieve said the tow truck guy would take at least _____.
2. Rory told Daniel it would take _____ for her car to get fixed.
3. Andrea told August she would see them in _____.
4. Andrea and Zoey had to wait _____ for the next train.

C 🔘 Make it personal In threes, share your experiences of planning things that didn't work out. Tell the class the best story.

Leo told us about a party he'd planned but no one came!

8

8.1 How important are looks?

1 Reading

A Is Photoshop a good thing? Have you used it? Would you use it?

> I use Photoshop to remove unnecessary objects from my photos – like trash cans!

> I've never used it. I like my photos to show reality.

B In pairs, take turns giving clues about the items in photos 1–5 until your partner guesses the item.

> It opens and closes. Her eyes? No, it's made of wood. Is it red?

C ▶ 8.1 Listen and read the introduction to the article. In pairs, how do you think Photoshop has changed the world? Brainstorm five ideas. Then read and match photos 1–5 to a paragraph. Were all your ideas mentioned?

How Photoshop HAS CHANGED THE WORLD

Adobe Photoshop is one of the most powerful image-editing tools in the world, and it has profoundly changed the art of photo retouching. What was once an expensive and time-consuming task is now a simple procedure with limitless possibilities. Here we take a look at how Photoshop has changed the way we view the world.

HOW WE THINK ABOUT IMAGES
"That must have been photoshopped!" [a _____] We even use "photoshop" as a verb to indicate that something doesn't look real.

HOW WE VIEW THE HUMAN BODY
A staggering 95 per cent of the human images we see are retouched. [b _____] The more camera-shy among us can photoshop away imperfections and it's great for simple things like removing red-eye. However, we are so used to photos being modified that seeing candid photos of celebrities, with all their imperfections, seems to shock us and many of these "un-photoshopped" images go viral.

HOW IT'S USED IN ADVERTISING
Look through any magazine and find an ad that hasn't been photoshopped. Good luck! Advertising has completely transformed since image manipulation. [c _____]

HOW IT'S USED IN THE TRAVEL INDUSTRY
Lots of vacationers wonder where the golden sand and blue skies are when they get to their destination. The sad fact is that travel companies doctor images. [d _____] This kind of manipulation only results in disappointed customers.

HOW WE VIEW HISTORY
Some of history's most iconic images were "photoshopped" before the software even existed! Photoshop has the power to alter the way we see history. [e _____] If not, they may be altered. With the recent craze of photobombing, politicians must be very grateful for Photoshop.

For better or worse, Photoshop is here to stay, and we are now so accustomed to seeing these images that often it doesn't even register that they've been photoshopped.

D ▶ 8.1 Complete the article with 1–5. Listen again to check. Has the article made you feel any differently about Photoshop?

1 Agencies can now just pay someone to make their ads for them without the need to take photographs!
2 As a result, Photoshop has changed our view of what is "normal."
3 For example, they might remove an ugly parking lot between your hotel and the beach.
4 Experts examine images in detail to make sure they give the right message.
5 These days, we are increasingly skeptical about the authenticity of images.

D **Make it personal** In groups, discuss 1–3.
1 Do you think Photoshop has had a positive or negative influence?
2 Do you think there should be more regulation of Photoshop in the media?
3 Has Photoshop affected your life in some way?

> *So you can keep me*
> *Inside the pocket of your ripped jeans,*
> *Holding me closer 'til our eyes meet,*
> *You won't ever be alone.*
>
> 8.1

> Well, I guess it depends on how you use it. If you work in the advertising industry, then it has had a positive influence.

2 Vocabulary Photography and photos

A Match the highlighted words in the article to the definitions.

1	_____	the red appearance of eyes in some photos
2	_____	to change something in order to deceive people
3	_____	describes someone who dislikes having his or her photo taken
4	_____	making small changes to a photo in order to improve it
5	_____	describes an image that has been manipulated by a computer program
6	_____	the activity of ruining someone else's photo by moving into view just before it is taken
7	_____	natural and informal

B Complete 1–7 with the correct form of the words from **A**.
1 Greta Garbo disappeared whenever a photographer appeared. She was incredibly _____.
2 _____ your vacation photos to make the weather look better is really easy!
3 My camera has a special flash mode to reduce _____.
4 The court discovered that the prosecution had _____ the image.
5 The photographer managed to get a _____ photo of the princess laughing.
6 The photo on the front cover had been _____ to make him look muscular.
7 Did you see that great photo from the Oscars a few years ago? Even celebrities are into this _____ craze.

Common mistake

Do you like ~~that people take your photo~~?
having your photo taken

3 Listening

A ▶ 8.2 Look at James Fridman's Instagram account and answer 1–2. Listen to check. Were you right?
1 What is funny / unusual about the photos?
2 Who do you think James Fridman might be, and what does he do on social media?

B ▶ 8.2 Listen again and correct the errors in 1–5.
1 James Fridman is well-known for taking people's email requests for image alterations.
2 Most of his images are shocking and cruel.
3 Fridman encourages people to retouch their images to meet today's often unrealistic beauty standards.
4 One heart-warming example of James's work is a photo sent to him by a woman who was suffering from anxiety and low self-esteem.
5 She asked James to make her look younger.

C 📶 **Make it personal** In small groups, go online and each find a good photoshopped image by James Fridman (or someone else). Show and explain your choice. Create a caption for it. Which are the funniest / cleverest?

> Look at this one. It looks like the giraffe is photobombing them!

> The caption could be, "I'm much better looking than him!"

99

8.2 Do you like watching illusions?

1 Listening

A In pairs, share what you know about Michael Jackson. Have you seen this video? Any idea how he did the illusion?

I know he was in a group with his family before he went solo.

Maybe there was a metal pole in his jacket.

B ▶8.3 Listen to two people guessing how they did the illusion. Did they mention your ideas? Do you think they are right?

C ▶8.4 Listen to someone explaining how the illusion was really done. Were the speakers in **B** correct? Did you guess correctly?

D ▶8.4 Listen again and complete 1–6. If there's time, watch the video!
1 The illusion appeared in the music video for _____.
2 The dancers were able to lean at an angle of _____ degrees.
3 The lean was performed by wearing a _____.
4 It had an opening in the _____. This attached to a _____ on the floor.
5 During a concert in 1996, Michael Jackson _____.
6 Someone bought the item for $_____.

E **Make it personal** Have you seen any spectacular performances by musicians?

Did anyone see Pink's Grammy performance? She sang while hanging from the ceiling on a ribbon!

2 Grammar Modal perfects

A Match the dialogue halves from **1B**. Then complete the grammar box.

1 How on earth did he do that?
2 Maybe it was something to do with his shoes.
3 Maybe he really could lean that far!
4 I guess his clothes were specially engineered.

a ☐ Yes, I suppose, he might have **put** mag**nets** on them and on the floor.
b ☐ He was good, but not that good! He can't have **been able** to do that. It's impossible!
c ☐ Yeah, he may have **had** special pants made!
d ☐ He must have **had** wires attached to his jacket. It's the only explanation, surely!

Common mistake

have gone
He might ~~went~~ to a party.

1 Sentences a–d in **A** refer to the **present** / **past**.
2 The green verbs are the **simple past** / **past participle** form.
3 Check (✓) the modal verbs with the same meaning as the underlined words in a–c below.

	must have	can't have	might have may have
a I'm <u>almost sure</u> this happened.			
b <u>Maybe</u> this happened.			
c I'm <u>almost sure this did not</u> happen.			

➜ **Grammar 8A** p. 152

B ▶8.5 Rephrase 1–6 using past modals. Listen to check.
1 You saw David Blaine live?! I'm certain the tickets were very expensive!
   The tickets must have been very expensive.
2 It wasn't possible for him to know my date of birth.
3 I don't know how he did that trick. Maybe he had the ring in a secret pocket.
4 I'm 100% sure he didn't levitate.
5 The illusion didn't work properly. Perhaps he didn't practice it enough.
6 I'm certain it wasn't comfortable in that block of ice!

♪ *It must've been love, but it's over now. It must've been good, but I lost it somehow.*

3 Pronunciation Contractions

A ▶8.6 Contractions are the norm in fast spoken English. Listen and repeat the answers in **2B** with contractions. Notice the links between *n't* and *'ve* /təv/.
The tickets must've been very expensive.

B In pairs, go to ▶8.3 on p. 171 and practice reading the dialogue, changing the full forms to contractions using /mʌstəv/, /kæntəv/, and /maɪtəv/.

C In groups, speculate about events 1–6. Choose your best theory for each. Then compare with others. Who has the most interesting idea?

1 You find a wallet lying on the ground close to a gas station.	4 Your classmate is wearing gloves on a hot day.
2 Your laptop is sitting open on your desk where you left it, but the screen is smashed.	5 Your teacher has come to class wearing a dinner jacket / evening dress.
3 You arrive home, and the floor is soaking wet.	6 You arrive at work, and your boss is extremely angry.

The driver might've put his wallet on the car roof when he was opening the door.

Yeah, I've done that with my phone!

And then he must've forgotten about it and started driving. What do you think?

D ▶8.7 Read about two illusions. In small groups, how do you think they were done? Listen to someone describing the tricks. Did you guess correctly?

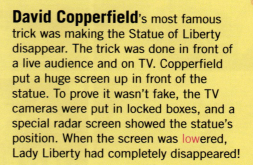

One of **David Blaine**'s first tricks to be shown on TV was levitation. Blaine positioned himself with his back to the audience, raised his arms, and to the crowd's amazement, appeared to lift off the ground at least 30 cm! He stayed there for a few seconds before returning to earth.

David Copperfield's most famous trick was making the Statue of Liberty disappear. The trick was done in front of a live audience and on TV. Copperfield put a huge screen up in front of the statue. To prove it wasn't fake, the TV cameras were put in locked boxes, and a special radar screen showed the statue's position. When the screen was lowered, Lady Liberty had completely disappeared!

E ▶8.7 Listen again. T (true) or F (false)?
1 It doesn't really matter where David Blaine stands.
2 The trick is more effective in front of a large audience.
3 What Blaine wears will affect how well the trick works.
4 David Copperfield used distraction techniques.
5 The audience thought they were sitting still.
6 The trick was performed in partial darkness.

F **Make it personal** 🔊 In small groups, find out how other well-known tricks or illusions are done. Describe / Mime it for the class to guess how it must have been done.

I found a video where David Blaine pulls out a girl's teeth! Then her teeth reappear when he blows on them!

8.3 Have you ever cut your own hair?

1 Listening

A In groups, answer 1–4. Do you all feel the same way about birthdays?
1. How do you like to celebrate your birthday?
2. What's your best birthday memory?
3. Which birthdays are significant in your country?
4. Have birthdays become too commercial?

I like to have a special meal out, blow out my candles, then go dancing.

B ▶8.8 Read the TV review. How do you think the critic rated the show? Listen and notice his tone of voice.

> *My Super Sweet 16* shows you all the fun, glamor, and excitement as kids prepare for their most important birthday celebration," says the MTV ad. OK. I get it. Your teenager is officially growing up. Fine. But there's nothing really sweet about *My Super Sweet 16* or *Quiero Mis Quinces*, its Latin version. Both shows are basically about a bunch of spoiled teens trying to look and act like adults as they prepare for their fifteenth or sixteenth birthday extravaganza. So don't waste your time. And be sure to keep your kids away from the TV—the show might give them some pretty expensive ideas.
>
> **BY JOEY MINOR**

C ▶8.9 Listen to Brandon telling Courtney about his birthday party. True (T) or false (F)?
1. His party was inspired by the show.
2. His mom suggested a movie party.
3. It'll be an outdoor party.
4. He liked the suit his father bought.

Wasn't Paris Hilton a little like that as a teen?

D ▶8.10 Listen to the second part and the activities 1–6. Do you know any teens like Brandon?

E ▶8.11 Match the two columns. Listen to extracts 1–6 to check.

1 Dad hired a fashion designer and	☐ I **signed** all 200 invitations myself.
2 Your hair looks awesome! Tell me,	☐ we still need to have the cake **made**.
3 I spent four hours at the sal**on** and	☐ we're going to have a new suit **made**.
4 The pool's dirty and	☐ I got my nails **done**, too.
5 Mom can't cook so	☐ Dad hasn't gotten it **cleaned** yet.
6 I'm exhausted!	☐ did you have it **dyed**?

Hey, Courtney, awesome news. So, I'm having a party ...

F 🔴 **Make it personal** In pairs, role-play Brandon and Courtney's dialogue. Read ▶8.9 and ▶8.10 on p. 172 and use the photos in **D** to prepare. Do you like feeling spoiled?

2 Grammar Causative form

A Read the grammar box. Then answer 1–3.

> Use **have / get** + **object** + **past participle** to talk about services or actions that other people do for you.
> In causatives, **have** and **get** mean the same, but **get** is more common in spoken English.
> To emphasize that you did something without help, use a **reflexive pronoun**.
> - "Where did you get your hair cut?"
> - "Oh, I cut it **myself**, actually."
> - "We couldn't get anyone to redecorate, so we did it **ourselves**."
>
> → **Grammar 8B** p.152

🎵 Now he's getting a tattoo, yeah, he's getting ink done. He asked for a "13" but they drew a "31."

8.3

a   b

1 Which preparations for the party did Brandon do himself?
2 Who did the other activities? Which do you think was the most expensive?
3 Match pictures a and b to the phrases.
   ☐ I had my photo taken with Zac Efron.
   ☐ I took a photo of Zac Efron.

B In pairs, remember the preparations for Brandon's party using the photos in **1D**. Then role-play **1D** again, switching roles. Be careful with causatives.

> *I can't remember. Did he have his hair dyed, or cut, or just dried?*

C ▶8.12 Complete comments 1–5 from Brandon's very spoiled friends with the causative of these verbs. There's one extra. Listen to check. Do you know anyone like this?

| build | cover | do | get | make | redecorate |

⚠ Common mistakes

get my hair cut
I usually ~~cut my hair~~ at Hairway to Heaven.

have your eyes checked
Did you ~~check your eyes~~ last week?

had this tattoo done
I ~~did this tattoo~~ when I was 16.

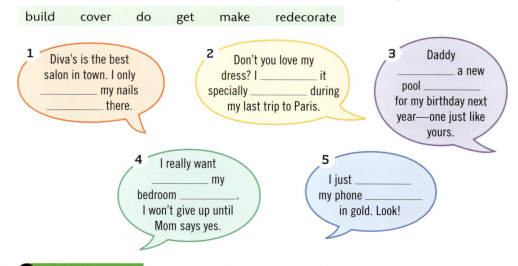

1. Diva's is the best salon in town. I only _____ my nails _____ there.
2. Don't you love my dress? I _____ it specially _____ during my last trip to Paris.
3. Daddy _____ a new pool _____ for my birthday next year—one just like yours.
4. I really want _____ my bedroom _____. I won't give up until Mom says yes.
5. I just _____ my phone _____ in gold. Look!

Could you fix a broken faucet?

I'd probably try to do it myself. And then get someone to do it for me!

Really? I don't know how to. I'd have to get it fixed.

D 🗣 **Make it personal** In groups, ask and answer to find out who's the most self-sufficient. What would be different if you had a lot more money? Who would survive best on a desert island?

HOW SELF-SUFFICIENT ARE YOU?

Do / Could / Would you do these activities yourself?

Do / Would you get them done for you?

iron / clothes   fix / broken faucet   paint / house   build / home
                                         make / dinner   clean / windows
change / flat tire   clean / bedroom   wash / car   grow / food

103

8.4 Do you have a lot of furniture in your room?

1 Vocabulary Furniture

A ▶8.13 Listen. Which bedroom is the designer describing? Match items a–k to these words.

☐ bookcase ☐ chair ☐ closet ☐ **com**forter ☐ dresser
☐ double bed ☐ lamp ☐ mirror ☐ nightstand ☐ pillow ☐ rug

B In pairs, use words in **A** to describe ten differences between rooms 1 and 2. If necessary, use a dictionary for the other items of furniture.

You can see a closet in room 1, but not in room 2.

C 🔵 **Make it personal** Which bedroom do you prefer? Why? Is either similar to yours? What does each one tell you about its owner?

I imagine the first one belongs to a woman because …

2 Listening

A ▶8.14 Listen to two friends talking about the second bedroom. What has happened?

B ▶8.15 Listen to the second part of the dialogue. Why did they do it?

C ▶8.15 Listen again. Check what they have done in the room.
☐ changed the rug   ☐ painted some furniture
☐ replaced the lamps   ☐ bought new pillows and a new comforter
☐ bought a new mirror   ☐ had the bookcase made
☐ painted the walls   ☐ had the windows cleaned

🖌 Common mistake

　　　　much
How ~~many~~ furnitures do you have?

D 🔵 **Make it personal** In pairs, answer 1–4. Any surprises?
1 How would you feel if this were done to you?
2 Have you ever made a nice surprise for someone like this? Has anyone ever done it for you?
3 Which room in your house would you most like to change? How? Why?
4 What would your ideal bedroom look like?

I can't stand my living room. The paint is a horrible color. I'm going to have it repainted one of these days.

♪ Well, I've heard there was a secret chord
That David played and it pleased the Lord
But you don't really care for music, do you?

③ Grammar Tag questions

A ▶8.16 Listen to the extracts and complete 1–6 with these phrases. There's one extra.

| did you? | don't you? | hasn't it? | isn't it? | was it? | won't he? | have you? |

1 You haven't done anything crazy, _____?
2 It's great, _____?
3 He'll love it, _____?
4 You didn't do it all yourself, _____?
5 That rug wasn't there before, _____?
6 You know he's going to be over the moon, _____?

B Look at **A** and complete rules 1–5 in the grammar box with these words.

| negative | ask for agreement | positive |
| check information | do | statement | verb |

1 Use a tag question to _____ or _____.
2 A tag question goes at the end of a _____.
3 Use the same auxiliary _____ and tense in the tag question as the statement.
4 In statements without an auxiliary verb, use _____ in the tag question.
5 With + statements, use a _____ tag. With − statements, use a _____.

→ Grammar 8C p. 152

Common mistakes

Your dad loves tennis, ~~no~~? *doesn't he*
You're not hungry again already, ~~do~~ you?
You were here yesterday, ~~was~~ you? *are* / *weren't*

④ Pronunciation Intonation in tag questions

A ▶8.16 Read the information, then listen again and mark ↗ or ↘ in **3A**.

> Tag questions can have two different functions depending on your intonation.
> Rising ↗ intonation is usually a real question. It means "I'm not sure, so I'm checking."
> Falling ↘ intonation is more like a statement. It means "I'm not really asking. I just want you to agree."

B ▶8.17 Listen to Tom's reaction. How many tag questions do you hear? Did he get upset?

C ▶8.17 In pairs, try to complete 1–4. Listen again to check.
1 But _____ you'd be discharged tomorrow, _____?
2 You _____ about doing this, _____?
3 You _____ serious, _____?
4 That's the rug _____ in the department store, _____?

D Complete 1–4 with tag questions and select the best answer for you.

1 You really like **action movies**, _____?
  a Yeah, I love them.
  b They're OK, I guess.
  c Actually, I hate them.

2 You're **from the capital**, _____?
  a Uh-huh.
  b How could you tell?
  c Nope.

3 You've never **been to the U.S.**, _____?
  a No, never.
  b No, but I'd love to.
  c Yes, I have.

4 You didn't **go out last night**, _____?
  a No, I didn't.
  b I did, actually.
  c Why do you ask?

E 🗣 Make it personal Replace the **bold** words in **D** with your own ideas. In pairs, ask and answer. Vary the verbs / tenses, and add follow-up questions. Share your best exchange with the class.

You really like baseball, don't you?   *It's OK, I guess, but I prefer basketball.*   *Why's that then?*

8.5 Is your listening improving?

Skills Predicting

A In pairs, compare the logo makeovers. Do you prefer the old or the new versions?

I prefer the old iTunes logo.   *I don't know. I kind of like the new one.*

My guess is they won't mention ...

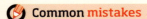

> **Common mistakes**
>
> ~~I guess they're not going to mention why.~~ **they won't**
>
> Use *will* when it's just a guess / there's no evidence.
>
> ~~Look at those clouds – it'll rain.~~ **it's going to**
>
> Use *going to* when it's probable / there's clear evidence.

B ▶8.18 In pairs, guess what will not be discussed in a college lecture on logo makeover, and why. Listen to check. Were you right?

☐ why the logos changed   ☐ consumers' reactions   ☐ the cost involved

C ▶8.19 Read about predicting. Then look at 1–6, listen to the second part, and predict what the lecturer will say after each beep.

> Predicting what the speaker is about to say is a very useful listening strategy. Here are three clues to listen for:
>
> 1 Use of adverbs:
>   *Dad was rushed to the hospital. <u>Fortunately</u> …* — You know it's good news.
>
> 2 Use of linking words:
>   *The economy was good last year. <u>However</u> …* — You know it's a contrast.
>   *Electric cars are greener. <u>In addition</u> …* — You know it's another point.
>
> 3 Intonation:
>   *"Would I like to live abroad?" "Hmm …"* ↘ — You know the answer is probably no.

Instagram
1 She'll mention something **positive** / **negative**.
2 She'll talk about **original** / **new** users.
3 She **likes** / **doesn't like** the logo transfor**ma**tion.

Starbucks
4 Customers **liked** / **didn't like** the new logo.
5 She'll give **her opinion** / **a suggestion**.
6 She'll **explain what she said** / **make a new point**.

D ▶8.20 In pairs, predict what happened to the Gap logo transformation. Use these questions. Listen to check.

1 How old was the logo?
2 How did people react?
3 Why did Gap want to change it?
4 What happened to the company president?

E ▶8.21 Predict how many words you will hear in gaps 1–3. Contractions count as two words. Listen to check. Order the four logos from most to least successful.

1 To mark the occasion, _____ thought: "Hey, let's create a new logo and drop the words 'Starbucks Coffee'."
2 However, Instagram was trying to attract new users—you know, people _____ visited the site before.
3 They _____ create something modern and contemporary, but, boy, were they wrong.

What's the hardest part of language learning?

8.5

ID in Action Expressing preferences

A *Logo Game!* Draw an authentic logo for 1–6. Compare in small groups. How many are the same? Score one point for each unique logo. Who's the class "Picasso"?

Awesome! I didn't know you could draw so well.

| 1 a sports clothing company | 3 a car manufacturer | 5 a TV channel |
| 2 a fast food chain | 4 a tech company | 6 a fashion label |

B In pairs, think of two companies for categories 1–6 in **A** and answer 1–3.
1 Which has a simpler logo?
2 Which is more famous? Does the logo help?
3 Do you prefer one company over the other? Why (not)?

I prefer Ray-Ban. Their designs are cooler.

C ▶8.22 Listen to two students leaving the lecture on logos on p. 106. Which logo(s) do they both like?

D ▶8.22 Try to remember the missing words. Listen again to check.

1 I love this class. It's really _interesting_.	4 I think I like the old one better _____ the new one.
2 Which one do you like _____?	5 I don't really like _____ of them.
3 _____ are OK, I guess.	6 I actually prefer the second one _____ the first.

Common mistakes

I like ~~more~~ grammar ~~than~~ pronunciation. *(better)*

I prefer English ~~than~~ French. *(to)*

I think both channels ~~is~~ great. *(are)* (both = they)

Pizza or pasta? I don't want ~~both~~ for lunch. *(either)*

E Study *Common mistakes*, then correct 1–4. Do you agree with these opinions?
1 Both Facebook and Twitter has good logos, I think.
2 I like Chrome best than Safari.
3 Beyoncé or Shakira? Hmm ... I don't like both of them.
4 I prefer cats than dogs. Actually, I can't stand dogs.

Let's see ... First one ... Yeah, I think so. I mean, they're so recognizable.

F 👤 **Make it personal** *English-learning preferences.* Interview three students and check (✓) their preferences. Use these words to help.

Which one are you better at: grammar or vocabulary?

easy   fun   good at   helpful   irritating   useful

Learner profile	1	2	3
grammar OR vocabulary			
listening OR reading			

Learner profile	1	2	3
pair work OR individual work			
speaking freely OR being corrected			

G 👤 **Make it personal** Report back to the class. Any major differences?

Two people in my group prefer grammar to vocabulary.

Well, here everybody likes vocabulary better.

♫ *I know someday you'll have a beautiful life,
I know you'll be a star
In somebody else's sky,
But why can't it be mine?*

Writing 8 — An opinion essay

'Cause all of me loves all of you. Love your curves and all your edges, all your perfect imperfections.

A Read Damir's opinion essay and check the best title for it.
- ☐ Beauty in the media
- ☐ Beauty: the good and bad sides
- ☐ Five steps to being more attractive

It is usually said that beauty is hard to define. At the same time, being beautiful, or at least being worried about the way you look, has become increasingly important in our society. Is this positive or are people getting obsessed with appearance?

On the one hand, taking care of your appearance has many advantages. In general, this leads both men and women to become more interested in a healthier lifestyle. **For instance**, they try to exercise and adopt better eating habits. All this, of course, has a positive effect on looks. **In addition**, these days it is much easier and cheaper to have beauty treatments that can boost your self-esteem and therefore make you feel happier.

On the other hand, some people are fanatical about having wonderful hair, the thinnest body, and the most attractive face. Many end up wasting a small fortune trying to do so. This false concept of perfection is usually imposed by the media, which makes us want to look like actors, sports stars, or supermodels. This image, of course, is not realistic for most people. **So**, the desire to look absolutely gorgeous can lead to stress, eating disorders, and even serious illness.

To summarize, I strongly believe that emphasizing perfection and physical attractiveness at all costs has extremely negative effects. It would be much better if people were more concerned about feeling good and taking care of their health.

B Which of structures 1–3 does Damir use to organize his opinion essay?
1. introduction + argument(s) for or against only + conclusion
2. introduction + one argument for + several arguments against + conclusion
3. introduction + argument(s) for + argument(s) against + conclusion

C Read *Write it right!* and match 1–6 to the highlighted conjunctions in the text.
1. Introducing arguments
2. Contrasting
3. Adding
4. Exemplifying
5. Summarizing
6. Expressing consequences

✓ Write it right!

In opinion essays, use a variety of conjunctions to organize and contrast your arguments.
- It's important to take care of your appearance. **However**, you should not become obsessed.
- **Even though** mass media, **like** TV, are important, they also have a negative influence, **so** be selective and don't just follow what others do.

Some conjunctions are followed by commas.
- However, / In addition to that, / Therefore,

Some mean the same.
- **Although / Even though** she looked great, she had plastic surgery.
- **Despite** his doctor's recommendations, he went on a radical diet.

D Match 1–5 to an equivalent expression.
1. It is usually said that
2. So
3. For instance
4. In addition
5. To summarize

- ☐ Moreover
- ☐ In short
- ☐ Therefore
- ☐ For example
- ☐ People believe that

E Circle the correct option (a or b). Sometimes both options are correct (c).
1. _____ some models are dangerously thin, fashion magazines still use them.
   a Although   b However   c both
2. Fruit and vegetables are healthy. _____, they're sometimes cheaper than processed food.
   a In addition   b Moreover   c both
3. Doing aerobic exercises, _____ cycling and swimming, helps you stay in shape.
   a such as   b like   c both
4. Some people follow ridiculous diets. _____ they can get sick.
   a Therefore   b Although   c both
5. _____, feeling healthy is more important than being attractive.
   a To summarize   b In conclusion   c both

F *Your turn!* Write an essay in 120–180 words entitled *You have to spend a lot of money to stay fit and healthy.*

Before	Note some arguments for and against. Choose a structure from **B** and organize your notes.
While	Write four paragraphs following the tips in *Write it right!* Try not to repeat any conjunctions. If you're writing on a computer, turn spell check off.
After	Ask a colleague to check spelling and formality or turn spell check on and see how many words you got wrong. Check conjunctions and punctuation before sending it to your teacher.

8 Small talk and smart phones

 Café

1 Before watching

A Match the get phrases to their meanings.

1 have a manicure
2 have a pedicure
3 permit someone a luxury
4 visit a barber / stylist
5 have your car serviced
6 complete a project
7 have a "2 for 1"

a get two things (done) for the price of one
b get something difficult done
c get your fingernails done
d get your hair done
e get a tune up
f get / be pampered (a spa day, a special dessert)

B 🔘 Make it personal Which of 1–7 in **A** have you done recently? How is / was your experience?

I got a pedicure done once. Never again! It really hurts.

I love being pampered. I get my nails done every week.

C Look at the photo. Guess five phrases from **A** you think you will hear.

2 While watching

A Watch up to 2:06 to check. What else did you pick up?

B Watch the video and complete 1–6 with the correct form of *get* or *get* + past participle. Watch again to check. Who said 1–6? What else did you hear?

1 You had to _____ that video _____.
2 It wasn't easy _____ all those martial arts shots.
3 This is heaven. I love _____ my nails _____.
4 I'm going to _____ my hair _____.
5 I should have _____ a tune-up long ago.
6 We never _____ to talk the other night!

C Watch the rest. How many voicemail messages are there? What good news does each of them get?

D Order the events 1–6. Watch again from 2:06 to check.
☐ Dr Moreno calls Zoey about her job application.
☐ Genevieve submitted a song for Daniel's TV show.
☐ Lucy changes her mind.
☐ Lucy says she doesn't want to ruin her nails.
☐ They all find out they got the jobs they applied for.
☐ Zoey and Genevieve listen to their messages.

E 🔘 Make it personal Do you still use voicemail? How often do you a) put off answering messages immediately? b) use flight mode? c) switch your phone off completely?

I sometimes put off difficult messages.

3 After watching

A True (T) or false (F)? Correct the false statements.
1 Lucy took Genevieve to a spa to thank her for her help.
2 Andrea and Paolo obviously don't like each other.
3 Zoey comes to the spa for a "two-for-one."
4 Genevieve put off getting a tune-up and got stranded at the mechanic's.
5 Zoey got a call about a job in the History department.
6 Lucy didn't want to answer her phone because she'd just gotten her nails done.

B Match 1–8 to their meanings a–h.
1 I owe you one.
2 They had on-camera chemistry.
3 That's putting it mildly.
4 It was a total disaster.
5 I should've gotten a tune-up.
6 I kept putting it off.
7 I ended up paying an arm and a leg.
8 It went from bad to worse.

a ☐ Everything went wrong.
b ☐ I delayed doing it.
c ☐ I spent too much money.
d ☐ It needed to be checked and fixed.
e ☐ It's not an exaggeration.
f ☐ They seem compatible on screen.
g ☐ It's my turn to help you.
h ☐ It started bad then became horrible.

C *Role-play.* In threes, create a "salon dialogue". Include at least two phrases from **1A** and **3B**. Role-play it for the class to spot which phrases you use.

Hi, Ale. What are you doing here?   *I'm getting my …*

R4 Grammar and Vocabulary

A *Picture dictionary.* Cover the words and definitions on the pages below and remember.

pages	
87	8 phrasal verbs
88	5 common objects
89	4 reported speech stories
97	5 transportation words
99	7 photography words
102	6 party preparations
104	11 bedroom items
161	2 words for each sound in lines 3 and 4 of the consonants chart (not the picture words)

B In pairs, describe Sam Soccer's pre-match ritual. Which action is different? Why?

> OK, so he has his uniform dry-cleaned before each match.

uniform / dry-clean

cleats / check

hair / cut and dye

photo / take

C *Role-play.* A: Interview Sam about his game day ritual. B: You're Sam. Be creative!

> So, Sam. On game days, what time do you get up?

> Well, for away games we normally sleep in a hotel. We get woken up at …

D ▶R4.1 Listen to the three tongue twisters. Which underlined ending is different? Listen again and practice saying the twisters.

1 a ask<u>ed</u>   b park<u>ed</u>   c start<u>ed</u>
2 a a<u>cc</u>use   b a<u>cc</u>ident   c e<u>xc</u>uses
3 a a<u>cc</u>elerate   b a<u>cc</u>ommodate   c e<u>x</u>periment

E ▶R4.2 Order the words in 1–7 to make sentences. Add the correct punctuation.

1 you / this / works / show / Can / how / me / phone / ?
2 you / this / stops / know / Do / where / bus / ?
3 I / if / tomorrow / it / will / wonder / rain
4 take / sugar / you / don't / milk / You / and / do / ?
5 forget / email / won't / will / You / to / you / send / that / ?
6 this / for / you / tell / me / Could / what / cable / is / ?
7 you / off / know / turn / Do / to / this / how / machine / ?

F In pairs, imagine what five pieces of news the people in photos 1 and 2 could have just received.

> He might have gotten a message from an old girlfriend.

G In pairs, plan a surprise birthday party for a friend. Discuss what you need to do / have done and who is doing what.

> Are we going to make a cake?

> No, let's have one made.

H Correct the mistakes in each sentence. Check your answers in units 7 and 8. What's your score, 1–10?

Common mistakes

1 I asked to you don't turn on it. (3 mistakes)
2 Why you didn't say me hello? (2 mistakes)
3 Could you tell to me what does it say? (2 mistakes)
4 Do you know where is mall? (2 mistakes)
5 It depend of many things. (2 mistakes)
6 I don't know where is he. He might went to work. (2 mistakes)
7 I painted my nails at the salon. Don't they look great? (2 mistakes)
8 You should to cut on down screen time. (2 mistakes)
9 He likes more the cars than the motorbikes. (2 mistakes)
10 "I prefer rock than pop." "Really? I don't like both." (2 mistakes)

Skills practice

I wonder, when I sing along with you, if everything could ever feel this real forever, if anything could ever be this good again.

R4

A Quickly reread the Photoshop text on p. 98. Then listen to ▶8.1, pausing every 12 seconds to write down the last five words you hear. Then reread to check.

B ▶R4.3 Listen to five extracts from ⒟3 and count the words in each. Contractions count as one word.

C ▶R4.3 Listen again and write the full extract. Check in pairs. Which words are hardest to understand?

D List eight electronic items you own. Order them from the most to the least important. In pairs, compare and explain.

> *I couldn't live without my refrigerator. It's too hot here not to have cold drinks.*

E In pairs, think of three things each person could be saying. Share the funniest with the class.

"I told you …"   "I thought you said …"

F Read the article opposite. True (T), false (F), or not mentioned (N)? Have you had a bad experience with builders?
1 Emreth installed the new items himself.
2 The bathroom cost more than he expected.
3 Emreth owns this small apartment.
4 Both the bath and the shower were dangerous.
5 When the bath fell it nearly killed Emreth.
6 Workers at WallsUp blame Emreth.
7 All the characters in the story are male.

G 🎧 **Make it personal** *Getting things done?*
Choose three verbs and write questions about the services people use. Ask four classmates and report the results.

clean	check	cut	(re)decorate
deliver	do	dye	iron	repair
renovate	service	test

> *When was the last time you had your eyes tested?*
> *She said she'd had them tested a month ago because she couldn't see the TV!*

H *Role-play.* Using smart phones
A: Imagine you're a Martian and have no idea what a smart phone is.
B: Explain three functions to the Martian. Then change roles.

Hello, human. What's that in your hand?

I ▶R4.4 🎧 **Make it personal** *Question time!*
In pairs, listen to the 12 lesson titles in units 7 and 8. Pause after each one and guess what your partner's answer will be. Correct each other's wrong guesses. Any surprises?

> *Does technology rule your life?*
> *I think you'll answer, "No, I actually love technology."*
> *You're right! And your answer will be …*

Expensive bath

An L.A. **home**owner has learned the hard way that you have to be careful when you get home reno**va**tions done. Emreth Jones, 42, paid $15,000 for a new bathroom, and another $10,000 to fix the mistakes after a building ins**pec**tion. "It's terrible," he said. "I wanted to get a new bath and shower put in upstairs. I thought it would be simple."

The building ins**pec**tor noticed that the workers had seriously **weak**ened the floor when they installed the bath and shower.

"The bath might have come through the floor at any moment," said Jones. "If it had hit me, that would have been it."

The manager of WallsUp declined to comment, although an employee claimed it was Jones' fault.

"He asked us if we could do it cheaply. And he didn't tell us he would get an inspection."

111

9

9.1 Does crime worry you?

1 Vocabulary Crime and violence

A ▶9.1 Quickly match the text types to extracts 1–6. Then listen and read to check. Which type do you read the most?

☐ a tweet ☐ a discussion forum for students of English
☐ a newspaper article ☐ a discussion forum for travelers

I'm always tweeting.

1 I spent four days in São Paulo. Lots of locals told me to be careful. I was, and it was cool. I heard a few crime stories, from credit card fraud to kidnapping. Maybe they're exaggerating. Anyway, enjoy your stay there. The food and nightlife are amazing!

2 Organized crime in Chicago has seen a fall. Statistics released recently show a 20% decrease in burglaries between June 2017 and 2018.

3 **Murder of millionaire shocks Jacksonville. Ex-husband main suspect.**

4 Got stopped for speeding. Actually thought about offering the cop $100, but remembered bribery is also a crime. Must slow down in future. #stupid
↩ Reply   ⇄ Retweet   ★ Favorite

5 **89-YEAR-OLD BOXING GRANDMA SENT TO PRISON FOR DOMESTIC ABUSE AND DRUG DEALING.**

6 OK, I think I can help you. Theft is a noun, and it is when someone takes something from you without you knowing. So, for example, if you were walking down the street and I ran by and stole your purse, that would be theft. So, in a way, tax evasion and music piracy are forms of theft, too. Robbery is a noun, too, but that's different: it usually involves violence or fear. Steal is a verb. Someone steals something from you. Hope that helps! 😊

☐ a newspaper headline ☐ a headline from a satirical news website

B ▶9.2 Match the highlighted words to pictures a–g. Listen to check.

C Complete 1–4 with other crimes from the texts. Then, in pairs, mime a noun from **B** or **C** for your partner to say it.

1 credit card f_____   3 tax e_____
2 domestic a_____   4 music p_____

Ha ha. That's brilliant! A burglary.

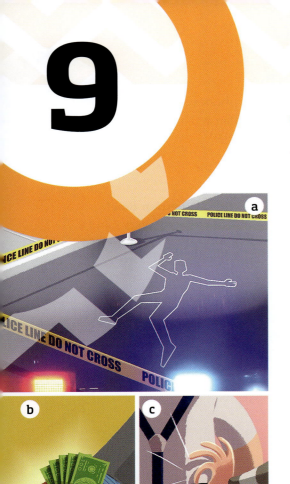
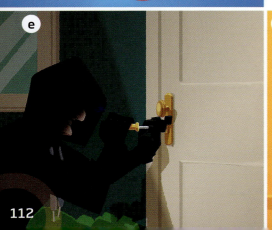

D Complete 1–4 with the words below. There are two extra.

burglary   robbery   robs   steal   stealing   thefts

1 There was an armed _____ at the gas station last night. Three men threatened the staff with guns and stole $6,000 in cash.
2 Unfortunately, we have had several _____ of personal property in the building recently.
3 They were so poor, they had to _____ food in order to feed themselves.
4 Many people install alarms to protect their houses against _____.

🎵 *Everybody wanna steal my girl*
Everybody wanna take her heart away,
Couple billion in the whole wide world,
Find another one 'cos she belongs to me.

9.1

E **Make it personal** Choose the three most and least serious crimes in **B** and **C**. In groups, compare your lists. Can you reach a consensus?

To me, credit-card fraud is the least serious crime.

Well, it depends on the amount of money you steal, doesn't it?

Common mistakes

~~stealing~~
I saw you ~~robbing~~ my wallet!

stolen
Help! My cell phone was ~~robbed~~!

robbed
Have you ever been ~~stolen~~?

robbed
What? Your grandmother ~~stole~~ a bank?

2 Listening

A ▶ 9.3 Listen and match short interviews 1–5 to the questions. There's one extra question.

Which of the crimes listed
☐ do you worry about the most?
☐ do you worry about the least?
☐ have / has affected someone you know?
☐ will probably increase in the next 10 years?
☐ would you like to eradicate for ever?
☐ shouldn't be considered a crime?

B ▶ 9.3 Listen again. True (T) or false (F)? Correct the false ones. Who do you empathize with?
1 He doesn't think people should pay for digital content.
2 People saw a robber in his neighborhood last year.
3 A middle-aged man broke into her neighbor's house.
4 The government is introducing new laws next year.
5 She has taught her kids to yell if a stranger approaches them.

Certainly not the first guy. I produce digital material myself!

3 Grammar Review of verb families

A Match the examples in 1–4 to the forms below, and name the four tenses. Then add a past example to each category, 1–4.

English verbs fall into four categories:
1 Simple (states, habits, single actions): *I study* English.
2 Continuous (progress): *I am studying* English.
3 Perfect (links a point in time with a previous action): *I have studied* English.
4 Perfect continuous (progress before a point in time): *I have been studying* English.

Knowing how each one works can help you make different past, present, and future verb combinations more easily.

➡ **Grammar 9A** p. 154

Example 1 is in the ... tense.

A past example for aspect 1 could be "I didn't study English at school."

☐ S + be + -ing   ☐ S + have + been + -ing   ☐ S + have + past participle   ☐ S + verb

B Name the tense in audio extracts 1–4. Order them from easiest to hardest for you.
1 I've lived in this neighborhood for, what, two years ...
2 You're simply downloading a song!
3 What has the government been doing to change things?
4 I don't see any way out.

C **Make it personal** Use the survey in **2A** to interview two classmates. What are the most common answers?

Most students, four out of five actually, think credit-card fraud has increased.

The crime everybody I asked would eliminate forever is ...

113

9.2 How could your city be improved?

1 Reading

I believe it's the second biggest city in Colombia.

A ▶ 9.4 In pairs, brainstorm what you know about Medellín. Listen and read the introduction. Then cover it. What can you remember?

Medellín Reinvented

Twenty years ago, if someone had said they were going on vacation to Medellín, Colombia, you'd have called them crazy. *Time* magazine once called it "the most dangerous city on earth." Civilized society had been destroyed, drug cartels ruled, and violence was part of everyday life. Fast-forward to the present and things couldn't be more different. Medellín is a city with plenty to celebrate and is fast becoming a hot destination! But why? Well, here are five things that I believe have brought a dramatic change to this fascinating city.

Maybe this cable car has made traveling much safer?

B ▶ 9.4 In pairs, look only at the photos and captions in the rest of the article to guess how each feature has helped reinvent Medellín. Then listen, read, and check. Were your guesses correct?

Public transportation

The public transportation network can take some credit for bringing peace to the city. MetroCable, the network of cable cars, connects poor and middle-class Medellín, both literally and symbolically, and this helped to reduce urban violence. Also, until 2011, the residents of Comuna 13, one of Medellín's poorest neighborhoods, had to climb 500 steps to get home. The commute has been reduced to five minutes thanks to outdoor escalators. These escalators gave people a sense of dignity and pride, which I think also had an impact on crime.

MetroCable

Innovation

Another reason I was impressed by Medellín is its urban development. It won the prestigious Lee Kuan Yew World City Prize award in 2016. This award is known as a kind of "Nobel Prize" for urbanism. It recognizes Medellín's transformation into a model of sustainable urban innovation. As well as the famous escalators and cable cars, Medellín's art galleries and public spaces were praised.

Art in Botero Square

Street art murals in Comuna 13

The arts

Medellín's art scene is also flourishing. Renowned artist Fernando Botero was born here and donated lots of his distinctive art to his home city. This also brings tourists to the area. Back in Comuna 13, previously the most notorious area, fantastic street art can be found. Local residents act as tour guides, giving them work and pride in their neighborhood. They explain with passion the personal stories told by the colorful murals. The tour really gave me an understanding of the history and transformation of Medellín.

Nature

Colombia is second only to Brazil for its biodiversity. It is home to 10% of the world's species! Protected areas are being expanded all the time. Some of these areas are accessible by MetroCable, including Arvi Park, where you escape urban life by walking, biking, and horse-back riding.

Arvi Park

Flower Festival

The "City of Eternal Spring"

Colombia is one of the world's biggest flower exporters, and billions of dollars' worth of flowers are exported every year. Medellín is in bloom all year round. The weather is a perfect 22–23 degrees Celsius whatever the season, and there are flowers everywhere you look all year round: on balconies, terraces, gardens, and parks. Thousands of tourists visit during "Feria de las Flores," and it was one of the most joyful and creative things I've ever seen. The festival will definitely be put on my list of favorite things to do in Latin America.

C Reread and answer 1–5. Practice the pink-stressed words.
1 How has public transportation helped to reduce crime in Medellín?
2 How does the flower festival help the economy?
3 Why was Medellín awarded the Lee Kuan Yew World City Prize?
4 How do the street art tours help visitors learn about the city?
5 How is Medellín protecting its biodiversity?

🎵 *Sweet dreams are made of this, who am I to disagree? I travel the world and the seven seas …*

9.2

D **Make it personal** In small groups, discuss 1–4. Any disagreements?
1 Which things do you think best explain Medellín's transformation?
2 Have any of the things in the article happened in your city?
3 Which other improvements could make your city better?
4 What would you put on your list list of favorite things to do in Latin America?

For me, it was because the violence ended.

2 Grammar Passive voice

A Study the underlined phrases in **1B**. Then read the grammar box and circle the correct alternative in rules 1–3. Is the form similar in your language?

> Use the passive voice when the "doer" of a verb is unknown, unimportant, or obvious. It is often used to move important information to the front of a sentence.
> 1 The passive voice is formed with *have* / *be* + the **simple past** / **past participle**.
> 2 The verb *be* can go in **the present or past** / **any tense or form**.
> 3 *For* / *By* is used to show who did the action.
>
> ➡ Grammar 9B p. 154

Common mistakes

Roses, carnations, and orchids are ~~growing~~ in Colombia.
     grown

                              ignored by
This story has been ~~ignoring for~~ the press.

B Complete the tweets about the article with these forms. There's one extra. Which are relevant where you live? In pairs, add a tweet of your own.

| will be | are being | can't have been | has been | should be | to be |

@PedroH: Outdoor escalators! Wonderful idea. I really think they ¹_____ adopted as a model for lots of other cities!

@grumpyoldman: Places really can change! It's incredible how much crime ²_____ reduced because of things like this!

@donnamaria: It's amazing how the arts can help. Two new art galleries ³_____ built right now. Kids need art in their lives. #arttherapy

More natural areas need ⁴_____ protected. If Medellín keeps improving, the tourist industry will take over.

Honestly? I doubt these changes ⁵_____ sustained. These things take too much time and money.

C ▶9.5 Complete the quotes about cities with the verbs in parentheses. Listen to check. In groups, choose your favorite. Which is the most popular?
1 Buildings do not make a city. A city _____ (make) by the people who live there.
2 Cities are places where money _____ (make), but life _____ (lose).
3 By its nature, a city provides what otherwise _____ (could / give) only by traveling.
4 Villages and towns _____ (swallow up) by cities. Soon there will be no countryside at all.
5 The way you view the future _____ (change) by living in any big city.

Our favorite quote is … because …

D Look at **2B** on p. 113. Say 1–5 in the passive voice.

E **Make it personal** *Passive Favorites!* In pairs, ask and answer full passive voice questions about your favorites in each square. Any coincidences?

Who's your favorite device made by?

It's made by Samsung. It's my phone.

115

9.3 Have you ever been to court?

POP CRIME?

Back in July, 22-year-old Chicago student Michael Lewis was driving home very late from a friend's house. He was listening to loud music in his car. Oh, with his windows down, naturally. The neighbors weren't happy, of course, and they called the police. Michael was <mark>sent to jail</mark> for the night, but was <mark>released</mark> the next day—free as a bird to terrorize the neighborhood again! A week later, more loud music at 2 a.m. This time, Michael was <mark>charged with</mark> disorderly conduct and <mark>taken to court</mark>, but there was no evidence against him, so Michael was acquitted. Free as a bird, again. Third week, more loud music. Trouble is, there was a police car patrolling the neighborhood. So Michael had to face the judge again, but this time things got serious: Michael was convicted. He was <mark>sentenced to</mark> three days in jail and had to pay a $1,000 fine. But, for some reason, the judge decided to give him an alternative. The judge asked Michael what his least favorite kind of music was. It turns out that Michael was not a fan of classical music. The judge's alternative was to listen to classical music for thirty hours. Easy choice, right? Not for Michael. After twenty minutes of Mozart and Beethoven, he chose the original punishment.

1 Vocabulary Crime and punishment

A In pairs, imagine the story in the pictures. Then read to check. Were you close?

> *A guy was leaning on his car at night listening to loud music …*

B ▶9.6 Match the <mark>highlighted</mark> words and phrases to the pictures. Listen to a dramatized version of the text to check. What kind of music would be a punishment for you?

> *I'd hate to be forced to listen to …*

C 🗣 Make it personal In pairs, use only the pictures to remember Michael's story. Take turns describing each scene.

2 Listening

A ▶9.7 In pairs, look at the punishments and guess the crimes. Listen to check.

B ▶9.7 Listen again and match the phrases to 1 and 2. Fair punishments?

- ☐ charged with
- ☐ sentenced to
- ☐ taken to court
- ☐ ordered to pay
- ☐ sent to jail
- ☐ released

C Complete extracts 1–11 with these prepositions. Then check in ▶9.7 on p. 173. How do you try to learn prepositions?

> 🎵 Breaking rocks in the hot sun.
> I fought the law and the law won.

9.3

| at | from | in (x2) | on | to (x4) | under | with |

1 Thirty-two-year-old Shena Hardin was caught _____ camera driving on a sidewalk.
2 The judge sentenced her _____ an embarrassing punishment.
3 She was told to stand _____ a busy intersection.
4 Just to add _____ her humiliation ... she was ordered to pay $250 _____ court costs.
5 It was an ordinary morning _____ San Francisco's District Court.
6 Bring it _____ me now.
7 All 42 people present were charged _____ disturbing the peace.
8 All 42 people present were sent _____ jail.
9 The judge was permanently removed _____ office.
10 He said he had been _____ a lot of stress.

> *I memorize a personal example: I work **in** Quito, **in** Bellavista, **on** Av. 6 September **at** number 347.*

> ⚠️ **Common mistakes**
> of / about   in
> Think ~~in~~ me when I'm ~~to~~ jail.

D 🎤 Make it personal 📡 In pairs, search online for a crime story in the news. Figure out how to summarize it in simple English. Then tell the class.

> *A woman was caught on camera pushing someone else's car out of a parking space with her car so she could park there. She damaged the car and was charged with reckless driving!*

3 Pronunciation -ed

A ▶9.8 Listen how *-ed* links to vowels and consonants. Is the *-ed* sound clear or does it link? Listen again and repeat.

-ed = /ɪd/		clear	links
1	... be arrested unless I get that phone now!		
2	... decided to give him an alternative.		
-ed = /t/			
3	... were released, of course.		
4	... be sentenced to a week in jail.		
-ed = /d/			
5	... no one confessed at all.		
6	... was permanently removed from office.		

> Remember: The pronunciation of *-ed* depends on the last sound (not spelling) in a regular verb.
> • /d/ after a voiced consonant – lived /lɪvd/
> • /d/ after a vowel sound – studied /stʌdiːd/
> • /t/ after an unvoiced consonant – liked /laɪkt/
> • /ɪd/ after /t/ or /d/ – wanted /wɒntɪd/

B ▶9.9 *Celebrity gossip!* Write full sentences for 1–5. Listen to check. Do you know any similar stories?

1 Justin Bieber / arrest and release / bail for $2,500 / driving dangerously
2 Axl Rose / order / pay a huge fine after biting a man's leg
3 Lindsay Lohan / sentence / 10 days' community service
4 Michelle Rodriguez / send / jail / 18 days
5 Lauren Hill / confess and serve / three months in jail / tax evasion

> *Wasn't Josh Brolin arrested for fighting back in 2013?*

C 🎤 Make it personal In groups, decide on the right punishment for each crime. Do you all agree?

> **Man arrested for burglary after breaking into house to use bathroom**

> **Teen charged with kidnapping after taking girlfriend on surprise trip**

> ⚠️ **Common mistake**
> *I think he should ~~to~~ do 100 hours' community service.*

> **Elderly woman faces robbery charge after trying to rob a bank with a banana**

> **20-year-old hacks into college computers and changes own grades**

> *We've agreed the bank robber should be sentenced to at least five years.*

> *No, that's not fair. I mean, what if she dies in prison?*

9.4 Where will you be living ten years from now?

"You borrowed $27,000 over the years to study computer sciences. According to our files, you now owe us $1.83."

Hmm ... I don't know. It might've been a mistake.

1 Listening

A ▶9.10 In pairs, look at the cartoon and answer 1–4. Then listen to part one of a radio show to check your answer to question 4. Were you right?
1. Who / Where are the cartoon characters?
2. Guess what happened to the man's debt.
3. What do you imagine will happen next?
4. Will cybercrime get better or worse in the future?

B ▶9.10 Listen again and complete 1 and 2 with numbers.
1. The radio show host gives _____ examples of cybercrime.
2. He says it will be the world's biggest problem some time before _____.

C ▶9.11 Listen to part two. How worried is Deniz Kaya?

D ▶9.12 Using the photos, think of three reasons why cybercrime will get worse. Listen to part three to check. Any correct guesses?

Common mistake
By
~~Until~~ 2040 I'll be retired.

E ▶9.12 Listen again. True (T), false (F), or not mentioned (N)?
1. Deniz says some hackers are teenagers.
2. The Facebook Messenger virus starts when you watch a video.
3. It was created by Facebook.
4. Future e-devices won't need protection.
5. Cybercriminals often hack computers for fun.
6. Currently, 20 percent of all phones are under attack.

F Match the highlighted words to the definitions.
1. By 2025, cyber attacks will have become the world's top **threat**.
2. He'll be telling us if we should take these **warnings** seriously.
3. Cybercriminals will be **carrying out** attacks wirelessly, and we won't be protected.
4. They will have developed the ability to **spread** viruses across multiple devices very, very easily.
5. Cybercriminals will have **targeted** 20 percent of all the world's smart phones.

☐ to perform, conduct
☐ to try to attack someone or something
☐ to affect more items / to increase / to develop fast
☐ a person or thing that could cause serious problems
☐ messages that tells us about a possible danger

G 🎤 Make it personal In pairs, have you ever had a major cyber problem? How do you protect yourself from cyber attacks? Any novel ideas? Who's more careful?

A year ago, I lost all my data. The worst part was losing my photos.
I try to create really difficult passwords.

H ▶9.13 Listen to part four and Deniz's advice on how to protect yourself. Did he mention any of your ideas?

118

2 Grammar Future perfect and continuous

🎵 *We'll be raising our hands, shining up to the sky 'Cause we got the fire, fire, fire, yeah we got the fire, fire, fire.*

9.4

A Reread 1–5 in **1F** and complete the rules in the grammar box with these words.

> be   have   continuous   perfect

> Use the future ¹_____ for an action completed before a point in the future.
> Form: will / won't + ²_____ + past participle
>
> Use the future ³_____ for an activity in progress at a point in the future.
> Form: will / won't + ⁴_____ + -ing verb
>
> → Grammar 9C p. 154

B Complete 1–5 with the *future perfect* or *continuous*. What will you be doing in ten years?

I won't be working in ten years. I'll have retired.

FIVE CAREERS FOR 2030

PRIVACY MANAGER:	NANO MEDICS:	BOOK-TO-APP CONVERTERS:	3D PRINTING ENGINEERS:	TURBINE SPECIALIST:
If you think you've lost some of your privacy, get ready. By 2030, you ¹_____ most of it. (lose)	Good news! In the next few years, you ²_____ nanotechnology to treat most of your health problems. (use)	In five years, you ³_____ paper books. Everybody will use an e-device. Just wait and see. (not read)	By the end of the decade, the demand for 3D printing ⁴_____. (double)	We ⁵_____ using electricity, but we will be getting more from green sources such as wind turbines, which need a lot of maintenance. (not stop)

⚠ Common mistakes

I will graduate from college by 2022. ~~by~~ *in*

When we celebrate our next anniversary, we will be married for 50 years. ~~be~~ *have been*

I'll be studying this weekend while everyone else ~~will be~~ relaxing. *is*

C Match 1–5 to photos a–e. Write full sentences in the *future perfect* or *continuous*.

> **The Optimist's Guide to the Next 20 Years**
> 1 ☐ soon / most people / work from home
> 2 ☐ we / stop / global warming / by 2040
> 3 ☐ scientists / discover / a cure for the common cold / by 2040
> 4 ☐ in next few years / most people / drive / electric cars
> 5 ☐ by / end / decade / all public places / install / free Wi-Fi

a  b  c  d  e

D 🗣 **Make it personal**   In pairs, use the photos in **C** and the phrases below to make predictions.

> I'm pretty sure (that) …   It's possible (that) …   I doubt (that) …

It's possible that we'll all be driving electric cars by 2030.

Really? I doubt that very much. I think lots of people will have stopped driving completely.

9.5 Do you watch TV crime dramas?

ID Skills Identifying sarcasm

A Quickly read the article and match 1–4 to the crimes in **1B** and **1C** on p. 112.

CRIME DOESN'T PAY. ESPECIALLY IF YOU'RE A DUMB CRIMINAL.

1 24-year-old Harry Zimmerman walked into the local convenience store with a gun and told the cashier to put all the money in a bag. On his way out, Zimmerman saw a bottle of Scotch behind the <u>counter</u> and told the cashier to put it in the bag, too, which the woman re<u>fused</u> to do because she suspected he might be under 21. So, <u>to prove his age</u>, Zimmerman, <u>a man of principles</u>, showed her his driver's license, took the bottle, and ran away. A few minutes later …

2 Forget "the dog ate my homework." Today's kids have <u>infinitely better ideas</u>. Like 22-year-old Brazilian student Susan Correia, for example, who was charged with reporting a false crime. One day, Susan called her mother in tears and told her that she'd just managed to escape from an old de<u>ser</u>ted house, where three armed men had held her <u>cap</u>tive for a whole day. <u>In despair, her mother called the police</u>, who soon discovered that Susan had actually spent the day at a friend's house. At the police station, Susan admitted that …

3 Rashia Wilson of Tampa, Florida, was sentenced to 22 years in prison for buying a $70,000 sports car and giving her one-year-old son <u>a relatively inexpensive</u> $40,000 birthday party—you know, <u>just like the ones your parents used to throw</u>. Unfortunately, the self-pro<u>claimed</u> queen of fraud (yes, that's what she called herself — <u>subtle, huh?</u>) took lots of photographs revealing how she'd been using <u>tax</u>payers' money and, believe it or not …

4 Today's <u>ultra-smart criminals</u> come from Iowa. Police had an easy time finding wanted criminals Joey Miller and Matthew McNelly. Before breaking into an apartment, these <u>masters of disguise</u> decided to hide their real identities. How did they do this? Well, <u>they covered their faces in permanent marker pen</u>. The thing about permanent marker pen is that … <u>it's permanent</u>.

First one ... Well, let's see. Maybe he left his driver's license at the store and went back to get it?

B ▶9.14 In pairs, match the titles to stories 1–4 in **A**. Predict how they end. Listen to check. Did you guess them all?
- ☐ How to make your mark
- ☐ Old enough to break the law
- ☐ Nope, it never happened
- ☐ Social media mistake

C Read the information. Then mark the underlined items in **A** sarcastic (S) or not sarcastic (N). Is sarcasm common in your community?

> Detecting sarcasm in writing, without intonation or facial expressions, isn't easy. Here are four tips:
> - If a sentence looks sarcastic, read it out loud. You might "hear" the sarcasm.
> - Ask yourself, "Does it make sense in this context?" *"Thanks, American Air, for losing my bags again this year!"* is a clear example of sarcasm.
> - Look for examples of exaggeration: *"Aren't you the greatest cook in the world?"*
> - Consider the style. Informal writing usually contains more sarcasm.

Well, my friends and I are sarcastic with each other. A lot!

Yeah, but when people don't understand you're joking, they can get upset.

D 🎤 **Make it personal** In pairs, answer 1–4. Any surprises?
1. In your opinion, who was the dumbest criminal?
2. What punishments should the people in **A** receive?
3. Have you ever committed a small crime?
4. What would you do if you were Susan's mom or dad?

I think all of them were pretty stupid, but the guy who showed his ID was the worst.

Are you good at making excuses?

9.5

ID in Action   Giving excuses

A In pairs, imagine the story behind the five headlines. Then change partners. Were any of your ideas the same?

Maybe they thought the mayor was corrupt and wanted to access his computer to prove it?

- [ ] ARMED GANG BREAKS INTO MAYOR'S HOUSE
- [ ] BURGLAR FALLS ASLEEP IN VICTIMS' BED
- [ ] TERROR THREAT ON FLIGHT 207
- [ ] 70-YEAR-OLD ARRESTED FOR FLYING WITH SNAKE
- [ ] 14-YEAR-OLD DRIVER SCARES JACKSONVILLE

B ▶9.15 Listen and match the headlines to dialogues 1–3. There are two extra headlines.

Common mistake

say / tell them
He will ~~tell~~ he's sorry.

C ▶9.16 Guess each person's excuse. Listen to the dialogue endings to check. Were the excuses believed? Were any of the stories similar to yours in **A**?

I think the burglar is going to say he entered the wrong house.

D ▶9.17 Complete 1–5. Listen, check, and repeat, copying the stress and intonation.

1	This is not what it looks _____.	4	It's not what it _____.
2	Just _____ me out, please!	5	_____, I can explain.
3	It's not what you're _____.		

E ◯ Make it personal   **Not guilty!**
1. Brainstorm what's happening in each photo, and why. Which other people might be in each situation?
2. In pairs, choose and role-play a photo.

Hey, what do you think you're doing?

Just a minute! This is not what it looks like. I was just …

♪ *I don't wanna close my eyes, I don't wanna fall asleep,*
Cause I'd miss you, baby, And I don't wanna miss a thing.

121

Writing 9 A formal letter

♪ *Don't it always seem to go,
That you don't know what you've got till it's gone;
They paved paradise,
And put up a parking lot.*

A Read the headline from a local newspaper article and the letter written in response to it. Answer 1–4.

**White Rose Park Set for Closure!
Town council seeking to sell land to construction company**

1. Who's Melissa writing to?
2. Why's she writing and how does she feel?
3. Find six reasons she thinks it's a bad idea.
4. What are her two suggestions?
5. Who does she want to make contact with?
6. How does her home and place of work connect to the project?

Melissa Gil
23a White Rose Lane
Grangetown
melgil@electromail.com
202-555-0152

The Editor
The Evening Post
Mill Lane
Grangetown

Dear Editor,

Re: White Rose Park Set for Closure

1. I'm writing to you ¹_____ express my huge disappointment after reading your article.. The whole community must be saddened to hear about the possible closure of White Rose Park. What is the town council thinking? How can they close one of the few safe play spaces ²_____ the area simply in order to make quick, easy money by selling the land?

2. Closing the park would affect the entire community. White Rose Park has been used for sports and recreation by local children and families for generations. In the summer, it is used to host concerts and the very popular annual folk festival.

3. People are always complaining that children have far too much screen time. How are they supposed to spend time outdoors if there is nowhere to go? What will the younger members of our community be doing ³_____ five years' time with no safe space to play? My little nephew will be extremely sad when he hears about this.

4. Perhaps local residents could set up a charity organization to raise funds to maintain the park. We could also start a petition and get as many people as possible to sign it. We can then present this ⁴_____ the town council.

5. I'd be very interested to hear ⁵_____ other people who are interested in getting involved to help save the park.

Yours faithfully,

Melissa Gil
Melissa Gil
Second grade teacher, White Rose Elementary School

B Complete 1–5 in her letter with the prepositions.

from   in (x2)   to   with

C In which paragraph, 1–5, does Melissa:
- ☐ suggest possible solutions/ideas?
- ☐ ☐ describe her opinion on the news story and express her feelings with examples?
- ☐ request contact from other readers?
- ☐ refer to the news story and explain why she is writing?

D Read *Write it right!* Then find three style errors in the letter.

✓ Write it right!

When writing a formal letter to a newspaper:
- put your full name, address, phone number, and email address at the top of the letter.
- refer to the article you are writing about with the headline and date of publication.
- keep your letter short and to the point. Make sure it only contains relevant information.
- use a formal style, no contractions, etc.
- you can ask questions or make suggestions.
- end the letter in an appropriate way.

E 👥 **Make it personal** In pairs, read the headlines from a local newspaper. Brainstorm possible solutions and ideas for each story.

> Language center to close all evening and mid-week English classes. Now weekends only!

> Historical buildings to be demolished to construct downtown highway.

> Train and bus prices to double!

> No more nightlife! All venues must close at midnight, even on weekends!

F *Your turn!* Choose a headline from **E** (or one from a real local newspaper) and write a "letter to the editor". Write 120–180 words.

Before	Note ideas for your letter.
While	Follow the tips in **C** and the tips in *Write it right!*
After	Share with a partner to check formality, spelling, and punctuation, then send it to your teacher.

9 A knight at the museum

1 Before watching

A 🔘 **Make it personal** Which of these have you visited? List three items you'd expect to find in each. What's the most interesting exhibit you've ever seen?
1. an art gallery
2. a natural history museum
3. a planetarium

I loved the recent Da Vinci exhibit. It was awesome!

B In which of 1–3 in **A** would you expect to find an exhibit on the items below?
- [ ] armor
- [ ] black holes
- [ ] bones
- [ ] dinosaurs
- [ ] fossils
- [ ] gemstones
- [ ] mammals
- [ ] mummies
- [ ] sculptures

C Use the photo, lesson title and the information in **A** and **B** to guess where August and Rory are. What are they saying? Who do they meet? What might happen next?

Maybe they're ... waiting to meet ...

2 While watching

A Watch and check all you hear.
1. [ ] It's museum week and August was given two free tickets.
2. [ ] Rory has never been to the museum before.
3. [ ] Genevieve is not bringing anyone with her.
4. [ ] Rory has always been fascinated by dinosaurs.
5. [ ] Rory was given a tour of the museum.
6. [ ] Genevieve says mummies are "kind of creepy."
7. [ ] August's text to Zoey didn't reach her.
8. [ ] Zoey got lost and was rescued by Paolo.
9. [ ] Today is the last day the film on black holes will be shown.
10. [ ] Paolo works in the museum.

B Watch again and complete 1–6 with the passive voice. What else did you hear this time?
1. Rory: Well, I _____ always _____ by dinosaurs as a kid.
2. August: You know where all the different bears and mountain lion exhibits _____ _____.
3. August: Mummies! These mummies _____ recently _____ in …
4. August: Since you're a biologist and your studies _____ _____ on animals.
5. August: Next thing I knew she _____ _____ in the crowd.
6. Genevieve: She says when she came back, August _____ _____. And she _____ _____ a tour of the museum by Paolo!

3 After watching

A Answer questions 1–7.
1. What had Genevieve done before she got to the museum?
2. Whose studies were focused on mammals and biology?
3. Who was Zoey with after she got lost?
4. Who is "kind of like a knight in shining armor"?
5. Where else has August seen Paolo, and how does he feel about him?
6. What did August do to try to find Zoey?
7. In which exhibit room did August get distracted?
8. Why does Rory think Paolo might be wearing armor?

B Match the phrases 1–6 to the functions. Can you remember how each phrase ends and who said it?

Describing an experience	Making a suggestion
☐ ☐ ☐	☐ ☐ ☐

1. It's my first time at …
2. I was fascinated by …
3. Let's go see …
4. One minute I was … and the next …
5. Maybe we should …
6. Do you want to go see an exhibit on …?

C *Role-play.* In pairs, imagine you're art critics at a museum. Show each other photos from your phones or from this book and comment on them.

This is an amazing photo. The light and colors are really impressive.

Yes, and the composition is perfect, too. A work of genius!

10

10.1 What drives you crazy?

1 Vocabulary Moods

A ▶10.1 Read and match the highlighted words to photos a–h. Listen to check.

What is your temperament?

Cool as a cucumber, occasionally moody, or chronically short-tempered?

1	Do you ever wake up feeling grumpy?	Y | N
2	Do you have nervous habits, like biting your nails or scratching yourself?	Y | N
3	Do you ever get fed up with activities and people you actually like?	Y | N
4	Do you ever get annoyed by people who are constantly in a good mood?	Y | N
5	Do you ever swear when other drivers do something stupid?	Y | N
6	Do you sometimes go from smiling to crying to singing in a matter of hours?	Y | N
7	Do you ever yell at people for no serious reason?	Y | N
8	Do you ever have to count to ten and take a deep breath, or else you'll explode?	Y | N

CALCULATE YOUR SCORE

For each *Yes* answer, give yourself the same number of points as the question number, e.g., 1 point for a yes in question 1, 3 points for question 3, and so on.

27–36: Hey, calm down! Being this explosive can be bad for you!

18–26: You're temperamental, but not dangerous. Learn to recognize your anger and relax.

9–17: You have your moments of madness, but, in general, you're pretty easygoing. Well done!

0–8: You're the king / queen of cool. Nothing can upset you. Or … Are you simply hiding your true self?

B ▶10.2 Listen, read, and take the quiz. Calculate your score and read what it means. Do you agree?

> I'm not convinced it's all true. I don't think that "nothing can upset me"!

C Match 1–4 to a highlighted word from **A**. Then write another example for your partner to match to the word.
1 "Keep your voice down. Do you want the whole building to hear you?"
2 "I love that you are always so happy. Nothing ever gets you down!"
3 "She was very calm and relaxed before her interview."
4 "Be careful, the tiniest little thing can make the boss angry."

✏️ Common mistakes

           mood
My boss was in a bad ~~humor~~ again.
She has no sense of humor.

           argue / fight
We respect each other and never ~~discuss~~.

D **Make it personal** Go back to your quiz answers. In pairs, ask follow-up questions to find out who is moodier? Any surprises?

♪ You're hot then you're cold, you're yes then you're no, you're in and you're out, you're up and you're down.

10.1

> You mean you're never grumpy? What's your secret?

> Life is short, and I'm just happy to be alive!

2 Listening

A ▶10.3 Listen to a couple talking about the quiz. Which three answers do they disagree on?

> Carlos reminds me of my brother. A bit grumpy!

B ▶10.3 Listen again. True (T) or false (F)? Do they remind you of anybody?
1 Carlos thinks Gloria is short-tempered.
2 Gloria is thinking of taking yoga classes.
3 She used to like her job.
4 She finds her job repetitive.
5 She's looking for a new job.
6 Carlos has seen Gloria swear at other drivers.

3 Vocabulary Binomials

A ▶10.4 Binomials are pairs of words connected by a conjunction or (e.g. *loud and clear*) a preposition (e.g. *step by step*). Try to complete 1–6, then listen to check. Are 1–6 true for you? Know any others?

1 I have my ups and _____, but I'm pretty stable.
2 Little by _____, I'm learning how to relax.
3 I'm sick and _____ of waking up early.
4 I need some peace and _____ in the morning.
5 I hate doing the same things again and _____.
6 Sooner or _____, I'll need to start looking for a new job.

> Not me. I'm much more emotional than that.

B Work in pairs. Take turns to say part of a binomial for your partner to complete.

> Peace and ...   ... quiet. Sooner or ...   ... later. More or ...   ... less. Again and ...

C **Make it personal** Which of these items affect your mood the most? Choose your top three, and then share ideas in groups. What's the most influential factor?

☐ what you eat   ☐ the time of day   ☐ other people's moods
☐ the weather   ☐ the day of the week   ☐ the news
☐ exercise   ☐ the season   ☐ your workload

> I definitely have my ups and downs, but I'm usually in a better mood in winter, when it's cooler.

125

10.2 What do you love to hate?

1 Grammar Gerunds and infinitives

A Read the definition. Does the example annoy you? Do you have a pet peeve?

> **Pet peeve** noun [C] – something that annoys you very much or makes you extremely angry. One of my pet peeves is people eating with their mouths open.

> Yes! When someone talks during a film and then asks, "Who's he?" "What happened?" etc.

B ▶10.5 Complete 1–10 with a–j. Listen to a radio show to check.

a interrupting you   e being the first   h knocking first
b playing with   f to call you   i using the word
c ringing the bell   g to pick   j not returning
d to put their trash

PEOPLE'S TOP PET PEEVES
We asked and you voted! Here are the results:

1 People who are addicted to _____ their phone.
2 _____ to arrive at a party.
3 When someone uses a finger _____ their teeth.
4 People who are too lazy _____ in the trash can.
5 People who promise _____, and then they don't.
6 Friends who honk instead of _____ when they come to pick you up.
7 Bad phone habits, like _____ texts or phone calls.
8 People who keep _____ "like."
9 When people keep _____ when you talk.
10 People who suddenly open the door without _____ first.

C In pairs, match 1–10 in **B** to the rules in the grammar box.

Use a gerund	Use an infinitive
• as the subject of the sentence: ☐	• to express purpose: _____
• after certain verbs: ☐☐☐	• after adjectives: _____
• after prepositions: ☐☐☐	• after certain verbs: _____
Form the negative by adding *not* before the gerund.	Form the negative by adding *not* before the *to*.

➔ Grammar 10A p. 156

D Complete 1–5 with the gerund or infinitive form of the verbs in parentheses.
1 _____ (not know) who a text message is from is really annoying.
2 I get really mad when I find it difficult _____ (sleep).
3 People who use social media _____ (show off).
4 I don't like people who avoid _____ (make) eye contact.
5 People telling you _____ (not use) your phone and then theirs rings!

E In pairs, compare your feelings about the pet peeves in **B** and **D**. Which are your top three?

F 🟢 **Make it personal** In groups, brainstorm more pet peeves. Use 1–5 to help. Choose your group's favorite.
1 People who _____ without / after / before _____.
2 People who try to _____ by _____.
3 _____ing in the middle of the night / early in the morning.
4 People who keep / enjoy / avoid / insist on _____.
5 People who are too _____ to _____.

> People who change the TV channel without asking.

> Yeah, and taxi drivers who keep talking about themselves!

⚠ Common mistakes

of not
Dad's afraid ~~of don't~~ finding a new job.

to
Students who are too lazy ~~for~~ do their homework.

not to
I asked you ~~to not~~ keep interrupting.

not to
We told you ~~to not~~ chew gum.

I can't stand … 😖
I don't like … 😕
I don't mind … 😐
… doesn't bother me. 😐

🎵 'Cause we were just kids when we fell in love
Not knowing what it was
I will not give you up this time

10.2

2 Listening

A ▶10.6 Listen to an anger management group and match the four people (Jim, Mia, Julia, and Vince) to the pet peeves in **1B**.

B ▶10.6 Listen again and circle the correct alternative.
1 Julia **is** / **isn't** new to the group.
2 Mia **agrees** / **disagrees** with her employers' opinion of her.
3 Jim's girlfriend says he is too **sociable** / **aggressive**.
4 Jim responds to Vince's criticism **sincerely** / **sarcastically**.
5 The coach wants to **change the subject** / **use the argument as an example**.

3 Vocabulary   Common expressions with *for* and *of*

A ▶10.7 Listen and repeat extracts 1 and 2. Notice the stress and the weak forms, then circle the correct alternative in the box.

> /əˈfreɪdəv/   /wɒnə/   /fər/
> 1 I'm afraid_of losing my job.   2 I want_to thank you for being so honest.
> The prepositions *of*, *for*, and *to* are usually **stressed** / **unstressed** and the *o* is pronounced /ə/.

B ▶10.8 Try to complete extracts 1–6. Listen to check. Then repeat.
1 She accuses me _____ _____ aggressive.
2 I'm sick and tired _____ _____ that kind of English.
3 I apologize _____ _____ your sensitive ears!
4 There's just no _____ _____ bad grammar.
5 Remember there are ways _____ _____ with this.
6 We are responsible _____ _____ our anger.

C Complete the mind maps with the examples from **B**.

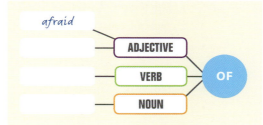

> *My Spanish teacher used to say that a lot.*

D ▶10.9 Guess what they are saying. Listen to compare. Were you right? What would you have said / done?

> *I'd have told him to forget the wedding!*

You should apologize … I'm sick and tired …

I'm afraid … There's an easy way …

⚠ Common mistakes

~~of~~
I'm afraid ~~about~~ flying.

for helping
Thank you ~~to help~~ me with my project.

E 🗣 **Make it personal** In groups, role-play your own anger management session. Choose your pet peeves and elect the coach. Who's the angriest student?

> *Mario, welcome to the group. What brings you here?*   *Well, I'm sick and tired of …*

127

10.3 How assertive are you?

1 Listening

A In pairs, answer 1–3. Any disagreements?
1 What mistake has the teacher made?
2 Why does no one want to tell him?
3 Can we train people to be more assertive?

> Yeah, I think so. A friend of mine took a course like this once.

B ▶10.10 Listen to the first part of a training course on assertiveness. Answer 1–2.
1 What is their definition of assertiveness?
2 What are the benefits of being assertive?

C ▶10.11 Listen to the whole course and complete the notes. Is it all good advice?

"Not ME. YOU go tell him it's misspelled."

> **Common mistake**
> tell
> I can't ~~say~~ the difference between X and Y.

Assertiveness

- Assertiveness is a way of ¹_____
- It's difficult to tell the difference between ²_____
- Assertive people are good at ³_____ because they can reach a compromise
- You shouldn't expect other people to ⁴_____
- You can control your own actions, but you can't ⁵_____
- It's important to ⁶_____ when confronting people you disagree with
- You have to learn to say ⁷_____
- Try saying "I will" instead of ⁸_____

2 Grammar Verb + gerund or infinitive

A Look at the highlighted items in ▶10.11 on p. 175. Underline the gerunds and circle the infinitives after *stop*, *try*, and *remember*. Then complete the grammar box with *-ing* or *to*. Does your language make this distinction?

> **Common mistakes**
> chatting
> Please stop ~~to chat~~ on your phone at lunch. Turn ~~it~~ off ⓘt.

Gerund and infinitive after *stop*, *try*, and *remember*

If you use two verbs together, the second one can be either a gerund or an infinitive. Sometimes there's no difference in meaning:
- I **began** to study / studying English when I was six.
- I **like** to listen to / listening to classical music while I'm driving.

But there are a few important exceptions.
Stop + _____: Not do something anymore.
Stop + _____: Interrupt what you're doing in order to do something else.

Try + _____: Make an effort to do something.
Try + _____: Do something and see if it works.

Remember + _____: Remember that you did something in the past.
Remember + _____: Remember that you should do something.

➜ Grammar 10B p. 156

B ▶10.12 Read a questionnaire from the training course. Match a–h to 1–8 and circle the correct alternative. Listen to check and practice the highlighted words.

♪ *I am not afraid to keep on living*
I am not afraid to walk this world alone **10.3**

a stop **talking / to talk** to her
b try **staring / to stare** at them
c try **crying / to cry** or something
d stop **standing / to stand** there politely
e stop **showing / to show** up for these family dinners
f he'll probably **trying / try** to find a way to get the money
g instead, you write a "Remember **calling / to call** Jane" note
h hey, I remember **lending / to lend** you some money a while ago

TEST YOUR ASSERTIVENESS

1 An uncle you meet regularly at family dinners is very critical of you and your career. You:
☐ say nothing and be friendly. Who wants conflict in the family?
☐ ¹_____. Forever. And tell everyone why.
☐ ask your uncle why he keeps criticizing you.
☐ ²_____. Maybe a little drama will work. Who knows?

2 A close friend has just broken up with her boyfriend. She needs some emotional support. The phone rings, and you see her number. You're finishing an urgent report at work. You:
☐ don't pick the phone up. ³_____.
☐ ⁴_____. The report can wait.
☐ say you're busy and can only talk for five minutes.
☐ are tough. Tell her she should stop crying and forget about him. Then hang up.

3 Your cousin borrowed $1,500 and promised to pay you back by April 30. It's October, and you still haven't heard from him. You:
☐ say nothing and accept the fact that you'll never see that money again.
☐ want to talk to him, but you keep putting it off. Give him a few more months. ⁵_____.
☐ explain why you need the money and negotiate a payback plan and a new deadline.
☐ call him and, in the middle of the conversation, say "⁶_____," as if you'd just remembered.

4 You're standing in line at the bank, and someone cuts in front of you. You:
☐ smile and say, "Excuse me, perhaps you didn't realize there is a line."
☐ ⁷_____—perhaps they'll notice how annoyed you are.
☐ just stay where you are. A few more minutes won't make any difference.
☐ ⁸_____—push back in front of them.

C In pairs, choose the most assertive reaction to 1–4 in **B**. What would your personal response be? Are your answers similar?

In the first one I'd probably stop going to those family meals.

D 🔘 **Make it personal** In groups, say what you would do in situations 1–5. Who's the most assertive? Is it possible to be too assertive?

1 The passenger next to you is playing a loud video game. The flight attendant has already asked him to turn it off.

2 You find out that someone at work / school has been spreading rumors about you.

3 The waiter brings your food after a very long wait, and, when it finally arrives, it's cold.

4 You have a friend who is consistently 15 to 20 minutes late when meeting you.

5 A coworker / classmate you interact with for hours and hours has bad breath.

I'd start _____ing / to _____.
I'd stop _____ing / to _____.
I'd try _____ing and see if it worked.
I'd try to find a way of _____ing.
I'd _____.

10.4 How similar are you to your friends?

I must admit a couple of my friends sometimes drive me crazy.

Me too. I have a friend who's a terrible gossip.

1 Listening

A ▶10.13 Do all your friendships make you happy? Why (not)? Imagine what "a toxic friend" is. Listen to / Watch the start of a vodcast to check.

B ▶10.13 Listen / Watch again and check all the points you hear. Imagine what you will hear in the next part.
1. ☐ In a relationship, both people's needs have the same importance.
2. ☐ Friends and significant others should try to make you happy.
3. ☐ Toxic relationships take away our energy.
4. ☐ Sometimes even close friends can be toxic.
5. ☐ Toxic relationships can impact all aspects of our lives.
6. ☐ The program will suggest ways to escape from toxic relationships.

C ▶10.14 Listen to / Watch the rest of the vodcast and match the two columns.

Antitoxic step	Main idea
1 Diagnose the relationship.	☐ Establish certain limits and be firm.
2 Recognize your role.	☐ Ask other people for advice.
3 Build **boun**daries.	☐ Stay away from people who treat you badly.
4 You can't change other people.	☐ Res**pect** yourself, and others will respect you.
5 Get a second opinion.	☐ Ask yourself how this person makes you feel.
6 Look out for yourself.	☐ Do you put other people before yourself?

Common mistakes
relationship
I'm in a stable ~~relation~~.

look out for / look after / take care of
You have to ~~look for~~ yourself.

D In pairs, summarize the video's advice from the pictures.

Some relationships can take away our energy and …

DON'T WORRY ABOUT ME. I'M NOT IMPORTANT!

E 🗣 **Make it personal** What are the most important things in a friendship? Write your top five. Compare with a partner. Agree on three.

Sharing the same sense of humor has to be one of them.

Oh, angel sent from up above
You know you make my world light up
When I was down, when I was hurt
You came to lift me up

10.4

2 Vocabulary Phrasal verbs

A Complete the definitions with the highlighted phrasal verbs. How many are literal meanings?

- Friends are supposed to give you energy and lift you up when you're down.
- How do you know if a friend is bringing you down? Well, in much the same way that you know you're coming down with a cold.
- If a friend or partner is stealing your sunshine, you need to figure out what you're doing to allow them to do this.
- Are they constantly bossing you around?
- Once you know the boundary that you want to set, stick to it! Draw your line in the sand.

1 _____ sb _____: tell somebody what to do
2 _____ sb _____: make somebody feel happier
3 _____ sb _____: make somebody feel sad
4 _____ sb / sth _____: find the answer, understand
5 _____ sth: continue, not change your mind
6 _____ sth: become sick with something

B 🔘 **Make it personal** Complete 1–4 with verbs from **A**. In pairs, ask and answer. Any surprises?

WHEN WAS THE LAST TIME ...
1 you couldn't _____ how to use a machine without reading the manual?
2 you missed school / work because you _____ a cold?
3 negative feedback (from a teacher, boss, or friend) _____ you _____?
4 you made a resolution? How long did you _____ it?

3 Grammar Separable and inseparable phrasal verbs

A Read the grammar box, and then write separable (S) or inseparable (I) next to 1–6 in **2A**.

> When a phrasal verb needs an object, sometimes you can separate the verb and particle (you can split them up), and sometimes you can't.
> 1 Most phrasal verbs with one particle are separable. If you use a pronoun, it always goes in the middle: Turn on the TV. / Turn the TV on. / Turn it on.
> 2 But some common phrasal verbs with one particle are inseparable: I'm looking for a job. If you're not sure, say it out loud, separating the verb and the particle. If the verb is inseparable, the sentence will sound really strange! I'm looking a job for (!)
> 3 Phrasal verbs with two particles are usually inseparable: She cut down on sugar.

➜ **Grammar 10C** p. 156

Common mistake

When you buy new shoes, try on them first.
              ^them

B Reread the questionnaire in **2B** on p. 129. Underline six phrasal verbs and mark them S or I.

C Complete 1–6 using *it / them* and the particles below. Do you like tests like these?

with (x3)   to   up (x2)

FRIENDSHIP TEST
1 I never argue with my friends. I have never fallen out _____.
2 If one of my friends is feeling sad, I know how to pick _____.
3 I consider some of my friends to be like family. I get along so well _____.
4 If I make a promise to a friend, I will stick _____.
5 If the phone rings and it's a friend, even if I'm really busy, I'll always pick _____.
6 I don't see some of my friends often enough. I'd like to hang out _____ more often.

D 🔘 **Make it personal** In groups of four, ask and answer the friendship test. Add follow-up questions, too. Any unusual stories or perspectives?

Do you ever fall out with friends?   *Hardly ever, but there was this one time ...*

10.5 What do you find hardest about English?

That's not me at all. I find writing hard, especially spelling.

For me, it's speaking. The most difficult thing is pronunciation.

I'm bad at listening. It's really hard to understand native speakers.

Common mistakes

I have difficulty ~~to pronounce~~ *pronouncing* new words.

I have ~~a problem to use~~ *trouble / difficulty using* the present perfect.

I ~~have facility~~ *find it easy* to remember new expressions.

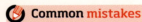

Skills Proofreading

A Mark 1–6 with S (same as / similar to me) or N (not like me). In groups of four, compare ideas. What's the most difficult skill?

	Easy		Difficult
1	I think I'm good at grammar	4	I find it hard to read fast
2	I have no trouble remembering new words	5	I have trouble expressing my ideas
3	I'm comfortable writing in English	6	I have a lot of difficulty understanding native speakers

B ▶10.15 Now write 1–6 from **A** in the gaps in the messages. Then listen to check.

C In pairs, read each message, ignoring the blanks for now, and find …
1. two unnecessary words (cross them out).
2. two missing words (insert them).
3. a missing *s* in a word (add it).
4. a misuse of *-ing* (correct it).

Feeling frustrated with your English? Worried you might not be making enough progress? Wondering what the best way forward is? Send us your message, and we'll try to help you in next week's podcast.

1 My name's Bruna, I'm have twenty-three years old, and I'm from Bucaramanga, in Colombia. I've studied English four years, and some things are easy, but others are very hard! For example _____ (I love rules!), but when I have to interact with other people, _____ and I hesitate a lot. My teacher says that I'll get better, she say it's only a matter of time. But sometimes I thinking I never to become fluent.

2 I'm Byung-Sang, from Seoul. I have studied English since I was a little boy, but, to be honest with you, I don't like English. I can communicate well, _____ (especially emails), but listening is nightmare. _____. Once I spent two week in London, and I am felt really lost. Do you know about if there anything I can do to improving my listening?

3 When I read, I try understand each and every word on the page, but people saying this is a bad habit. I have a friend who she is a teacher, and she told me do not worry about all the new word. But, honestly, _____, for general comprehension. What do you think? There's another problem: How can I use the new vocabulary? _____, but it's hard for me to use them. Any suggestions? Omar, from Istanbul.

D 🔒 **Make it personal** Complete 1–4 with the phrasal verbs in the correct form. Then discuss them in pairs. Are you good proofreaders?

pick up   figure out   look up   put off

1. I _____ all of the mistakes in **B**.
2. I always _____ words in the dictionary if I'm not sure of the spelling.
3. I proofread my work immediately. I never _____ (it) until later.
4. I always check my grammar and _____ any mistakes myself.

132

Are you going to take an English exam?

10.5

ID in Action Making recommendations

A In pairs, list two ways to improve your listening, speaking, reading, writing, grammar, vocabulary, and pronunciation. Share with the class.

To practice listening, watch TV first without subtitles, then again with subtitles to check.

B ▶10.16 Listen to the podcast. Check the two recommendations the teacher makes to each student. Do you agree?

BRUNA
1. ☐ Spend some time abroad.
2. ☐ Don't worry too much about mistakes.
3. ☐ Find someone you can practice with.
4. ☐ Think carefully about what you want to say.

BYUNG-SANG
1. ☐ Watch both easy and difficult videos.
2. ☐ Increase your vocabulary.
3. ☐ Don't use subtitles.
4. ☐ Improve your pronunciation.

OMAR
1. ☐ Vary your reading strategies.
2. ☐ Take a reading course.
3. ☐ Use a monolingual dictionary.
4. ☐ Learn expressions, not isolated words.

C ▶10.17 Match the two columns. Listen to check and repeat.

Making recommendations	
1 Try to focus …	☐ learning "make an effort" instead of "effort"?
2 Have you thought …	☐ of practicing is watching Internet videos.
3 A good way …	☐ consider giving pronunciation a little more attention.
4 You should …	☐ reading slowly all the time.
5 Try to avoid …	☐ on expressing your ideas fluently.
6 How about …	☐ about asking a friend to practice with you?

D Paircheck. A: Cover the first column and remember the full sentence. B: Check. Then change roles.

E Role-play the recommendations for the students as a dialogue.
A: You're a student. B: You're the teacher.
Change roles and suggest extra ideas.

So, Bruna, are you pleased with your progress?

Well, yes and no. I still have difficulty speaking. What do you suggest?

F 🔴 **Make it personal** Think about your English, and note your strengths and weaknesses in two columns, plus any action ideas. Compare in groups, make more recommendations, and note down the best ideas.

My English

Strengths	Weaknesses	Action plan
grammar (verb tenses)	pronunciation – "th" sound	Say "thirty-three thieves" every day. Listen for "th" words in movies and echo them. Ask the teacher to correct me more often.

♪ *I'm only human. I make mistakes. I'm only human. That's all it takes. Don't put your blame on me.*

I'm OK with grammar—especially verb tenses. But I find pronunciation hard, like the "th" sound.

Have you thought about using a pronunciation book with audio to practice? Or finding some pronunciation videos on YouTube?

Writing 10   A forum post

Go, go, go
Figure it out, figure it out, but don't stop moving
Go, go, go
Figure it out, figure it out, you can do this

A Read the forum post, ignoring any mistakes. What advice does Lara ask for? Does she get a good response?

LaraVenice

Good English school in the center of Edinburgh?   Sep 5th, 19:02

Hi, I'm planning to come to the UK ~~for learning~~ *to learn* English during four weeks. I'm not sure which city would be a good place to stay. I'm thinking about Edinburgh. What do you suggest? Also, if you was me, what would you do about accommodations? Do you think it's better stay with a host family or in a hostel or an apartment?
Could you suggest a good school in Edinburgh? Is a good city for students? I'm 23 years old.
What do you advise me doing?
Thanks in advance.

CatCrazy21

Re: Good English school in the center of Edinburgh   Sep 6th, 07:31

Have you thought about to contact the British Council? They are the country's cultural ambassadors. They have offices all over the world and will help you figure out where to go. You should have a look at schools on ARELS (Association of Recognized English Language Services), too.
IMO Edinburgh is a great place for study! There's a university and lots of things to do and places to explore. You ought to contact the University. They probably have courses and plenty of informations for overseas students. As far as accommodation is concerned, how about stay with a host family? You'll learn much more about the culture and also get used to the Scottish accent faster! 😊 Good luck!

B Reread, find, and correct
1. five more mistakes with the use of gerunds and infinitives.
2. five more common mistakes.

C Underline five phrases used for asking for advice and circle four phrases for giving advice.

D Match the sentence halves.

1. You ought
2. You shouldn't
3. How about
4. Have you thought
5. Why don't you

☐ about speaking to your tutor?
☐ leave the door unlocked.
☐ go to bed early tonight?
☐ hiring a bicycle?
☐ to call your mother.

E Read *Write it right!* Then find examples of indirect questions in the forum posts.

✓ Write it right!

- Internet forums are useful places to share / get information.
- Forums have rules, so make sure you check and follow them.
- Acronyms such as OP (original poster) and TBH (to be honest) are often used to make communication faster. These are informal.
- Use indirect questions when asking for information to sound more polite.
- You can use more direct questions when you are familiar with the person you are chatting to online.

F What do you think the acronyms in 1–5 mean? Use these words to help you.

as (x2)	at	by	in	laugh	loud
moment	my	opinion	out	possible
soon	the (x2)	way

1. BTW, have you thought about asking your tutor?
2. I'm a bit busy ATM. I'll call you later.
3. IMO, the Scottish accent is difficult to understand.
4. I'll think about it and let you know ASAP.
5. That's the funniest photo ever! LOL.

G 🎤 **Make it personal**   In pairs, what advice would you give to someone coming to study language in your hometown?

H *Your turn!* Write a forum post asking for advice on one of the following topics.

- Help! I'm giving a class presentation.
- Nice places to walk my dog
- Best restaurant for a family celebration

Before	Decide what advice you want to ask for.
While	Follow the tips in *Write it right!*
After	Use more direct questions when you are familiar with the person you are chatting to online.

134

10 Mad men

 Café

1 Before watching

A Match 1–6 to their definitions a–f.
1. brood and mope around
2. knock some sense into people
3. watch chick flicks and cry your eyes out
4. work your fingers to the bone
5. yell like Tarzan
6. stereotyping

a ☐ to work incredibly hard
b ☐ to cry a lot watching a rom-com-type movie
c ☐ to make someone behave more logically
d ☐ to label something as "typical" in a negative way
e ☐ to express anger or emotion in a loud, primitive way
f ☐ to obsess about what makes you unhappy

B 🔘 Make it personal In pairs, share your experiences of 1–7.

When her boyfriend doesn't call, my sister broods and mopes.

2 While watching

A Watch to 2:00 and answer 1–4. Check all you hear.
1. According to the guys, on a girls' day out, they …
   ☐ cry their eyes out.   ☐ shop.
   ☐ watch a "chick flick." ☐ sit in a spa.
   ☐ complain about men.   ☐ gossip.
   ☐ get their nails done.   ☐ laugh at men.
   ☐ do their hair.
2. What really annoys August the most?
   ☐ that he's tired of competing
   ☐ that Paolo is always the "hero"
   ☐ that he's scared
   ☐ that he's not a knight in shining armor
3. Seeing a shrink means you have to
   ☐ sit in an office.   ☐ talk about your life.
   ☐ work out your problems. ☐ pay unnecessarily.
4. What makes Rory angry?
   ☐ losing a game   ☐ cooking for other people
   ☐ sitting on the bench   ☐ having no confidence

B Watch the video again and order what happened, 1–10.
☐ The guys talk about how to solve their problems.
☐ Rory wonders what a "girls' day out" is all about.
☐ August complains about Paolo's heroic behavior.
☐ Daniel says he's pretty happy and confident.
☐ Daniel explains what he thinks women do when they are out together.
☐ August reminds Rory about how cooking was a disaster.
☐ Daniel recommends that August talk to a therapist.
☐ Rory realizes that Daniel is right.
☐ Rory thinks that stereotyping is a bad idea.
☐ They end up relaxing by playing video games.

C Complete the excerpts. Who says them? Watch again to check.

beating	boxing	brooding	chasing
competing	complaining	experiencing
jumping	moping around	using

1. What if the science foundation starts _____ my ideas without my permission?
2. Rory, you're mad because of the time you wasted _____ after Genevieve.
3. I've seen you both _____ the extremes of emotions. Some days practically _____ for joy, other days _____ and _____.
4. _____ stinks!
5. Stop _____.
6. Yep, nothing's ever so bad that a little _____ can't cure.
7. _____ you two at video games makes me feel the number one winner.

3 After watching

A True (T) or false (F)? Correct the false statements.
1. August needs to build up more muscles and more confidence.
2. Daniel tells Rory and August to stop complaining.
3. Daniel thinks video games are a bad solution.
4. August says that yelling like Tarzan is a great therapy.
5. Rory tried punching an avatar to deal with stress.

B 🔘 Make it personal Do you use video games to relax? In groups, share suggestions for working out anger or stress. Which works best for you?

Dancing is a great way to de-stress.   *Hmm … For me, yelling and exercising is much better.*

C 🔘 Make it personal Which ID Café characters do you like the most and the least: Andrea, August, Daniel, Genevieve, Lucy, Paolo or Zoey?

I really like Genevieve. I'd love to be a musician, and she seems really confident.

135

R5 Grammar and Vocabulary

A *Picture dictionary.* Cover the words on the pages below and remember.

pages	
112	7 crimes
116	Michael's story
118	3 cybercrime risks
119	5 optimistic predictions
124–125	8 mood words and phrases
127	6 expressions with *of* and 6 with *for*
130	4 pieces of advice from the video
131	6 phrasal verbs from the definitions
161	2 words for each sound in lines 5 and 6 of the consonants chart (not the picture words)

B Rewrite 1–6 using the *passive voice.* Do you remember which units of D 3 refer to them?
1 Millions of Americans watch late night talk shows.
2 Technology is killing our creativity.
3 Dyson invented the first cordless vacuum cleaner.
4 Disney gave the cast of *Avengers: Infinity War* fake scripts.
5 Do you think our voices will operate more technology in the future?
6 Brandon is holding his party outside.

C Complete signs 1–6 with *to, for,* or *of.* In pairs, think of two places where you might see each of them.

1 **All thieves will be taken ____ court.**

2 **If you're afraid ____ change—give it to me.**

3  **Thank you ____ not smoking.**

4 **Tired ____ being single?**

5 **Ticket machine under maintenance. We apologize ____ any inconvenience.**

6 **Not responsible ____ personal items left in vehicles.**

The first one looks like it's in some kind of store.

D 🔵 **Make it personal** Circle the correct alternative. In pairs, ask and answer. Any surprises?
1 How many times do you stop **to have / having** a break at work or school?
2 Do you worry about **to be / being** robbed online?
3 Can you remember **to learn / learning** to ride a bike?
4 Have you ever tried **to camp / camping**?
5 Do you always remember **to wash / washing** your hands before **to eat / eating**?

I stop maybe three or four times a day. *And what do you do on your break?*

E 🔊 R5.1 Listen to three dialogues and match verbs 1–7 to the particles. Listen again and find one more phrasal verb in each dialogue.

1 get ☐ with
2 figure ☐ down
3 stick ☐ into
4 lift ☐ out
5 come down ☐ to
6 bring ☐ up
7 boss ☐ around

F Make ➕ or ➖ predictions about these topics 20 years from now. Compare in pairs. Any different opinions?

climate change   colonize the moon
discover time travel   end poverty   over-population
pandas disappear   use house phones

I guess we'll be starting to colonize the moon. *Really? I don't think we'll have started by then.*

G Correct the mistakes in each sentence. Check your answers in units 9 and 10. What's your score, 1–10?

Common mistakes
1 They tried to steal the shop but didn't rob anything. (2 mistakes)
2 This photo was took secretly and has been showing on the Internet. (2 mistakes)
3 Hurry up! By the time we get the theater, the movie will start. (2 mistakes)
4 People shouldn't to go in prison for theft. (2 mistakes)
5 Do you worry with not to pass the final exams? (2 mistakes)
6 Remember locking the doors after to leave. (2 mistakes)
7 I like the people who are smiling all the time. (2 mistakes)
8 Do you want to go with me out to a party this night? (2 mistakes)
9 I'm good with speaking but I have difficulty to understand. (2 mistakes)
10 Is it easy for to use correctly prepositions? (2 mistakes)

Skills practice

*Hey, Jude, don't make it bad
Take a sad song and make it better
Remember to let her into your heart
Then you can start to make it better*

R5

A Listen again to the four stories ▶9.14 on p.120 one at a time. After each one, reread and underline any words that were difficult to hear. Are they:
 a unfamiliar?
 b words with unexpected pronunciation?
 c words which "disappear"?
 d difficult for another reason?

B 👤 **Make it personal** In groups, which do you think is the worst, and why?
 1 a bribery   b tax evasion   c music piracy
 2 a Mondays   b rainy days   c getting up early
 3 a preparing food   b washing dishes   c ironing
 4 a big hands   b big feet   c big head
 5 a being tired   b being thirsty   c being hungry

C Read and order the paragraphs in this article.

Cup of History

☐ In 1966, the Jules Rimet was on display in London, ahead of the World Cup there. On Sunday, March 20, the security guards noticed that the cabinet ¹_____ (open) and the trophy ²_____ (steal). The police ³_____ (start) an investigation, but the trophy ⁴_____ (find) a week later by a man walking his dog.

☐ In 2018, the World Cup ⁵_____ (hold) in Russia, a historic first for the "new" trophy! It ⁶_____ (win) by France for the second time, making them one of only six teams to ⁷_____ (win) it more than once.

☐ Italy won the competition in 1938 and so the trophy ⁸_____ (display) in Rome. When the country ⁹_____ (occupy) by the German army, an Italian FIFA official ¹⁰_____ (hide) the cup in a shoebox under his bed to keep it from the Nazis.

☐ Since the World Cup started in 1930, there ¹¹_____ (are) two trophies. The original, the Jules Rimet, ¹²_____ (give) permanently to Brazil in 1970, after they won their third tournament. This cup has many interesting stories around it.

☐ In 1983, the cup was stolen again, this time in Rio de Janeiro. It ¹³_____ (never / find) to this day.

D Complete **C** with the correct form of the verbs in parentheses. Past or present? Active or passive? Simple or perfect?

E Complete 1–5, then share in pairs. Any similarities?
 1 I'm sick and tired of _____.
 2 _____ is getting better, little by little.
 3 Most _____ have its / their ups and downs.
 4 I go to _____ when I need some peace and quiet.
 5 It annoys me when I have to _____ again and again.

I'm sick and tired of this weather. When will it change?

F ▶R5.2 Order the story, 1–5. Listen to check.

 a ☐   b ☐   c ☐   d ☐   e ☐

G ▶R5.3 **Dictation**. Listen and write six extracts from **F**. Listen again, and repeat.

H ▶R5.4 👤 **Make it personal** Listen to these pet peeves and react in pairs. How do they make you feel?

Oh, I really hate it when people do that.   *Really? It doesn't bother me much.*

I *Role-play*. In pairs, choose a pet peeve.
 A: You are doing this action.
 B: You are annoyed by it. Complain to **A**.

 PLAYING LOUD MUSIC   ENTERING WITHOUT KNOCKING
 CELL PHONES AT THE MOVIES   BITING NAILS   EXCESSIVE PESSIMISM
 CHEWING WITH MOUTH OPEN   SINGING OFF THE BEAT

J ▶R5.5 **Question time!**
In pairs, listen to the 12 lesson titles in units 9 and 10. Pause after each one and tell each other the **opposite** of your normal answer. Ask follow-up questions, too, for fun.

Does crime worry you?   *No, not at all. I love it when people rob me.*

Grammar Unit 6

6A Restrictive relative clauses

Restrictive relative clauses identify the word(s) they refer to. They are essential for meaning and don't need commas.

Sentence 1	Sentence 2	Subject of relative clause
A guest sang last night.	The guest was Rihanna.	The guest *who* sang last night was Rihanna.
The class is meeting now.	It's in room 3.	The class *that* is meeting now is in room 3.
The man's dog is so smart.	He lives next door.	The man *whose* dog is so smart lives next door.

Sentence 1	Sentence 2	Object of relative clause
We bought a new apartment.	It's in Dubai.	The new apartment *that* we bought is in Dubai.
She's in love with a movie star.	He's Will Smith.	Will Smith is the movie star *that* she's in love with.
I met a man.	His sister is in my class.	I met a man *whose* sister is in my class.

Use relative clauses to connect two ideas with a relative pronoun.
- Shh! The game show *that* we're all addicted to is on now.
- The contestant *who's* winning is from Atlanta.

Relative pronouns

	Subject	Object	Possessive
People	who, that	who, whom	whose
Things	that	that	

Note: *that* can only be used in restrictive relative clauses. It is optional when it refers to the object of the sentence.
- The soap opera she's addicted to is *Another World*.

6B Non-restrictive relative clauses

Non-restrictive relative clauses are not essential. They add extra information and need commas.

Subject	Non-restrictive clause	Phrase
Calvin Harris,	who is from Scotland,	is my favorite DJ.
My favorite band,	(which is) One Direction,	is from the UK.
The party I went to,	which was last Saturday,	was really fun.
The girl in my class,	whom I had never met before,	was from Argentina.
Shakira,	whose voice is amazing,	is a world-famous singer.

Use non-restrictive relative clauses to give additional information.
- Lady Gaga, who sang at 9 p.m., was unable to leave the theater.

Form non-restrictive relative clauses with **who / whom**, **whose**, and **which**.
The non-restrictive clause always comes between two commas or a comma and a period.

Note:
- do not use *that* in a non-restrictive clause.
- do not repeat the subject or object pronoun in the clause.

Miami, which is one of the most exciting cities in the world, is an expensive place.
NOT ~~Miami, that is one of the most exciting cities in the world, it is an expensive place.~~

The movie that we want to see is playing at 9 p.m.
NOT ~~The movie that we want to see it is playing at 9 p.m.~~

"The editor who turned down the first Harry Potter book, say hello to the publisher who took a pass on Stephen King."

Unit 6

6A

1 Complete the dialogue with *who, that,* or *whose* when necessary.

A: So tell me about the concert ¹_____ you went to yesterday.
B: It was great! There were two performances ²_____ were perfect.
A: Really? Wow! Who performed?
B: The first singer ³_____ I heard was Bruno Mars! He's awesome.
A: I love him! Isn't he touring with ... oh, what's the name of that band ⁴_____ lead singer is from New Jersey?
B: That's Bon Jovi. They're the band ⁵_____ Bruno sang with! There were lots of people in the audience ⁶_____ were amazed by their performance.

2 Which gaps, 1–6 in **1**,
  a) could also be *which*?
  b) are correct with no relative pronoun?

3 Combine the two sentences with *who, that, which,* or *whose*.
  1 I'm sick of that talk show host. She complains too much.
  2 We always watch the international news. It's on at 6 p.m.
  3 Meghan's not interested in the guy. His ex-girlfriend just broke up with him.
  4 *Star Trek* is a sci-fi show. It has been popular since the 1960s.
  5 There are a lot of movies. They are based on superheroes.

6B

1 Correct the mistakes in 1–5.
  1 This movie, that is based on a novel by Virginia Woolf, won many awards.
  2 My favorite author, which I've liked since grade school, is J.K. Rowling.
  3 They speak a language, that is called Basque, we hadn't heard before.
  4 I saw Emma Stone, who's latest movie was brilliant, in the mall this morning.
  5 He loves dancing to "Gangnam Style," that is a popular music video from South Korea.
  6 Tom Cruise who's one of world's richest actors, he has three children and three ex-wives.

2 Match columns A, B, and C to make non-restrictive relative clauses.

A
1 The first book I read,
2 Cardi B,
3 That TV show,
4 My first teacher,
5 The time machine in *Back to the Future*,

B
☐ which was set in 1985,
☐ which was canceled after three episodes,
☐ who I remember well,
☐ which I really loved,
☐ whose real name is Belcalis Marlenis Almánzar,

C
☐ performed for a huge audience.
☐ was Mrs. Rodriguez.
☐ was called *Zero Hour*.
☐ was a Delorean.
☐ was *Harry Potter*.

3 Order the words in 1–5 to make relative clauses. Remember to use commas in the non-restrictive clause.
  1 the movie / saw / which / that / I / Academy Awards / two / favorite / won / my / is / .
  2 known for / has / shows / which / Canada / great / is / its / locations / popular / TV / a lot of / .
  3 one of / famous / Johnny Depp / is / who / actors / in his fifties / most / Hollywood's / .
  4 is / J.K. Rowling / who / the / of / crime / author / the / novel / Robert Galbraith / really / is / .
  5 last / superheroes / *The Avengers* / movie / which / about / is / was / summer / released / a / .

4 🎤 **Make it personal** Describe your favorites in these five categories. Use non-restrictive relative clauses to give additional information.

movie   movie star   movie character   novel   TV show

My favorite TV show is Brooklyn Nine-Nine, which is set in New York, I think it is really funny.

149

Grammar Unit 7

7A Reported speech

Direct speech	Subject	Reporting verb	Reported speech
I **go** there every day.	I		he / she **went** there every day.
I **am working** here.	You		he / she **was working** there.
We'**ll travel** tomorrow.	He	**said** (that)	you / they **would travel** the next day.
I **would try** if I **could**.	She	**told** (me, him, her, etc.)	he / she **would have tried** if he / she **could have**.
They **went** to the U.S.	We		they **had gone** to the U.S.
I **was talking** to her.	They		he / she **had been talking** to her.
We **had done** this before.			you / they **had done** that before.

Use **Reported speech** to report what someone said / told (you).
Form:
- a Simple past reporting verb (*said, told*, etc.).
- the main verb moves one tense back.

In reported speech, also remember to change:
- pronouns (*I* → *he / she*; *we* → *they*)
- place and time expressions (*this* → *that*; *here* → *there*, *tonight* → *that night*; *yesterday* → *the day before*, etc.)

The most common reporting verbs are: *describe, emphasize, explain, mention, observe, recommend, report, say, speculate, state, suggest, tell (someone)*.

Note: use an object (*you, me, her, John*, etc.) with **tell**.
She **told me** she was traveling. NOT ~~She told she was traveling.~~

7B Indirect questions

Expression	*if* / *whether* / *wh* word	Statement
	if	I could leave my luggage here?
Do you have any idea	whether	there's free Wi-Fi in the lobby?
	what / which	payment methods I can use?
Do you know / remember	when	the restaurant opens?
Could you tell me	where	the restroom is?
	why	I can't get my keycard to work?
Can you tell me	how	to get to the nearest bank?
	who	is in charge here?

Use indirect questions to sound more polite.
For *yes / no* questions, use *if* or **whether**. **Whether** is more formal.
Form:
Indirect question expression + *if* / *whether* / *wh* word + inversion of auxiliary and subject.
Note: don't use a question mark with the indirect question expressions *I wonder* or *I'd like to know*.

7C Reported questions, commands, and requests

Reported questions

Use expressions like *He asked me* and *They wanted to know* to report questions.
▸ "Do you know the answer?" → I asked him if he knew the answer.
▸ "What time does the flight leave?" → They wanted to know what time the flight left.
▸ "Where did I leave my purse?" → She wondered where she had left her purse.

Form:
- as in reported speech, the main verb moves one tense back and there are changes to pronouns and place and time expressions.
- use the same word order as a statement.
They asked us who the man was. NOT ~~They asked us who was the man.~~
- reported questions end with a period, not a question mark.

Note: use an object with *ask*.

Reported commands and requests

Use *ask* when reporting requests and *told* when reporting commands.
▸ "Can I see your passport, please?" → He asked to see my passport.
▸ "Place your bags on the X-ray machine." → She told me to place my bags on the X-ray machine.

Form:
- commands and requests are usually reported using **(not) + to + infinitive**.
▸ "Please remember! Don't forget the homework!" → He told us **not to forget** the homework.
- *ask* and *tell* are followed by an object.
▸ She **asked / told them** to help her.

Unit 7

7A

1 Correct the mistakes in 1–7.
1 He said he doesn't know where was the parking lot.
2 She mentioned that she won't be back in time for the party.
3 She said she not know where was David.
4 They never told us where is the party.
5 He explained why there will be an extra charge on the bill.
6 He said me that he wasn't going to Lima.
7 They told they would be late.

2 Complete 1–5 with the correct form of these verbs.

| be | learn | locate | mention | not know |

1 The teacher promised that we _____ Spanish in three weeks!
2 He told us he _____ if he could fix the Internet connection.
3 We wondered where the restrooms were _____.
4 She _____ that the concierge would not be back until 1 p.m.
5 The manager said that the elevators _____ broken.

7B

1 Complete 1–5 with the words below.

| what | when | whether | where | who |

1 Do you know _____ the changing rooms are?
2 I'd like to know _____ or not the flight will be on time.
3 Could you tell me _____ the Internet is going to be working again?
4 Do you have any idea _____ he was trying to say?
5 Could you tell me _____ I have to contact to solve this problem?

2 Match 1–5 to a–e to form indirect questions.
1 I wonder if you can
2 Could you please
3 Do you happen to know
4 Could you tell me whether
5 Do you have any idea what

a ☐ what time the train leaves?
b ☐ this button on my phone is for?
c ☐ this bus is going downtown or not?
d ☐ tell me where I put my keys.
e ☐ remind us when the next flight leaves?

3 You're a polite tourist in a hotel. Prepare indirect questions to ask about five of these things.

| ATM | cheap stores | free parking | free Wi-Fi |
| good restaurant | gym | restroom | safe |
| swimming pool |

Could you tell me where the restroom is?

7C

1 Order the words in 1–6 to make sentences.
1 asked / knew / if / he / get / to / repair / how / shop / I / to / a / .
2 she / me / take / Main Street / left / a / to / told / on / .
3 not / for / late / the / told / they / us / to / be / lecture / .
4 actor / reporter / asked / what / was / favorite / the / his / movie / the / .
5 her / asked / instructor / what / in / time / hand / could / she / the / paper / the / .
6 soccer player / the / time / training / what / started / new / asked / the / coach / the / .

2 Complete 1–4 with reported questions.
1 A: Excuse me, is there an ATM nearby?
   B: Sorry, what did you ask me?
   A: I asked _____.
2 A: What's your rate for a single room?
   B: Excuse me, I didn't understand what you said.
   A: I asked _____.
3 A: Do you know where the bus station is?
   B: Pardon me? I didn't catch what you said.
   A: I asked _____.
4 A: Did you talk to your girlfriend about it?
   B: What did you say?
   A: I asked _____.

3 Report the instructions using *You told us (not) to*.
1 Don't blame me.
2 Keep calm and carry on.
3 Don't worry, be happy.
4 Enjoy yourselves but don't go crazy!

151

Grammar Unit 8

8A Modal perfects – *must have, can't have, might / may have*

Use **Modal perfects**:
1 to speculate about the past.
- You **must have** been really upset when that happened.
- It **can't have** been easy to give up chocolate!
2 to express possibility or uncertainty.
- They **might have** left the party early ... I don't see them!
- Do you think the area **may have** flooded?

Form:
Subject + modal + *have* + past participle.

Note:
must have = we're sure something **did** happen
can't have = we're sure it **didn't** happen

8B Causative form

Use the **Causative** form to talk about services / actions that other people do for you.
- Do you know where I can **have my car fixed**?
- She doesn't **get her hair styled** by a professional.
- You **got your teeth whitened**, didn't you?
- Are you **getting your computer fixed**?
- We're going to **have a class photo taken** at school tomorrow.

Form:
Subject + *get* / *have* + object + past participle.
Remember: *get* / *have* can be in any tense.

Note: when other people do bad things to you, it's more common to use *have* instead of *get*.
- He **had** his car stolen last night.
(He didn't ask / pay anyone to do it = not a service.)

8C Tag questions

Tag question	
⊕ **Statement**	⊖ **Question tag**
We're crazy to be doing this,	aren't we?
She has already traveled to Europe,	hasn't she?
I think Chris and Sue went to the beach,	didn't they?
He had planned on coming over,	hadn't he?
I'm sure you'll be fine,	won't you?
⊖ **Statement**	⊕ **Question tag**
She didn't do this correctly,	did she?
You have no idea what I'm talking about,	do you?
They weren't married, I think,	were they?
I haven't told her anything,	have I?
He would never ask her out,	would he?
We've got nothing to lose,	have we?

Form:
- Subject + ⊕ statement + comma + ⊖ auxiliary + subject?
- Subject + ⊖ statement + comma + ⊕ auxiliary + subject?
- Keep the tenses the same.

Use:
- rising intonation to check information that you are not sure about.
- falling intonation to state your opinion and invite the other person to comment.

Note:
- a **question tag** is the "mini-question" after the comma.
- a **tag question** is the whole sentence, plus the "mini-question."
- even when the verb in the statement is ⊕, if its meaning is ⊖ because of words like *never, no, nothing, nobody*, etc., the **question tag** should be ⊕.
- You never enjoyed sports at school, **did you**?

"But in your business, being laughed at is *good*, isn't it?"

Unit 8

8A

1 Complete 1–5 with *can't have, may have, must have,* and the past participle of the verb in parentheses.
1. You drove from Chicago to L.A.! That _____ a long time! (take)
2. I don't know why the traffic is so slow. There _____ an accident. (be)
3. That loud sound _____ all the animals. (scare)
4. "What was that noise?" "I don't know, it _____ a cat or something." (be)
5. Well, she _____ too hard for her keys. They're on the table! (look)

2 Prepare at least two sentences about each photo a–d, using *must have / might have / can't have* to apologize, criticize, or sympathize.

A: *Excuse me, but this bill can't have been calculated correctly. It's too expensive.*
B: *Sorry, but you might have forgotten this is a French gourmet restaurant.*

8B

1 Complete 1–5 with the correct form of *have / get* of these verbs.

break   change   check   install   rebuild   steal

1. Do you go to Dr. Smith to _____ your teeth _____?
2. This neighborhood is getting dangerous. Joe _____ his car _____ last night.
3. Their kitchen looks really nice now, after they _____ it _____.
4. My car sounds a little strange. I think I need to _____ the oil _____.
5. Grandpa _____ his house _____ into, so he _____ an alarm _____ and now he feels more secure.

2 Describe two things you can get done by these people.
a. a beauty technician
b. a mechanic
c. a doctor
d. a construction worker
e. an artist

You could get your nails done by a beauty technician.

8C

1 Complete 1–6 with the correct tag.
1. This coat doesn't make me look overweight, _____?
2. You were going to say "yes," _____?
3. I'm not very good at managing these files, _____?
4. That's absolutely incredible, _____?
5. They haven't gone home yet, _____?
6. She got her car fixed before the trip, _____?

2 Look at photos a–d and make tag questions using the words in parentheses.

He / can't

You / not like

You / not study

It / hot

3 Correct the mistake in these tag questions.
a. That boy's too young to drive, isn't it.
b. Lots of kids don't eat enough vegetables, don't they?
c. You'll never speak English if you don't practice, won't you?
d. There are too many plastic bottles in the world, aren't they?

Grammar Unit 9

9A Review of verb families

Time \ Family	Simple	Continuous	Perfect	Perfect continuous
Present	+ He **studies** English. − They **don't work** together. ? **Does** she **live** near here?	+ I'm **writing** an essay. − She's **not working** today. ? **Are** you **kidding** me?	+ I've **lived** here since 1998. − You **haven't seen** her for a long time. ? **Has** she **bought** anything since then?	+ Global warming **has been getting** worse recently. − We **haven't been waiting** for long. ? How long **has** she **been working** here?
Past	+ We **danced** all night long yesterday. − I **didn't go** to Mary's party. ? **Did** you **hear** what she said?	+ They **were fighting** again. − She **wasn't crying** because of you. ? **Were** they **talking** about her?	+ I'd **left** by the time they arrived. − They **hadn't arrived**. ? **Had** they **called** you before you left?	+ We'd **been trying** that before she called. − They **hadn't been talking** to each other. ? **Had** he **been living** with her before she moved to the U.S.?

9B Passive voice

Simple passive

Present	am / is / are (not)	Past participle	The chefs here **are known** for their amazing dishes.
Past	was / were (not)		These sweaters **were made** in Ireland.
Future	will / won't		**Will** the construction **be completed** by 2030?

Perfect passive

Present	have / has (not)	been Past participle	Has the bank **been authorized** to send money?
Past	had / hadn't		I wanted to buy that painting but it **had already been sold**.
Future	will / won't have		It **won't have been built** by next month.

Continuous passive

Present	am / is / are (not)	being Past participle	How cool! You're **being followed** on Twitter. The website **is being watched** by the authorities.
Past	was / were (not)		In January 2019, Facebook **was being used** by over 2.25 billion people.

In the active voice, the subject does the action and the object receives the action.

In the passive voice, the receiver is the subject and the "doer" is optionally included as the object.

Active: Tony washed the dishes.
Passive: The dishes were washed (by Tony).

Use the passive voice:
1. to emphasize that receiving the action is more important.
2. if you don't know (or don't want to mention) who does the action.

9C Future perfect and continuous

Future perfect

Use the **Future perfect** to talk about a future action that will be finished before another future time or action.
▸ By next week, we'**ll have been** together for six months!
Form: *will (not) have* + **past participle** + phrases like *by the time, by the year (2030), in (hours)*.

Future continuous

Use the **Future continuous** to talk about an action in progress at a certain future time.
▸ By this time tomorrow, **we'll be lying** on a beautiful beach.
Form: *will (not)* + *be* + verb + *-ing*.

154

Unit 9

9A

1 Complete 1–6 with *Present* or *Past*, *Simple* or *Continuous* form of the verbs in parentheses.
1. We _____ our time this morning. There's no need to rush. (take)
2. I _____ at the light when the bike ran into my car. (wait)
3. She _____ to download that file but her laptop froze halfway through. (try)
4. Students always _____ new words on that language website. (pick up)
5. We _____ in dangerous areas at night. (not walk)
6. _____ you _____ TV when I texted you? (watch)

2 Complete the dialogues with the correct form of the verbs. Use contractions where possible.
1. A: What _____? (you / do)
   B: Well, I _____ this show about the history of crime. It's so interesting. (watch)
2. A: Really? I _____ you _____ into history. (not know) (be)
   B: Yeah, I guess I _____. _____ the story of Al Capone? (be) (you / hear)
3. A: Oh, yeah! _____ he the guy who _____ alcohol back in the 20s? (be) (sell)
   B: Yep, that _____ him. He _____ one of the most notorious criminals in history, until he _____ in 1947. (be) (be) (die)

3 Describe pictures a and b. Use as many verb tenses as you can.

9B

1 Complete 1–6 with *has / have / had + been*.
1. We're sorry. The phone number _____ changed.
2. I tried to download the song, but the site _____ shut down.
3. Lately it seems like books _____ replaced by digital texts.
4. The movie _____ nominated for three awards, but didn't win any.
5. They _____ (not) _____ notified of the flight's cancellation and are still waiting at the airport!
6. Excuse me, ma'am. _____ your passport _____ stamped?

2 Correct the seven mistakes.

Welcome to the **ALCATRAZ NATIONAL PARK**. Our website is designing to help you understand the history of Alcatraz.
Our visitors' center has just being renovated and guided tours being given every hour. Alcatraz prison is built in 1933 and have been one of the most famous federal prisons in the U.S.
The National Park Service is being dedicated to keeping the park up to date, clean, and accessible for all visitors. The park will be not held responsible for cancellation due to weather.

9C

1 Complete 1–5 with the *Future perfect* or *Future continuous* of the verbs in parentheses.
1. The new student center building _____ by the time school starts. (not finish)
2. I really don't know what I _____ next week. (do)
3. By next June, I _____ in this town for five years. (live)
4. I think the government _____ this problem for years to come. (debate)
5. Don't worry, they _____ the exhibit before you see it. (not take down)

2 🔘 **Make it personal** Describe what you think will be happening or have happened in the future to at least five of these.

extinction of animals   genetically-modified food
new forms of transportation   growing old
living in space   soccer players' salaries

By 2050, I think people will be living on Mars.

155

Grammar Unit 10

10A Gerunds and infinitives

Use **gerunds**:
1 as the subject of a sentence
2 for an activity in progress
3 after prepositions or adjective + prepositions
4 after specific verbs

- *Listening* to music always calms him down.
- I really don't like **looking** at your mess.
- She never asks **before using** my computer!
- We are sick **of standing** here and **waiting** for tickets.
- She got angry **without knowing** the whole story.

Verb + gerund

admit	deny	imagine	regret
adore	dislike	keep	risk
advise	enjoy	mind	spend (time)
avoid	fed up with	miss	suggest
can't help	feel like	practice	understand
consider	finish	quit	waste (time)

Use **infinitives**:
1 to express purpose
2 after adjectives
3 after specific verbs

- I'm studying hard **to get** good grades.
- It will be impossible **to finish** this on time.
- I was stupid **not to tell** the truth.

Form: must have = we're sure something **did** happen
can't have = we're sure it **didn't** happen

Verb + infinitive

afford	demand	offer	remember
agree	expect	plan	seem
appear	fail	prepare	stop
arrange	forget	pretend	wait
ask	hope	promise	want
decide	manage	refuse	wish

10B Verb + gerund or infinitive

Using the gerund **G** or infinitive **I** after *forget, remember, stop,* and *try* changes the meaning.

Forget

I not do something that you should do / have done.	I forgot **to bring** my ID!
G a planned activity that is canceled.	Well, you can forget **coming** to my party! I'm uninviting you.

Remember

I remember something you should do.	He never remembers **to lock** his car.
G remember an event or action in the past.	I remember **seeing** her at the party.

Stop

I interrupt an activity to begin another.	She was lost so she stopped **to get** directions.
G interrupt or quit something.	She stopped **smoking** last year.

Try

I make an effort to do something.	He'll try **to go** to your party, but he's very busy.
G do something and see if it works.	I'll try **talking** to her about it. She might change her mind.

After certain verbs, there is little change in meaning.
- She doesn't like **talking** / **to talk** about her problems.
- I prefer **working** / **to work** alone.

Verb + gerund or infinitive

begin	continue	like	prefer
choose	hate	love	start

10C Separable and inseparable phrasal verbs

Separable phrasal verbs

Most phrasal verbs with one particle are **separable** and can take a direct object (*the book, your friend*) between the verb and the particle or after the particle. If the object is a pronoun, it **must** go between the verb and the particle.
- Mike was afraid to **ask** *Julie* **out**, but he finally **called** *her* **up**.
- We tried to **cheer** *the team* **up** by **taking** *them* **out**.

Mike finally called her up. NOT ~~Mike finally called up her.~~

Inseparable phrasal verbs

With **inseparable phrasal verbs**, objects (and pronouns) cannot come between the verb and particle.
She turned into a princess. NOT ~~She turned a princess into.~~
Verbs with more than one particle are usually inseparable and the object follows the second particle.
- I know what you're **going through**. It's a really hard time.
- Let's **catch up** when we're not so busy.
- You know he's not easy to **get along with**.

Separable	Inseparable
Don't **throw** the bottles **away**.	I'm **looking forward to** it.
Can I **try** your glasses **on**?	Will we ever **run out** of oil?
Can you **turn** the heat **up**?	If I make a plan, I **stick to** it.
Switch your phone **off**!	I'm sorry, we've **sold out**.
Plug it **into** the wall socket.	This sofa **turns into** a bed.
I **cut** salt **out** of my diet.	What's that statue **made of**?
I'm cooking. Please **keep** the cat **away**.	My car **broke down** on the highway.
Please **hear** me **out**!	The office was **broken into**.
Stop **putting** it **off**!	Nick hasn't **showed up** yet.

Unit 10

10A

1 Complete 1–5 with the correct form of these verbs.

avoid   call   like   promise   wake up

1 I _____ last night to ask for your advice.
2 She _____ answering texts or calls when she's having dinner.
3 I've never _____ playing video games.
4 We often _____ feeling too tired to work.
5 She always _____ to help me tidy up, but she never does.

2 Correct two mistakes in each of 1–6.

1 I don't mind to drive you for the train station.
2 She's not interested on listen to his problems.
3 It's a very interesting subject for talking about.
4 They got fed up with hear to neighbor's noisy party.
5 I hope you seeing again one day soon.
6 I usually prefer watch movies to read books.

10B

1 Circle the correct alternative in 1–5.

1 Lee's so afraid of **making** / **to make** a mistake that he doesn't try.
2 You can try **change** / **changing** my mind if you want, but it won't work.
3 After joining www.stopthejunk.com we stopped **to get** / **getting** spam.
4 Alex hadn't thought about **to do** / **doing** anything special for her birthday.
5 I can't stand people who bump into me on the street without **to apologize** / **apologizing**.

2 Match 1–5 to a–e to make sentences.

1 I'm looking forward to
2 They've planned on
3 We prefer not
4 She hopes
5 Don't forget

a ☐ to sit near the aisle.
b ☐ to turn on the security system when you leave.
c ☐ to graduate next year so she can get a job.
d ☐ seeing you next weekend! We'll have a great time.
e ☐ visiting the art museum this Saturday.

3 Describe photos a–d using *forget*, *remember*, *stop*, and *try*.

 a  b

 c  d

In the first photo, I hope she doesn't forget to pack her passport.

10C

1 Complete 1–6 with the correct separable or inseparable phrasal verb and an object.

cut down on   grow up   look at   pick up
run into   run out of

1 Jose _____ in a beautiful neighborhood of Buenos Aires.
2 Yumi needed bread but forgot to _____ after work.
3 They're mad at Jeff and hope they don't _____ at the party.
4 Lu eats too many sweets. She's trying to _____.
5 The pop star walked by and he couldn't stop _____.
6 My car's _____ so I can't drive you to the station.

2 Order the words in 1–5 to make sentences.

1 with / wants / she / boyfriend / break / her / to / up / .
2 put / can't / up / noise / I / all / on / weekend / with / that / the / .
3 that / should've / tried / you / sweater / on / .
4 he / can / he / call / any / time / up / us / wants / .
5 away / best / when / seven / was / my / I / old / moved / years / friend / .

3 🔵 **Make it personal** Correct the mistakes in 1–5. Then prepare questions for 1–5.

1 When I learn a new word, I try it on with my friends.
2 Tom is going to ask out her on a date.
3 It's difficult to figure it out what new words mean.
4 He always forgets to turn the lights before he goes to bed.
5 She'd been making a cake when she ran out eggs of.

How do you remember new words?

157

Verbs

Irregular verbs

Irregular verbs can be difficult to remember. Try remembering them in groups with similar sounds, conjugation patterns, or spellings.

Simple past and Past participle are the same

Base form	Simple past	Past participle
bring	brought /brɔt/	brought
buy	bought	bought
catch	caught /cɔt/	caught
fight	fought	fought
teach	taught	taught
think	thought	thought
feed	fed	fed
feel	felt	felt
keep	kept	kept
leave	left	left
mean	meant /mɛnt/	meant
meet	met	met
sleep	slept	slept
lay	laid	laid
pay	paid	paid
sell	sold	sold
tell	told	told
send	sent	sent
spend	spent	spent
stand	stood /stʊd/	stood
understand	understood	understood
lose	lost	lost
shoot	shot	shot
can	could	could
will	would	would
build	built /bɪlt/	built
find	found /faʊnd/	found
hang	hung	hung
have	had	had
hear	heard /hɜrd/	heard
hold	held	held
make	made	made
say	said /sɛd/	said
sit	sat	sat
swing	swung /swʌŋ/	swung
win	won /wʌn/	won

Base form and Past participle are the same

Base form	Simple past	Past participle
become	became	become
come	came	come
run	ran	run

No changes across the three forms

Base form	Simple past	Past participle
cost	cost	cost
cut	cut	cut
hit	hit	hit
let	let	let
put	put /pʊt/	put
quit	quit /kwɪt/	quit
set	set	set
split	split	split

Special cases

Base form	Simple past	Past participle
be	was / were	been
draw	drew /dru:/	drawn /drɔn/
fly	flew /flu:/	flown /floʊn/
lie	lay	lain
read	read /rɛd/	read /rɛd/

Simple past + -en

Base form	Simple past	Past participle
beat	beat	beaten
bite	bit	bitten
break	broke	broken
choose	chose	chosen
forget	forgot	forgotten
freeze	froze	frozen
get	got	got / gotten
speak	spoke	spoken
steal	stole	stolen
wake	woke	woken

Verbs

Simple past + -en

Base form	Simple past	Past participle
beat	beat	beaten
bite	bit	bitten
break	broke	broken
choose	chose	chosen
forget	forgot	forgotten
freeze	froze	frozen
get	got	got / gotten
speak	spoke	spoken
steal	stole	stolen
wake	woke	woken

Base form + -en

Base form	Simple past	Past participle
drive	drove	driven /drɪvən/
eat	ate	eaten
fall	fell	fallen
give	gave	given
ride	rode	ridden /rɪdən/
see	saw /sɔ/	seen
shake	shook	shaken
take	took	taken
write	wrote	written /rɪtən/

Base form ending in o + -ne

Base form	Simple past	Past participle
do	did	done /dʌn/
go	went	gone /gɔn/

i - a - u

Base form	Simple past	Past participle
begin	began	begun
drink	drank	drunk
ring	rang	rung
sing	sang	sung
swim	swam	swum

ow - ew - own

Base form	Simple past	Past participle
blow	blew /bluː/	blown
grow	grew	grown
know	knew	known
throw	threw	thrown

ear - ore - orn

Base form	Simple past	Past participle
swear	swore	sworn
tear /tɛr/	tore	torn
wear	wore	worn

Common stative verbs

Thinking / opinions

(dis)agree	imagine	realize	suppose
believe	know	recognize	think
depend	matter	remember	understand
guess	mean	seem	

Feelings / emotions

feel (=have an opinion)	(dis)like	prefer	wish
	love	promise	
hate	need	want	

Senses

see	taste	feel
hear	smell	

Others

belong	have	involve
contain	include	own

Use stative verbs:

▸ to describe states / opinions, not actions.
I believe in God. I hate spiders.
▸ in the simple form, even for temporary situations.
Sorry, we don't understand. NOT ~~We aren't understanding.~~

Note:
▸ Some verbs which are usually stative can be actions:
I think that's a good idea. (opinion).
It's lunchtime, so I'm thinking about food. (action)
We're having a 10-minute break.
▸ A few, especially *like* and *love* are increasingly used in speech as "actions":
I'm liking this burger.
I've been loving you for so long …

159

Sounds and usual spellings

S Difficult sounds for Spanish speakers
P Difficult sounds for Portuguese speakers

▶ To listen to these words and sounds, and to practice them, go to the pronunciation section on the Richmond Learning Platform.

Vowels

/iː/	three, tree, eat, receive, believe, key, B, C, D, E, G, P, T, V, Z	/ɜr/	shirt, skirt, work, turn, learn, verb
/ɪ/	six, mix, it, fifty, fish, trip, lip, fix	/ɔr/	four, door, north, fourth
/ʊ/	book, cook, put, could, cook, woman	/ɔ/	walk, saw, water, talk, author, law
/uː/	two, shoe, food, new, soup, true, suit, Q, U, W	/æ/	man, fan, bad, apple
/ɛ/	pen, ten, heavy, then, again, men, F, L, M, N, S, X	/ʌ/	sun, run, cut, umbrella, country, love
/ə/	bananas, pajamas, family, photography	/ɑ/	hot, not, on, clock, fall, tall
		/ɑr/	car, star, far, start, party, artist, R

Diphthongs

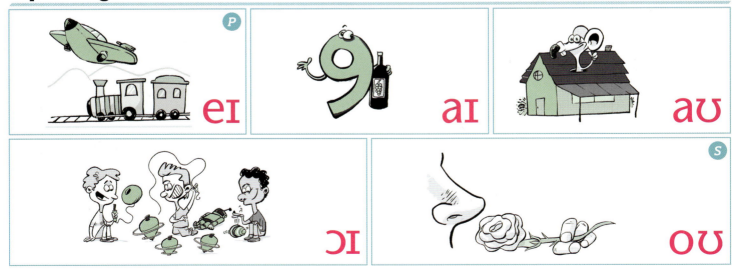

/eɪ/	plane, train, made, stay, they, A, H, J, K	/ɔɪ/	toys, boys, oil, coin
/aɪ/	nine, wine, night, my, pie, buy, eyes, I, Y	/oʊ/	nose, rose, home, know, toe, road, O
/aʊ/	house, mouse, town, cloud		

Sounds and usual spellings

☐ Voiced
☐ Unvoiced

Consonants

/p/	pig, pie, open, top, apple	
/b/	bike, bird, describe, able, club, rabbit	
/m/	medal, monster, name, summer	
/w/	web, watch, where, square, one	
/f/	fish, feet, off, phone, enough	
/v/	vet, van, five, have, video	
/θ/	teeth, thief, thank, nothing, mouth	
/ð/	mother, father, the, other	
/t/	truck, taxi, hot, stop, attractive	
/d/	dog, dress, made, adore, sad, middle	
/n/	net, nurse, tennis, one, sign, know	
/l/	lion, lips, long, all, old	
/s/	snake, skate, kiss, city, science	
/z/	zoo, zebra, size, jazz, lose	
/ʃ/	shark, shorts, action, special, session, chef	
/ʒ/	television, treasure, usual	
/k/	cat, cake, back, quick	
/g/	goal, girl, leg, guess, exist	
/ŋ/	king, ring, single, bank	
/h/	hand, hat, unhappy, who	
/tʃ/	chair, cheese, kitchen, future, question	
/dʒ/	jeans, jump, generous, bridge	
/r/	red, rock, ride, married, write	
/j/	yellow, yacht, university	

161

Audioscript

Unit 6

6.1 Notice the schwa /ə/ in the non-content words (for, to, a, the, of).

1 Ads for a movie, showing extracts of it are trailers.
2 Critics' opinions are reviews.
3 To pay regularly to receive something is to subscribe.
4 To really like something is to be into something.
5 All the episodes in one year of a series is a season.
6 On-screen translation of speech are subtitles.
7 Foreign movies spoken in the viewer's native language are dubbed.
8 When you are unable to stop doing something, you are addicted to it.

6.3 Notice the sentence stress and weak forms.

D = daughter F = father

D Hey, did you have a TV when you were a kid, Dad?
F Yeah, believe it or not. TV has been around pretty much forever. But it's changed a lot in my lifetime.
D What? TV's just TV, isn't it?
F No way! The first TV I remember was in black and white, and it was massive. TVs now, well, you can put them on the wall and they take up no space. When I was a kid, they were like a piece of furniture.
D Huh?
F And the way you guys watch TV is very different from my generation.
D I don't get it. What do you mean?
F Just think. When I was a kid, we watched TV together in the evening as a family.
D Watch TV with your parents? Yuck!
F Yeah, really, and there was no choosing. We watched what Mom and Dad wanted to watch! Now, you all just download or stream everything—sitcoms, movies, news programs—and watch what you want, when you want.
D Live music, soaps, yeah, that's true, I guess. Uh, I mean, I hardly ever watch TV in real time. Only big sports events.
F Or in the car on long journeys ... You never speak to us! Yeah, and TV is just about everywhere now—on tablets, computers, smart phones—you name it.
D Sure ...
F Hm, and even watching TV has changed.
D How? We still use our eyes ...
F Yeah, right, but instead of chatting to friends or family in the same room, everybody uses their smart phones to chat with their "cyber buddies," you know, somewhere else.
D Oh, come on, Dad! That's social TV! Twitter is the best place to talk about TV now.
F Uh-huh. But there's one thing I'm sure of. The word "viewer" will never mean the same again.

6.4 Notice /æ/, /ɒ/, and /eɪ/.

C = Clara E = Emilia

C So, have you been watching anything good recently?
E Yes! I'm really into Stranger Things at the moment. Have you seen it?
C No, not yet. Everyone is raving about it, but, I don't know ... it just sounds ... well ... strange ...
E Well, that's kind of the point. Oh, you've got to watch it. It's amazing.
C So, what's so good about it, then? What's it about?
E It's hard to explain. It's about this group of kids who discover lots of weird paranormal activity going on in their town.
C It's about kids? Isn't it really scary, though?
E It is pretty spooky, yeah, but that's the interesting thing about it. You know, it was rejected between 15 and 20 times by different TV companies before Netflix decided to make it. Apparently, other TV executives didn't like the fact that it was a story about children, but wasn't for kids' TV.
C I guess that is pretty unusual. Does it work?
E Totally! That's the best thing about it! The children's performances are amazing, and I got hooked on the spooky storyline immediately.
C I guess the industry didn't get the concept of a TV show starring kids that was actually for adults!
E That's it exactly. It's so unusual. And, of course, it gave Winona Ryder her big comeback. She plays a mother whose son has gone missing and she's going to do everything in her power to get him back. She's fantastic in it!
C Well, you've certainly sold it to me! I think I'll start watching tonight.
E Great ... I can't wait for the third season. You'll love the pilot episode when ...
C Stop! No spoilers!

6.7 Notice the pauses. //

DJ ... and, remember, today's prize is two front row tickets for Sia's October show. Wow! This week we've been talking about moviemakers who have changed American cinema. And we have Gloria on the line. Gloria, how's it going?
W I'm good, thanks.
DJ The first question is about Ryan Coogler, // who many people consider to be one of the finest new moviemakers around.
W Oh my gosh, I love Ryan Coogler! I think he's the best.
DJ So, here's our first question ... Are you ready?
W I guess ...
DJ Which box office smash did Coogler direct in 2018?
W That's easy. Black Panther!
DJ Correct! This movie made Coogler the youngest ever Marvel moviemaker.
W Oh, wow! What an achievement.
DJ Second question ... In 2013, Coogler directed a movie, which was called Creed. Creed, // which also starred Sylvester Stallone, // was a spin-off from a classic series of movies, Rocky. What are these movies about?
W Can you give me a clue?
DJ Well, // it's a kind of sport that involves two people and a ring.
W Oh, of course! I know, I know. Boxing?
DJ Did you say boxing?
W Yep.
DJ You're absolutely right. The movie, // which won Stallone a Golden Globe, // was highly-acclaimed by critics. I loved it! ... Anyway, here's our third question. Which famous person tweeted this after watching Black Panther: "I loved this movie and I know it will inspire people of all backgrounds to dig deep and find the courage to be heroes of their own stories"?
W Who said that? Oh ... That's a tough one.
DJ OK, Gloria. Time's up.
W Well, I guess another director said it. Erm ... Steven Spielberg?
DJ Good guess, but I'm afraid not. It was // Barack Obama.
W Wow! Imagine an ex-president saying that about your work!
DJ Pretty cool, huh? OK. Question 4 is actually about Steven Spielberg! Are you ready? What did ...

6.9

1 Notice /k/.

A And it's just such a powerful movie, you know, like how science could destroy us eventually. I really think it could be true. I think the whole trilogy is amazing.
B Yeah, some of the experiments they do on animals now, it's pretty sad. But didn't they use animals for the movie, too? I mean, that's bad as well, right?
A No, no animals. They are all actors. The cast members who play apes have to wear this special suit when they shoot the movie. It captures all the movements of the actor and then they can add everything else with computers. It's very clever. Imagine working as an actor, wearing that special suit and acting in front of a green screen all day!
B No way! So the actors actually move like apes? They look so real! Man, he should get an Oscar for that role! Acting like a chimpanzee! That is real acting!

2 Notice /eɪ/.

C Bah! I've got that song in my head again!
D Huh, I hate it when that happens. But that is a great song!
C I know, there's a reason it was so popular. I saw a clip of the video on a TV show last night about the power of the Internet. It's had billions of views. It was such a cool video and the song is so catchy!
D Huh, really? I didn't see that. But yeah, the video was great, wasn't it? And they made a few different versions of it. A Portuguese one ...
C Yeah, and of course the Justin Bieber version.
D I know! I wish I could sing in Spanish like him. They're all good, but I like the original.
C Of course!

3 Notice /ʒ/, /dʒ/, and /g/.

E Hey, I've got this movie from iTunes, do you wanna watch it with me?
F Uh ... What's it about? It's not filled with explosions like that last one you got, is it?
E Well, probably. It's about a bunch of superheroes defending the universe, so I guess there's going to be quite a lot of explosions!
F Oh, come on! You know I'm not into action movies. I like something with a bit of intelligence, you know?
E Duh, always the same. Why can't you just relax and enjoy the fun! All the big Hollywood names star in it!
F Why can't we watch my choice this time? What about that one with the woman who works as a cleaner in a government lab ... with the fish guy ... what's it called?
E The Shape of Water?! No, I'm not watching that ...

6.10 Notice the sentence stress and weak forms.

Here are some tips and tricks to making a short video. Plan your shoot. What is your video about? Sketch out

168

Audioscript

your **idea**. **Think** about what your **to**pic will be and **how** many **people** will be **in** it. **What** do you **want** the **final** video to **look** like?

Technologies: Decide what **media** you will be **using**: **digital camera, camcorder, webcam,** or **mobile phone**.

Capture your **clips: Press** the **record** button a **few seconds** before the **actual shoot**. The **pro**fe**ssionals** always say "**Keep** it **steady**." If **possible**, use a **tripod**. **Take** lots of **shoots** and **still images**— they **might come** in **handy**. **Try** not to **cut** off the **top** of the **subject's head**.

Lighting: Shoot in a **well-lit area**. **Make sure** there is **not** a **bright light** like the **sun** be**hind** the **subject**. Be**fore** your **final recording**, do a **test shoot** to **check** the **lighting**.

Length of **shoot: Plan** your **script** be**fore**hand. **Don't talk** about **one topic** for too **long**, as this may **lose** the **viewers' interest**. **Keep** the **video short** and **simple**.

Sound and **audio**: It's **best** to **use** an **ex**ter**nal microphone**. **Always** be **conscious** of background **noise**. **Always** do a **sound** check **before** the **actual shoot**.

Copyright: If you are **shooting outside**, make **sure** you don't **capture anyone** on **camera** with**out** their **permission**. It can be **difficult** to **use images** from the **Internet**, so be **adventurous** and take your **own**. **Always** gather **written** per**mission** from your **subjects**.

Accessibi**lity**: To **make** your **video accessible** to **all**: **Prepare transcripts**, use **subtitles**, record a **voice**over if you are **making** a **video** of **still images**. And **remember**, have **fun** making your **video**.

6.11 Notice /ɪ/ and /i:/.

S = Sue   J = Joe
S I can't get enough of Ellen. I think she's awesome.
J So do I. I'm a huge fan. She's a terrific host.
S Yeah, I can still remember the Sia interview a while ago.
J Oh, yeah? Mmm ... Sia's not my thing. I like a song or two, but that's about it.
S Really? I think she's amazing. She's written some fantastic songs. She's written a lot of songs which have been huge hits for other singers, too.
J Like what?   S   Oh, you name it! She wrote *Titanium ... Diamonds* by Rihanna.
J What? Get out of here! She wrote those?
S Yes! Everyone knows that ... Anyway, I'll never forget that interview ...
J Why? What happened?
S This is how it goes ... First Ellen asks her to explain why she doesn't like showing her face.
J Oh, I bet *nobody* ever asks her that!
S Ha, ha. Yeah. But Sia is so natural and so funny. She says that she hides her face so she can go to the grocery store or use a public restroom without being recognized.
J Like nobody would recognize her with that wig on!
S No, silly – she only wears the wig when she's performing! Anyway, then Ellen starts saying that they've made a deal that when Sia performs on the show, she'll take her wig off so everyone can see what she looks like. And she agreed to it!
J Really, you're kidding, right?
S Yeah, this was in the days when nobody knew what she looked like. So all the people around me start getting really excited and ...
J What do you mean the people around you?

S I was actually in the audience. I got two tickets for my birthday.
J No way! You were actually in the audience? You never told me that!

6.12 Notice the intonation. ↗↘

J No way! ↘ You were actually in the audience? ↗ You never told me that! ↘
S It's true! ↘ So, as I was saying .... ↘ They make this big deal over pulling the wig off ... ↘ and everyone's going crazy and then ... ↘
J What? ↘
S Nothing. ↘ It was all a dumb joke. ↘ She wasn't really going to reveal herself at all. ↘
J Are you serious? ↗ You mean they were just pretending? ↗ What a disappointment! ↘
S I know. ↘ Talk about an anti-climax! ↘ But, I guess it would spoil her image. ↘ Anyway, she performed live in the studio and I got to see that, which was amazing! ↘ She performed with the dancer, Maddie Ziegler, who's often in her videos and she hid behind this crazy long dress thing. ↘ Typical Sia. ↘
J My goodness! ↘ Yes, Maddie Ziegler is so talented. ↘ What a show. ↘ It must have been great to see her live. I wish I could have been there. ↘
S It was. ↘ I'm so glad I got tickets. ↘

6.17 Notice the reductions.

1 A Wanna come on over for spaghetti tonight? I'm cooking!
  B No way! You're making spaghetti?
  A Well, there's always a first time.
2 C I'm sick and tired of this SUV. Gonna buy a smaller car.
  D Get out of here! You want to buy a smaller car?
  C Yeah. What's wrong?
3 E Janet's turning 18 next week. Gonna get her a puppy.
  F What? You're going to get Janet a dog for her birthday?
  E Uh-uh.
4 G Love this chocolate diet! I've lost ten pounds in two weeks.
  H No way! You've lost ten pounds in two weeks eating chocolate?
  G Yeah. Isn't it amazing?

Review 3

R3.3 Notice the disappearing consonants.

1 I'm dead serious. Savejohnsmith.com is my last hope.
2 There must be a problem with your card machine.
3 Although it's supposed to be for kids, I loved it!
4 They ran out of money to pay for the statue.
5 "Shopping haul" videos are a huge trend.

Unit 7

7.4 (with addition in 7.6) Notice the intonation / emotion on *right*.

1 Notice stress and /ə/
A God, it seems that for every five letters I type, one comes out wrong.
B American keyboard layout, right?
A Well, the salesman said some of the keys were different, but it was basically the same thing, blah, blah, blah. Yeah, right! But how was I to know? He said I would learn fast. Guess he was wrong.

2 Notice stress and /ə/.
C Oh, Dad, you're wearing the watch I got you. How do you like it?
D Well, I'd like it better if it worked properly. I missed two meetings last week. Do you have the warranty?
C Warranty? No, he didn't give me one.
D What? No warranty? Where did you get it?
C Well, there was a guy in the market selling this watch really cheap. He said that it worked just as well as the famous brand.
D In the market! So, this isn't a Rolex?
C Uh ... no ... Maybe not. Oh no, look, it says Polex. He told me he was there every week and he could get me video games, too. Maybe we can ask him for a refund?

3 Notice /aʊ/.
E Oh, my ...!
F What in the name of ...
E Oh no ... There goes my Christmas present.
F But how ... how ... did it happen? You didn't ... you didn't put it up yourself, right? Right?
E Uh ... Well, the delivery guy told me I could mount it on the wall myself. How was I to know?
F But you're not a pro! You're a doctor! Doctors don't install TV sets. What were you thinking?
E But ... he said it was easy and it would only take ten minutes!

4 Notice /e/ and /eɪ/.
G Paula, we're OK, right? I mean, it's just that ... Well, you haven't returned any of my calls.
H Sorry, didn't get your messages—yours or anybody's. My phone's dead.
G Dead?
H I bought it from this site and it came straight from the States. Turns out I can't make or receive calls. Some sort of network problem ... Which is odd, because on the site it said I'd be able to use it in any country ... Guess they were lying. But how was I to know?
G Can't you get a refund or something?
H Oh yeah—easily. They told me that lots of people had complained and so on.

5 Notice /ʌ/ and /ə/.
I One of these days I swear I will throw this tablet right out of the window.
J Oh, come on! It's not so bad!
I You're kidding, right? The screen sucks and the software's full of bugs. To think I could've gotten a laptop! I bought it on ... on impulse, I guess. The store manager said it had just arrived and, you know, I couldn't resist it. But how was I to know?
J Well, try to control yourself next time.
I I know ... But she said that these tablets usually sold pretty quickly, so ...
J You were afraid they would sell out?
I Bingo.

7.7

1 Notice /ɑ/ and /u:/.
M = mother   W = William
M William Bonney Junior! What is this?
W It's my school report, Mom.
M I know what it is! But you told me you'd done well this year. You wait till your father sees this.

169

2 Notice /g/ and /k/.
V = Vanessa C = Chris

V Hi, Chris. So good that you could come. Come in, come in.
C Hi, Vanessa, yeah, it's gonna be a great party. And this must be Pickles. Who's a cute little dog, then? Huh?
V Pickles. Pickles, no! Bad dog, bad dog.
C Ow! Get it off! Get it off! Vanessa! I thought you said your dog was friendly.

3 Notice the contractions and the connections.
G = Geri J = Josh

G Hi, Josh, uh, nice shirt.
J Geri, what is this? James Bond night?
G Josh, it's a cocktail party, you are supposed to look smart.
J But ... but you told me the party was informal and ...
G No, I said "a few friends and drinks," I didn't say "wear your beach clothes."

4 Notice /iː/ and /ɪ/.
A = Andy Z = Zoey

A Please leave your message after the beep.
Z Andy! Where are you? I'm in the line and the movie is going to start soon. Andy, you said that you wouldn't arrive late.

⏵ 7.9 Notice the final /k/.
P = Presenter PB = Paul Le Bernard

P Good evening and welcome to *Tech Talk*, your weekly discussion program on what's new in tech. I'm joined in the studio this week by the editor of *Technology World* magazine, Paul Le Bernard. This week we are discussing young tech innovators. From medical breakthroughs, energy technologies, or engineering electronic devices. First, Paul, what makes someone an innovator?
PB Personally, I think innovators are persistent and inquisitive and they are easily inspired by what they see around them. Take our first example this week, Brazilian tech innovator, Neide Sellin. She's an ex-computer science teacher and she's spent most of her career inventing new technology to help improve the quality of life for people with disabilities.
P I see. We'd love to hear more. Can you tell us what her latest development is?
PB Well, do you have any idea how many Brazilian people have vision problems?
P No, I don't.
PB 6.5 million people. Do you know how many guide dogs there are in Brazil?
P Absolutely no idea.
PB There are only 100 guide dogs! The problem is that buying, training, and looking after a guide dog can cost thousands of dollars. This is impossible for many blind people.
P And this is where Neide Sellin comes in?
PB Exactly. Neide has invented a robot guide dog called Lysa. Her invention has five sensors and two engines. It can tell the user about risks and obstacles via recorded voice messages. With this device, blind users can be guided around indoor areas such as shopping malls and schools. By 2020, Neide hopes Lysa will be used outside, too.
P It sounds amazing, but I wonder if this is really a more affordable solution. Do you have any idea how much it costs?
PB Well, Lysa still costs around $3,000, but this is far cheaper than a real guide dog. At the moment, the device is available to private and public companies, such as airports and hospitals. Neide eventually hopes to improve the dog with artificial intelligence and GPS. Her greatest ambition is to offer dignity and independence to the 253 million blind and visually-impaired people around the world.
P Well, that certainly sounds very inspiring. Let's move on to our next young innovator ...

⏵ 7.11 Notice spellings of /n/, /t/, and /d/ endings.
A = Ann B = Bruce

A Cool phone, dude.
B Thanks. Mom was like, "What's wrong with the one we gave you last year?" and I was like, "Mom, that model is so last year," so she got me this one for Christmas.
A You like it?
B Are you kidding? I love it—especially Justin.
A Justin?
B Yep—my, what do they call it—personal assistant.
A Oh, speech recognition. Sweet. Does it, uh, tell the time, check the weather, and stuff?
B Yeah, and much more. This morning I told Justin I was bored—which I was—and I thought he was going to, like, ask me to repeat the command or whatever, and, guess what, he asked if he bored me.
A Get out! No way! Man, this is, like, so cool.
B Then I asked him if he was hungry and he, uh, he was like, "I'm a cell phone, not a person." Freaking unbelievable.
A Mine has voice recognition, too, but it's not so smart, you know? It'll, like, make calls, set the alarm clock ... and stuff. The other day I asked her to text someone and it took her, like, three minutes to figure out what to do.
B Her?
A Mine's not a dude—it's called Alice.

⏵ 7.12 Notice the weak h in *he* and *him*.

A Dude, I so want to try Justin.
B Here, have fun.

A Sweet ... Justin, where am I?
J I'm sorry, I don't know your name.
A And you said he was smart, right? I asked where, not who.
B He is smart, I'm telling you. Give it another shot.
A OK. Uh ... Justin, will the weather get worse?
J It looks like rain tonight. Here's the forecast for the next two days ...
A Wow ... Pretty awesome, dude. Justin ...
J Yes?
A Do you love me?
B AHAHAH—never tried to ask him that.
J I'm not ready for that kind of commitment yet.
B Isn't he amazing?
A Oh my God, I love him, I love him! Mmm ... What can I ask him now ... Justin, please call me an ambulance.
J OK. From now on I will call you Anne Ambulance.
A What? No way! Uh ... Justin, make me a coffee.
J Ahem, I'm just a phone.
B Don't you just love him?
A But was it, like, a joke? Or did he misunderstand me?
B I think he was kidding.

⏵ 7.16 Notice Mark's hesitation / repetitions and Nick's listening sounds.
M = Mark N = Nick

M What I don't understand is how, how is it that, on the 2001 NAEP history exam, 52% of high school seniors chose Nazi Germany, Imperial Japan, or Fascist Italy as our ally. Not the Soviet Union.
N Hi, I'm Nick Gillespie with Reason TV. I'm here today with Mark Bauerlein, author of *The Dumbest Generation*. A provocative new book that says "the digital age stupefies young Americans and jeopardizes our future." In fact, there's even a, uh, second uh, subtitle, which says "don't trust anyone under thirty." Mark, what's the premise of the book?
M Digital culture ... uh, means, means this to most teenagers. It doesn't open them up to the great big world ... of ideas and artworks and, and, and documents and politics and foreign affairs—which is all out there on the Internet, the potential is there. Instead, it gives them what ... teenagers really care about: other teenagers.
N Mmm hmm.
M Access to one another. They're not going to the Smithsonian Institution website. When Nielsen Ratings examined the most popular websites for young adults, nine out of the top ten, teenagers, nine out of the top ten were for social networking.
N Mmm.
M 55% of high school students spend less than one hour a week reading and studying for class. They spend nine hours a week social networking.
N Sure.
M And this, this is what brought me into this, this work. Studies of leisure habits by, by young adults. And one thing we can say is ... that ... the leisure reading people do, young people do, the visits to museums that they do.
N Mmm hmm.
M The library visits that they do, those have gone down. And that's, that's just natural, because the menu of leisure options for young, for teenagers and young adults, has gotten bigger. Reading is, is, is ... has a smaller portion on the menu ... uh, that they have. And when you go into the average fifteen-year old's bedroom now, it's a multimedia center. Yeah, there're a few books up there on the shelf. There's the laptop, the cell phone, video game console, Blackberry, iPod, and all those diversions give them something a lot more compelling ... than the story of Anthony and Cleopatra and Caesar!
N Mhm.

⏵ 7.17 Notice the stress, pauses, and /ɔɪ/.
H = host T = Tom B = Barbara

H ... which means, that, / yeah, the website was most probably hacked. // Speaking of the Internet, / I just got my hands on a book by a guy called Mark Bauerlein and ... // well, the book's called *The Dumbest Generation* and basically it says the Internet is making young people ... // stupid.
T Well, he has a point.
B Seriously, Tom?
T Yeah. I mean, / we can't deny that teens are buying fewer books and generally ...
H How old are you, Tom?
T 32 ... / We're not reading as much as people in their 40s or 50s, you know? // I mean, / bookstores are going out of business week after week. I find that ...

B Well, it depends on what you mean by **reading**. // It's ... / It's not that teens are reading less, / it's just that we're reading on our tablets ... or e-readers, smart phones, or whatever. // For example, I'm 19 / and I've got hundreds of digital titles downloaded.
H But how many of those have you actually **read**?
T That's a good point.
B I don't know, but, / you see, / the point is ... reading has been on the decline for ...
T Barbara, / but don't you think ...
B Hold on a second, let me finish. // Listen, / people have been reading less for **at least** 30 years, / long before the Internet ever existed. / So, / really, // we can't blame the Internet, can we?
H Well, you may agree or disagree, but he makes some valid points, / don't you think? // Young people have access to more information than we ever did, but, / honestly, how much are they actually / **learning**? I mean, I was talking to my son the other day and he thought Rome was a country ... / **a country**! / And he's a pretty smart boy, you know?
B My point **exactly**! / The book says teens are getting dumber ... / I totally disagree. // If anything, / people's IQs have gone up, / **not** down, / over the past 90 years or so.
T Mmm ... / That may be true, but don't you think there's something wrong here? / **Rome** / — a **country**? / Come on! // And you know what, / I also think the, uh ... / young people are starting to avoid face-to-face contact because of the Internet ...
B Yeah, / I couldn't agree more.
T I mean, / most of my friends spend hours and hours locked in their rooms, / chatting on Facebook. // I mean, this can't ...

Unit 8

▶ 8.2 Notice /ɪ/ and /iː/.

Sure, we all want to look better. Some people try makeup or even plastic surgery. Others choose Photoshop. Graphic designer and Photoshop expert James Fridman is well-known for taking people's Twitter requests for image alterations. James reads people's requests for changes to their pictures and does exactly what they ask him to do. Unfortunately for them, James does literally whatever he is asked.

Most of his images are silly and fun. People ask James to remove photobombers, make them look smaller or bigger, or add something to the picture. But Fridman does not encourage people to retouch their images to meet today's often unrealistic beauty standards. He now has thousands of online followers because of the creative way he doctors the "vain" photos shared on social media.

One heart-warming example of James's work is a photo sent to him by a young woman who was suffering from an eating disorder and low self-esteem. She asked James to photoshop her to make her look beautiful. He responded by making no change to the image and telling her that nothing could make her more beautiful than she already was.

▶ 8.3 Notice /ð/, /θ/, and /v/.

J = Jon E = Eliza
J I used to love Michael Jackson. *Smooth Criminal* had the coolest video ever!
E I know! I loved it, too. Remember that thing he did when he leaned right over. I used to try to do it and fall down ... a lot! How on earth did he do that?
J He must have had wires attached to his jacket. It's the only explanation, surely!
E Well ... maybe it was something to do with his shoes.
J Yes, I suppose, he might have put magnets on them and on the floor.
E Magnets?! To hold up the weight of a man, they must have been very strong!
J True, but it's possible, isn't it? Or maybe he really could lean that far!
E He was good, but not that good! He can't have been able to do that. It's impossible.
J I bet Michael Jackson could!
E Or, I guess his clothes were specially engineered.
J Yeah, he may have had special pants made!

▶ 8.4 Notice /ʌ/, /uː/, and /ʊ/.

Fans all over the world tried to copy Michael Jackson's smooth moves. However, there was one move in particular that left everyone wondering just how he did it: that famous lean from *Smooth Criminal*. Jackson and his dancers leaned forward at an angle of 45 degrees with their feet flat on the floor and then returned to an upright position. So just how did they manage to defy gravity like that?

The truth is that Jackson had a special shoe designed. The shoe had a triangular opening in the heel which attached to a metal hook which emerged from the floor at exactly the right moment. This anchored the dancers to the floor and stopped them from falling over.

This clever shoe did the job perfectly apart from one mistake in 1996. Jackson's heel came loose from the hook during a concert and he fell flat. Luckily, the star wasn't injured, and the shoe was redesigned to make sure it didn't happen again. The shoe was sold for $600,000 after Jackson's death and is now in the Hard Rock Café in Moscow.

▶ 8.7 Notice /tʃ/, /ʃ/, /ʒ/, and /kt/.

What David Blaine is actually performing is an optical illusion called Balducci levitation. This method involves the illusionist positioning themselves approximately three metres away from their audience and at a 45-degree angle. The audience should be a small one so that they are always in this limited field of vision. The audience will only see the back of one foot and most of the other foot. It's also important to wear long pants which obstruct the view of the illusionist's feet. This increases the effectiveness of the trick. The performer, of course, uses various methods to misdirect and distract the audience. Then they simply stand on the toes of one foot and raise the other foot. To the audience it looks like they are really levitating.

David Copperfield had a performance area of a stage with two towers and an arch to support a huge curtain. The TV cameras and the audience could only see the statue through the arch. The curtains were closed and Copperfield distracted the audience with enthusiastic chatter. While this was happening, the stage was actually slowly rotated! When the curtains opened again, the Statue of Liberty had disappeared! In fact, it was simply concealed behind one of the towers and the audience didn't realize they had been moved. The lights on the stage were also so bright that the audience would have been partially blinded anyway!

▶ 8.9 Notice s = /s/ or /z/.

B = Brandon C = Courtney
C No way! You're kidding! You mean just like the one on *My Super Sweet 16*?
B Yeah, but, like, a thousand times better ... Mom was like, "Sweetheart, why don't we have an ice-skating party?," and I was like, "Mom, that is so last year."
C Yeah, totally.
B So ... We're having a movie party.
C Yay! Awesome!
B There'll be a massive outdoor screen by the pool and ... Well, you'll see. It'll be, like, the most fun you've ever had ... Ever. I hope it doesn't rain.
C Brandon, this is so exciting! What will you be wearing?
B Dad bought me this pathetic gray suit and tie ...
C Yuck!
B Yeah, I know! So I told him, "Dad! Hello? This is a movie party, not a fairy tale!"
C Duh!
B And I wanna look just like Alden Ehrenreich.
C Who?!
B You know, the actor who plays Han Solo in the *Star Wars Story* movie.
C Oh yeah, he always looks great!

▶ 8.10 Notice s = /s/ or /z/.

B And I wanna look just like Alden Ehrenreich.
C Who?!
B You know, the actor who plays Han Solo in the *Star Wars Story* movie.
C Oh yeah, he always looks great!
B So Dad hired—wait for it—a fashion designer and we're going to have a new suit made.
C Specially for you?
B Of course.
C That is so cool! And your hair looks awesome! Tell me, did you have it dyed?
B Yeah. I spent, like, four hours at the salon and I got my nails done, too ... Look!
C Oh, yeah! They look so good. So ... is everything ready?
B No! Can you believe it? My parents are, like, so incompetent. I mean, the pool's dirty and Dad hasn't gotten it cleaned yet. Hello? Does he expect me to do it? And Mom can't cook, so we still need to have the cake made. This is all so stressful! I'm exhausted!
C Who wouldn't be?
B And, get ready for this, I signed all the two hundred invitations myself. It took me, like, one hour.
C Humph! Like you had nothing better to do.

▶ 8.13 Notice the three-syllable words.

I love this bedroom. The double bed looks so comfortable. I like the color scheme. The dresser, mirror, and closet are the same color. It looks very fresh. The pillows and the comforter match, too. I also like the color of the walls and how it complements the color of the furniture. There are lots of cool accessories, too, and I love the light and the colorful bird hanging from the ceiling. They add a modern touch. Yes, I really like this bedroom.

▶ 8.14 Notice the intonation. ↗↘

B = Barry M = Mick
B Hey, you've gotta come and see what we've done in here.
M Done? Hmm, you haven't done anything crazy, have you? ↗
B No, of course not! Come and have a look.
M Oh, wow! When did you do all this? It looks fantastic!
B I've been doing it evenings and weekends for the last few weeks. This room really needed some attention. It's great, isn't it? ↘
M Well, what a surprise for Tom! He'll love it, won't he? ↘
B I hope so!

8.15 Notice the intonation. ↗↘

M I can't believe it! You didn't do it all yourself, did you? ↗
B No. I got some of the guys to come over and help me last weekend. We gave the walls a fresh coat of paint, painted some of the furniture. I had the bookcase on the wall made by a friend of mine. I remember Tom saw one like that in a magazine and really liked it.
M It's very cool. That rug wasn't there before, was it? ↘
B No, that's new.
M Tom's been talking about doing this for ages. You know he's going to be over the moon, don't you? ↘
B Let's hope so! I wanted to surprise him when he got out of the hospital.

8.17 Notice the intonation. ↗↘

B = Barry   T = Tom
B Hey, look who's here! Welcome home!
T Hi, Barry. Man, it's good to be back.
B But you said you'd be discharged tomorrow, didn't you? ↗
T Yeah … but they let me out early, thank goodness, so here I am.
B So, how are things?
T Good. I'm feeling a lot better and it's so good to be home. The hospital bed was just … What in the name of …?
B Surprise!
T Oh, wow! What have you done?!
B You've been thinking about doing this, haven't you? ↘
T Yes, but I wasn't expecting this! You aren't serious, are you? ↗ I don't know what to say.
B I knew you'd love it. Just say "Thank you."
T Thank you so much. That's the rug I saw in the department store, isn't it? ↘
B Sure is!
T Thank you, Barry. This is awesome!

8.18 Notice /ʌ/, /oʊ/, and /ɒ/.

… and we will cover that in the next couple of days. So today, as part of our "image is everything" series, we're going to be looking at the reasons behind three different companies—global companies—altering their logos and how their target markets liked—or didn't like—the new versions. And trust me, some of the stories are fascinating. Our very first story involved the international …

8.19 Notice the sentence stress and weak forms.

So, as most of you probably know, Instagram's former logo was considered one of the most recognizable tech logos of all time. The retro brown and cream camera with a rainbow stripe that reminded us of instant Polaroid cameras was iconic, but one day, [beep – 1] for some reason, they sadly decided to change the logo! Users were not impressed and took to the Internet to share their opinions. The main complaint from original users was that it seemed no time or effort had been spent on the new logo. No one really got it, and it didn't make sense. However, [beep – 2] Instagram was trying to attract new users— you know people who might've never visited the site before, and wanted the new logo to reflect how the app had transformed since its creation. The new purple, orange, and pink icon is more colorful, sleek, and modern, but was it a good idea? Hmm [beep – 3], I'm not convinced it works.

Now, take a look at the second slide … As some of you may know, in 2011, Starbucks celebrated its, uh, its 40th anniversary. To mark the occasion, they must've thought: "Hey, let's create a new logo and drop the words 'Starbucks Coffee.'" Well, unfortunately, [beep – 4] most Starbucks customers were not crazy about the new logo … They preferred the old one and didn't quite understand why Starbucks took their name off. Well, personally, [beep – 5] I find the new green logo simple and elegant. You see, Starbucks and its logo are well-known all over the world, and the green circle … well, the green circle speaks for itself. In other words, [beep – 6] the logo doesn't need to tell the world that it's Starbucks Coffee—everybody knows that.

8.20 Notice /ə/ and /ɜː/.

Now, moving on to our third story … and the last one today … Gap released their new logo … yeah, this beauty … a few years ago. They must've tried to create something modern and contemporary, but, boy, were they wrong. The dark blue square of the original logo certainly looked very traditional, didn't it? It was used for more than two decades, and most people loved it. Then the new one comes along and, guess what, everybody … hates it. In a matter of hours, there are thousands—I mean thousands—of negative comments on Facebook and Twitter. A few weeks later, Gap discards the new logo, returns to the old one, and fires the president. How about that? Honestly, I think they were right to go back to the old one. Moral of the story? Well, if it ain't broke, don't fix it!

8.22 Notice /ʌ/, /ʊ/, and /ɔː/.

G = Guilherme   F = Fabi
G I love this class. It's really interesting.
F Yeah, it's really good, isn't it? I wish we'd had Professor Ford last year.
G Yeah. She's awesome.
F That Instagram logo is interesting, isn't it?
G Honestly, I don't like the new one. I really don't.
F Hmm … I kind of like it … It feels, I don't know, different … What about Starbucks? Which one do you like better?
G I don't know … Both are OK, I guess, but I think I like the old one better than the new one.
F Really? Oh, come on! It feels so … old, with the name and all … Well, I don't really like either of them … I'm tired of the green mermaid.
G Now, maybe I'm crazy, but remember the Gap logo?
F Uh-huh.
G I actually prefer the second one to the first.
F You mean the one that looks like it was drawn by a child?
G Exactly!
F You know what? Me, too. They shouldn't have gone back to the old one.

Review 4

R4.1 Notice the spellings of the repeated sounds.

1 I asked, then I parked, and then the problems started.
2 We accuse you of causing the accident. No excuses!
3 Should they accelerate, accommodate, or experiment?

Unit 9

9.3 Notice /ʃ/, /θ/, and /ð/.

1 … And I mean, it's just not fair. You're simply downloading a song! This is not theft! You're not a thief! Why should you go to prison? For using something that's out there for the whole world to use? Just last month they arrested this 19-year-old who'd been downloading CSI episodes. That's so unfair! That's why I really think songs, books, and music should be completely free. Also …
2 So this one's kind of hard to answer, but, uh … Gee, I don't know, maybe … armed robbery … I've lived in this neighborhood for, what, two years and I've never actually seen a robber. So, yeah, I mean, I never even think about it. I feel pretty safe here, actually. By the way, this is really for a school project, right? I mean, you're not going to share this on the Internet or anything, are you?
3 … Uh, yeah. Burglary. Our next-door neighbors went away for the weekend and someone broke into their house. I was watching TV, you know, and I saw the whole thing. The burglar was a woman in her 40s—yeah, a woman, a blonde woman wearing a mask. I called the cops, but when they got there, she'd already left, you know? So, I wonder …
4 Yeah, and call me a pessimist, but, really, I don't see any way out. People are turning to drugs for all sorts of reasons – it's never for just one thing. What has the government been doing to change things? No one knows for sure. And I … well, I think drug dealing is likely to get worse as the years go by. And you know what? The new legislation next year will probably make no difference. I mean, sending drug dealers to prison isn't enough. You see … Excuse me …
5 … Yeah. Well, not only me, but every mother in my neighborhood. I mean, my husband and I are doing OK: brand new car, nice house, we've just had a new pool built … So, you know, all eyes are on us. So, uh … I keep telling my kids to, you know, just run if someone they don't know gets too close … Run as fast as they can, no matter who—anyone can be a potential kidnapper, you know? Or, even worse, a murderer. So, yeah, that's something that worries me. A lot. Oh, and here's something else …

9.7 Notice /w/ and /ʷ/ when two vowels connect.

1 Thirty-two-year-old Shena Hardin was caught on camera driving on a sidewalk in order to go around a school bus that was dropping off children. She was taken to court and the judge sentenced her to an embarrassing punishment. She was told to stand at a busy intersection holding a sign which read, "Only an idiot would drive on a sidewalk to avoid a school bus." Just to add to her humiliation, the event was live-streamed by television crews. Hardin also had her license suspended and was ordered to pay $250 in court costs.
2 It was an ordinary morning in San Francisco's District Court, and then, without warning, someone's cell phone rang and broke the silence. Judge Robert Rather didn't like what he heard: "Whose phone is ringing? Bring it to me now!" Nobody did. "Everyone will be arrested unless I get that phone now!" Again, no one confessed at all. Judge Rather wasn't kidding: all 42 people present were charged with disturbing the peace and sent to jail. After suffering in prison for a couple of hours, they were released, of course. But the judge was permanently removed from office for abusing judicial power. In a recent interview, he said he had been under a lot of stress.

Audioscript

9.10 Notice /aɪ/.
Cybercrime. This is a term we are used to hearing in the news almost every day. In fact, experts predict that by 2025 cyberattacks will have become—are you ready for this—the world's top threat. Cybercrime covers a wide range of different offences. Cybercriminals can delete or change computer records, create fraudulent documents, and sell classified information. And there's nothing to stop them from one day saying: "I have an idea. Why don't we overheat some nuclear reactors?" With us on set this morning, we have Deniz Kaya, author, consultant, and technology guru. He'll be telling us if we should take these warnings seriously. But first, the shocking news about the tragic ...

9.11 Notice /ə/.
H = host D = Deniz
- H Joining us now is Deniz Kaya, senior editor of *Technology Today* and author of *Dark Times Ahead*. Deniz, thanks for being here.
- D Thanks for having me.
- H So ... is it that bad?
- D No.
- H Oh yeah?
- D It's catastrophic. And it'll get much worse.
- H Really?
- D I'm afraid so.

9.12 Notice /j/ and /w/.
- D For starters, there's a new generation of hackers out there, and some are as young as, what, 12, 13.
- H No way!
- D Yeah, and they're only kids, you know? But at some point you have to stop and ask yourself—what's gonna happen to these kids? Will they have become big-time criminals by the time they're 20, 25?
- H Exactly.
- D Here's another problem. Malware is getting more and more intelligent ...
- H Who's malware? A super villain or something?
- D No, that's not a person. Malware refers to, uh, to all sorts of viruses out there, you know? And some of them are pretty scary. Did you hear about the Facebook Messenger virus?
- H Yeah. The one with the video?
- D That's the one. By December, one out of 50 computers in New York will have been infected by that thing. Here's what it does: It sends a message, from a "friend," which says: "OMG! It's you?" and has a link to what looks like YouTube. However, when you follow the link, it downloads malware onto the computer. The same message will then be sent to more victims from your account.
- H Wow. That's awful. Do not open links to videos if you're not sure, then!
- D Bingo! But you know what really worries me? Cybercriminals will be carrying out more and more attacks wirelessly, and we won't be protected. They will have developed the ability to spread viruses across multiple devices very, very easily. They'll jump from phone to phone ... and then from phone to laptop, and then to tablet ...
- H Over wireless networks ...
- D Exactly. So you might be walking down the street and ... bang! And you know, there's actually some data suggesting that by the end of the decade, cybercriminals will have targeted 20 per cent of all the world's smart phones. And that's an optimistic estimate.
- H Wow. But is there anything we can do to protect ourselves?
- D Yep. There's all sorts of trouble you can avoid by taking a few simple precautions.

9.13 Notice /p/, /v/, and /b/.
- H So you've told us about the dangers we'll be facing in the future. Can you offer us some advice on what we can do about it?
- D Of course! The first thing is passwords! I know it's much easier to use the same password for all your accounts, but you're putting yourself at risk. Use a unique password for everything. Each one should have at least eight characters and be a combination of letters, symbols, and numbers. Also be very aware of what you click on. It's so easy to get caught out by just clicking on a link from someone you don't know. The consequences can be dramatic. Just don't do it. If you are attacked, you might lose all of your files. To prevent this, make sure you regularly back up your files. If you are targeted, you will have already stored your information elsewhere. Another important point is to always install the latest updates. Don't ignore the messages your computer sends you. By updating, your software will be easier to use.
- H Yes, essential rules we all need to follow. Deniz, thank you very much for your input today. Coming up ...

9.15 Notice the intonation. ↗↘
1
H = husband W = wife B = burglar
- H Oh, it's good to be home, isn't it? ↗
- W Sure is. ↘ I know that late flight was cheaper, ↘ but, boy, I'm exhausted! ↘
- H: Me, too. ↘ I can't wait to crawl into ...What the ...?! ↘ What's going on?! ↘ Who are you?! ↘
- B What, wait, hang on ...
- W Oh my goodness! ↗ I'm calling the police! ↗
- B No, wait ...

2
F = father D = daughter
- F Do you have any idea what time it is? ↗ Your mother and I were worried sick ab ... Wait a second ... Are those my car keys? ↗
- D What? ↘
- F Jennifer, what are you doing with my keys? ↘
- D Dad, uh, it's not what you're thinking.
- F Oh, that's good news. ↘ 'Cause I was starting to think my teenage daughter had stolen the family car. ↘
- D It's not what it seems. I swear. I was, uh, I was ...

3
F = flight attendant P = passenger
- F Excuse me sir, we're about to take off. ↘ I'm gonna have to ask you to put your bag in the luggage compartment. ↘
- P1 Uh, no, it's fine here, thank you. ↘
- F Sir, I'm afraid this is ...
- P2 Hey, is that bag moving? ↗
- P1 What? No, it's not. Of course not. ↘
- P2 Yes, it is. Something's just moved in that bag. ↘
- P1 Hold on, I can explain. ↘
- F Sir, I'm gonna have to ask you to ...

9.16 Notice the **sentence stress** and weak forms.
1
- W The police will be here any minute!
- B Wait a minute. This is not what it looks like!
- H Stay where you are.
- B Just hear me out! Please! I just ... I got kicked out of my accommodation and I saw the house was empty and ... I haven't taken anything, I promise.
- W No! We don't want to hear it! Just keep quiet until the police get here.

2
- F Jennifer, what are you doing with my keys?
- D Dad, uh, it's not what you're thinking.
- F Oh, that's good news. 'Cause I was starting to think my teenage daughter had stolen the family car.
- D It's not what it seems. I swear. I was, uh, I was just checking out your MP3 collection.
- F Yes, of course you were. I mean, that's just the kind of music you're into, isn't it?
- D No, but, but Dad ... You don't understand.
- F No ifs and buts, Jennifer. I don't want to get a phone call from the police. You stay out of my car unless you're with me. Do you hear me?
- D Yes, Dad, but ...
- F No!

3
- P2 Yes, it is. Something's just moved in that bag.
- P1 Hold on, I can explain.
- F Sir, I'm going to have to ask you to get off the plane.
- P1 Lucy's just six months old, she's not dangerous at all. Look!
- P2 Oh well, that makes me feel much better. Thank you.
- F Now sir, please stand up and come with me.
- P1 OK, OK. But really, she wouldn't hurt anybody, I promise.

Unit 10

10.3 Notice /j/ and /dʒ/.
C = Carlos G = Gloria
- G Hey, what are you doing home so soon?
- C Good to see you, too! What are you doing?
- G Some silly quiz ...
- C Cool as a cucumber, occasionally moody, or chronically short-tempered. Let's hear your answers then. This should be interesting ...
- G Hey, what's that supposed to mean? I have my ups and downs, but I'm pretty stable.
- C Well, yes, you do, but you're trying to work it out. How's the yoga class going by the way?
- G Really well. I think it's really helping. You know, little by little, I'm learning how to relax.
- C That's good. Let's have a look at the first question ... Do you ever wake up feeling grumpy? Yeah, I'd have to agree with that. You definitely do!
- G I know, I know, I'm grumpy in the morning, but I'm sick and tired of waking up early, Carlos! Five thirty feels like the middle of the night still!
- C I guess, it's easy for me to say. I don't even dare to talk to you before 7 a.m.
- G It's probably wise. I just ... I need some peace and quiet in the morning, that's all.
- C What about this one: Do you ever get fed up with activities and people you actually like ... What do you mean "no"? You're fed up with your job!
- G Well, yeah, but the question is about stuff I like. And I don't like working in retail.
- C But you did when you started, right?
- G Well, yeah, I did, but not anymore. "How can I help you today? That looks great on you. Have a nice day." Blah, blah, blah, blah, blah. I just ... I hate doing the same things again and again ...
- C ... and again and again. Yeah, I get it. You need variety.
- G Yeah. Sooner or later, I'll need to start looking for a new job.
- C Five ... Do you ever swear when other drivers do something stupid? Yep, that's right. You do.
- G How would you know that?
- C I've been told.
- G What?
- C It's a small neighborhood, Gloria.
- G Well, but you can't blame me, can you? I mean, you know what it's like to drive in L.A.!

173

C Do you ever yell at people for no serious reason? "No." You're kidding, right?
G Carlos, when did I ever yell at someone? Tell me!
C Whoa, whoa. OK, forget I said anything. You're really, really calm!

10.5 Notice the connections.
... and that just_about does_it for_us tonight. But before we go, here's the moment you've_all been waiting for: People's top pet peeves. Yes, we_asked_ and you voted! So, here_are the results.
At number 10, with 871 votes, people who suddenly_open the door without knocking first. Yep—we've_all done that before, haven't we?
Number 9, when people keep_interrupting you when you talk. Well, that's_just rude.
Number 8, people who keep using the word "like" all the time. Yeah, that_is_annoying.
Number 7, with_a_little_over 1,000 votes, bad phone habits, like not returning texts_or phone calls.
At number 6, with 1,234, people who honk, instead_ of ringing the bell, when they come to pick_you_up— especially late_at night. Hate that, too.
Number 5, people who promise to call you and then they don't.
Number 4—oh, I hate this_one—people who_are too lazy to put their trash_in the trash can. I mean ...it's right there.
Number 3, with_exactly 1,700 votes, when someone uses_a finger to pick their teeth. Well, that's_just gross. Don't do_it.
The next one kind_of surprised me—I didn't_expect to see_it near the top with_as many as 1,809 votes, number 2 being the first_one to_arrive_at a party— Well, I guess it_is pretty embarrassing, isn't it?
And finally, at number 1, something I think many_of_ us hate, it's people who_are addicted to playing with their phones. What do you think? Let_us know on ...

10.6 Notice /juː/ and /uː/.
C = coach   Mi = Mia   J = Jim   V = Vince   Ju = Julia
C ... the last time we met. So, anyway, let's give a warm welcome to anyone who's joining our anger management group for the first time—and that's, well, everybody except Julia. So, first of all, Mia, hi. Welcome aboard.
Mi Hi.
C So, Mia, why are you here?
Mi My name's Mia and my employers have told me I have to sort my issues out. They say I'm too demanding and impatient with my staff. They are probably right. If things aren't done the way I want them or immediately ... like, if I call and leave a message, and I don't hear from them in an hour, I get really mad and yell at them. You know, I really want to change, 'cause I'm afraid of losing my job.
C OK, Mia. Listen, I want to thank you for being so honest—that's the spirit! Jim, would you like to introduce yourself?
J OK, I guess.
C Go on ...
J Ah, yeah, well ... my girlfriend ... she thinks I'm, like, too possessive. You know, I just want to know where she is and, like, what she's doing.
C OK, is that it?
J Well, I don't like it when she talks to other people—she's constantly on the phone with her friends and on Snapchat and stuff—I mean, all the time, and it makes me jealous, you know, and then she accuses me of being aggressive. So, that's why I'm here.
C I see. Interesting. Thank you, Jim. OK ... Uh, next on the list is ... Vince. Hi. Why don't you tell us what brought you here?

V Well, actually, I'm afraid it's people like Jim that brought me here.
C What do you mean?
V I don't mean to be arrogant, but ... I'm sick and tired of hearing that kind of English. Didn't you learn anything at school?
J Excuse me? What are you talking about?
V "Like, like, like." How old are you? Like, 14?
J Wow! OK. Well, I am sorry! I apologize for upsetting your sensitive ears.
V So you should be! You know, there's just no excuse for bad grammar.
J Well, I guess we know why you're here now, don't we?
C OK, guys. I think we can talk about this reasonably.
Ju Reasonably? Do you think yelling at someone for the way they speak is reasonable?
V Hey! What's it got to do with you?
Ju Hey, didn't your mother ever teach you any manners?
C Julia! Vince! Everybody, calm down. Remember, there are ways of dealing with this ... carefully, step by step. We are responsible for controlling our anger. In fact, let's use this as a good example. Let's look at some strategies to help us face these feelings and ...

10.9 Notice /s/, /z/, and /ʃ/.
1
B = bride   G = groom
B I cannot believe that you said that. To my mother, Jose, my mother.
G Well, she just wouldn't stop talking about your ex-boyfriend, you have to admit it!
B Jose! Stop it! You should apologize for saying that or we're never going to ...
G Oh, or what? I'm sick and tired of hearing how wonderful Chris is! I don't think I'm being unreasonable.

2
G = grandmother   Gd = granddaughter
G Oh ... but ... what happens if I press the wrong button by accident? I'm afraid of losing everything.
Gd Oh, don't worry, you won't. Look, there's an easy way of saving this. I promise. Just click on the file here and save here.
G Is that really all I have to do? That's easy, isn't it?
Gd Of course! I told you it was. Now you have a go.
G OK, so I just click here and then ...

10.11 Notice the sentence stress.
Good morning everyone, and welcome to Assertiveness Training. I hope you're ready to learn some life-changing lessons! What is assertiveness? Any ideas? No? OK, assertiveness is a way of communicating your needs and wants but without hurting other people.
It's difficult to tell the difference between assertiveness and aggression. Aggression is about getting what you want without caring how you affect others.
Now, there are many benefits of being assertive. Assertive people are better managers. They get the job done but treat colleagues respectfully. They're good at negotiating because they can understand the opponent's argument and can reach a compromise more easily. They are also less stressed because they are more self-confident. Sounds good, doesn't it?
So, how do we become more assertive? First, you have to believe in yourself. Believe that you deserve respect. Next, identify what you need

and say that in a clear and confident way. You shouldn't expect others to know what you want! Accept that you cannot control other people. If someone reacts badly to you, this is not your fault (but remember to be respectful). Don't return their anger and resentment. Stay calm. You can control your own actions. If you are not offending others, you have the right to do as you wish.
Next, say what you're thinking even if it's difficult. However, say it constructively and with sensitivity. You can confront people who disagree with you but stay in control and be positive.
Accept criticism as well as compliments. It's important to take feedback even when it's negative. If you don't agree, that's fine and you can say so without being defensive.
A very useful tip next. Remember saying yes to every little thing you've been asked to do over the years? Well, stop it. You need to stop agreeing to everything and learn to say no more often. Understand your limits. Stop to think about how much you can manage realistically.
Change your language. Instead of saying "I could, or would," say "I will." Try using more "I" statements: say "I want, I feel, I need" rather than "You don't, you should, you never," etc. This can be very effective.
And finally, something simple. Listen. Listen and try to understand the other person's opinion. Try not to interrupt.
So, let's try putting some of this into practice. I'd like to try some roleplay. Let's get into groups of ...

10.13 Notice /ʃ/, /ð/, /θ/, and /f/.
Any true relationship between friends or significant others should be one between equals: you give and take equally. One person's needs aren't met over another's. Friends and partners are supposed to give you energy and lift you up when you're down, and want the best for you. But sometimes we get into relationships that drain energy from us. These are toxic relationships and they can negatively affect all aspects of our lives. On this week's WellCast, we're going to tell you how you can tell if you're even in a toxic relationship. And then we're going to help you extricate yourself from that unhealthy situation, pronto!

10.14 Notice the short (/) and long (//) pauses.
Step 1: // Diagnose the relationship. // How do you know if a friend or partner is bringing you down? // Well, / in much the same way that you know you're coming down with a cold. // Toxic relationships come with symptoms. // When you're around this person, / how do you feel? // Here are a few other questions you should ask yourself if you're thinking you might be in a toxic situation: // Does my friend put me down all the time? // Are they jealous when I spend time with others? // Do they constantly bring up parts of me that they want to change? // Do they take more than they give? // Am I only doing the things that they want to do? //
Step 2: // Recognize your role / in the relationship. // As Eleanor Roosevelt once said, / "Nobody can make you feel inferior without your consent." / All right, look, you know we got that from *Princess Diaries*, obviously. Moving on. // Listen, you have autonomy in every relationship in your life. // If a friend or partner is stealing your sunshine, / you need to figure out what you're doing to allow them to do this. // Are you being a doormat? // Are you putting this person's emotional needs ahead of your own health? //

Audioscript

Step 3: // Start to build boundaries for this relationship. // Does your friend invite themselves over at all hours of the night? // Are they constantly bossing you around? // Are they always borrowing money from you? // Once you know the boundary that you want to set, / stick to it! / Draw your line in the sand. //

Step 4: // Recognize that you can't change other people, / but you can stop being a doormat. // If you've determined that a friendship or relationship is toxic, / you know that you have to change the nature of that relationship. // Start by spending less time with that person / and do your best to detach yourself emotionally. // Setting boundaries will hopefully help you begin to phase this relationship out. //

Step 5: // Get a second opinion. // Especially if you're emotionally vulnerable, / the best thing you can do is surround yourself with people who love you / and who want you to be happy and healthy. // Use them as a lifeline during this time. //

Step 6: // Above all else, / look out for yourself. // Studies have shown that people with low self-esteem / are far more likely to find themselves in toxic relationships. // You will never be treated with love and respect / unless you absolutely believe that you deserve these things. // Remember: you teach people how to treat you. / So do yourself the favor of loving yourself!

◯ 10.16 Notice the connections that produce /w/ and /j/ sounds.

Welcome to *English for all*, the podcast for students who want to improve their English—fast! Last week, we asked you to tell us about your strengths and weaknesses, your successes and your frustrations. So, today we've chosen three messages to read on the air. The first one—where is it? Oh, here—was written by Bruna, a listener from Colombia—hi, Bruna—who says she's good at grammar, but finds it hard to express herself fluently. Listen, your English sounds fantastic and, you know, maybe you're much more fluent than you think. Anyway, here's what I think you should do: Try to focus on expressing your ideas fluently instead of speaking 100% correctly all the time. 'Cause, you see, the more you stop to think about what you're going to say next, the more you hesitate. And remember: People will still understand you if you make a few mistakes. And here's another suggestion: Have you thought about asking a friend to practice with you for a few hours a week? You probably have at least one or two friends who speak some English, right? So think about it: You can have fun and improve your English at the same time without having to, I don't know, live abroad or anything. Thanks for writing, Bruna, and good luck.

Our second message comes from South Korea. Our listener says he has trouble understanding spoken English ... Yeah, that's a common problem. Byung-Sang, listen, I have two suggestions. First, listen to as much English as you can outside the classroom. For example, a good way of practicing is watching Internet videos on sites like YouTube, Dailymotion, and so on, at least every other day, for about an hour or so. Religiously. Turn the subtitles on and off sometimes, too. But be sure to choose a variety of videos—both more and less challenging, OK? And who knows, you might even learn a new expression or two! And here's the second suggestion: If you want to improve your listening, you should consider giving pronunciation a little more attention. Yeah, I'm serious. Research has shown that students with good pronunciation tend to be much better listeners. How about that?

And our final message comes from Omar—where's he from?—oh, Turkey, wow. Omar says he's not comfortable reading quickly, for, uh, for general comprehension. Omar, listen, reading too slowly is not always a good idea. For example, if you take an international exam, you'll need to be able to read fast, without a dictionary. So here's what I think you should do: Next time you approach a text, read it once quickly first. Then, if necessary, read it again, more carefully, looking for information you need. But try to avoid reading slowly all the time. And about your vocabulary question, here's something that might help: learn words together. For example, how about learning "make an effort" instead of "effort"? Or "take a course" rather than only "course"? Our brains like these kinds of associations, you know? Well, that does it for us tonight. In the next episode, we'll be talking about …

Review 5

◯ R5.1 Notice /r/ and /h/.

1

R = Ron   H = Hanna

R   Hey, Hanna, what are you reading?
H   Oh, hi, Ron. Oh, this? It's a book Ralph lent me. He said it was really good, but I just can't get into it.
R   Huh, so, what's it about?
H   Well, uh, that's just it. Ralph said it was a really interesting detective story … but there's no crime, not much storyline, nothing really. I just can't figure it out.
R   Hmmm … Well, maybe it'll turn out better than you think. You know, keep reading!

2

L = Lenny   S = Sue

S   Lenny? Have you changed something … Your hair or something?
L   Nope, not my hair. But I'm on this diet right now. I've lost a little weight.
S   Ah! That must be it! Yeah, you look really good!
L   Oh, thanks, Sue. You know, it's pretty hard to stick to it, there are so many things I can't eat, but, you know, it really lifts me up when I hear things like that. So, thank you.
S   No problem! Yeah, stick to it, Lenny. Don't give up!

3

J = Jackie   B = Beth

J   What is it, Beth? You look kind of miserable. You're not coming down with anything, are you?
B   Oh, I don't think so … No, it's this work. I've got so much to do and so little time. I just don't know what to do. It's really bringing me down.
J   Oh, Beth, you poor thing. Look, tell me it's none of my business, I don't want to boss you around or anything, but you really need to look out for yourself. Take a break or something, you know?
B   Yeah, Jackie, maybe you're right. But then when will I finish this work?

◯ R5.2 Notice the /t/, /d/, and /ɪd/ endings.

William Watts was a thief. One day he was stealing some jewels from a shop and set off the alarm. The police arrived at the shop before William had finished, so he quickly jumped out of the window and ran away. Unfortunately for William, he turned the wrong way and saw the police station in front of him. He stopped running and tried to act naturally, but he was arrested. He was taken to court and convicted of burglary. When the judge read the sentence, William started to cry.

175

PAUL SELIGSON
TOM ABRAHAM
CRIS GONTOW

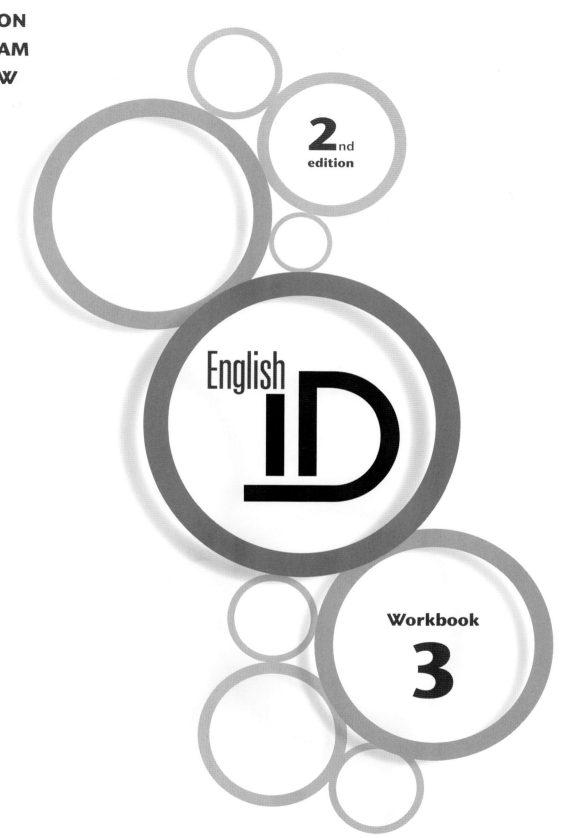

English ID
2nd edition
Workbook 3

Richmond

6.1 What are you watching these days?

1 Read the article and put the words in the title in the correct order.

Makes / What / Addictive / Ever / Than / Today's / Before / Series / More / ?

☐ Sitting down in front of the TV to watch your favorite show is becoming a thing of the past. Binge watching, which means watching several episodes one after another, is growing, and it seems to be how more and more of us want our TV. The best show creators are beginning to understand that, too.

☐ According to him, the majority of 20th-century shows, including great dramas like *The Sopranos* and *Six Feet Under*, had episodes that worked independently. If you missed one, it didn't matter too much. In the early 2000s, shows like *24*, a series by Fox, started to change that. Viewers really needed to watch every episode to understand the story and soon, the 12- or 13-episode serialized drama had become a new American art form.

☐ The adult themes, antiheroes, and the art direction make them look like movies. But, while older shows focused on the characters, today's also focus on what happens next. Series creators are beginning to create stories that are less obvious. Series like *Stranger Things*, for example, tell stories with more unexpected occurrences and a lot more suspense.

☐ After watching our favorite series, we feel relaxed, our brains rest and our bodies fill with endorphins, our natural "feel-good substance". Maybe that's why we feel happy as soon as we turn the TV on and then watch several episodes at once to satisfy our "addiction".

☐ Before DVDs and Internet streaming, TV viewers had two choices: (1) watch whatever happened to be on, no matter how idiotic; or (2) turn the TV off and feel frustrated. Now we have a third: watch the shows we like, whenever we like, and for as long as we like. Serialized, streaming TV is perfect for keeping the endorphins flowing, and TV writers know it.

2 Circle the correct alternative in a–e and insert the missing sentences in the paragraphs in **1**.

a TV producers **have** / **having** discovered this science, and by **use** / **using** new technology, they have given TV fans a third option.
b Apparently, **have** / **having** to watch more before you can understand what's going on makes modern series more and more addictive.
c How we watch TV **has** / **have** been changing in recent years.
d New series like *The Walking Dead* **is** / **are** similar to series from the past in some ways.
e D. B. Weiss, a writer for *Game of Thrones*, **told** / **said** *Newsweek* how he thinks things are changing.

3 Complete a–e with prepositions. Then reread the article. True (T) or False (F)?

a According _____ the article, some show creators have detected changes in traditional TV viewing patterns.
b Fox was very influential in changing TV shows at the end _____ the last century.
c Modern series usually have more complex storylines _____ series from the past.
d If you have to watch _____ a long time to understand a story, you get tired and stop watching.
e Today's viewers don't need to feel frustrated if there's nothing of interest _____ TV.

4 ▶6.1 Match both columns to form media words. Listen to check and mark the stress.

a sports   ☐ services
b medical   ☐ program
c reality   ☐ opera
d TV streaming   ☐ events
e soap   ☐ media
f talk   ☐ show
g music   ☐ drama
h social   ☐ TV

5 ▶6.2 Listen to five dialogues and match items a–h in **4** to the speakers. There are two extra items.

1 The man's addicted to ☐.
2 This lady just loves ☐.
 The guy prefers ☐.
3 Both of them really like ☐.
4 They are both addicted to ☐.
5 They're always watching ☐.

6 🎤 **Make it personal** In pairs. What TV shows do you like to watch? How do you watch TV? When do you like to watch it? Share your favorite TV show with a classmate. Any similarities / differences?

I watch TV on my tablet after dinner.
I normally watch soap operas!

I love music shows, like The Voice. *I watch it on my phone while I'm on the bus.*

6.2 What's your favorite TV show ever?

1 **Complete a–f with *a*, *an*, *the*, or prepositions. Read the article. True (T) or False (F)?**
   a ___ shows are ___ order ___ popularity.
   b ___ U.S. has made more seasons ___ *Survivor* than the UK.
   c ___ man ___ *The Bachelor* always proposes.
   d People have become interested in baking again largely because ___ *The Great British Baking Show*.
   e There is ___ range ___ different talents from contestants on *America's Got Talent*.
   f All ___ ___ celebrities ___ *Dancing with the Stars* are extremely famous.

The Five Reality TV Shows that Had the Biggest Impact this Century

20 years ago, with the exception of the news and documentaries, the people on TV were all actors who had learned from scripts. There weren't many "real" people, but everything changed in 1997 with a show called *Survivor*. Now it seems reality TV is here to stay. Here are some of our favorites, in no particular order.

Survivor
Since starting in Sweden in 1997, dozens of different countries and regions have used the show's format. A cast of strangers are sent to an island or jungle location and have to live without modern luxuries until the final winner gets a prize. The British version only ran for two seasons, although there have been 37 seasons in the U.S.!

The Bachelor
This show focuses on a group of women who live together and compete for a handsome guy's marriage proposal. There have been four proposals in the British version since the show started in 2003.

The Great British Baking Show
Starting in 2010, this show invites a group of amateur bakers to compete against each other. Contestants aim to reach the final round by showing off their baking skills. The success of the show, both nationally and internationally, has been credited with renewing an interest in home baking, with some participants going on to become professional bakers.

America's Got Talent
Since its debut in 2006, this giant talent show created by Simon Cowell has attracted a huge number of weird and wonderful contestants to compete with a range of talents, including singing, dancing, magic, comedy, and more. Acts are judged by a panel of celebrities who change each season, and the winner receives a large cash prize.

Dancing with the Stars
Who wants to see a celebrity dance salsa? Apparently, millions of us do. This show became an instant hit in 2004. Part of the success comes from showing a vulnerable side of celebrities, some minor and some big names, as they struggle to learn a new skill.

2 **Correct the mistakes in a–d and match them to the shows in 1.**
   a The contestant who she is leaving the island this week is Fifi.
   b The women who lives in the house want to get married.
   c The island what we chose is very beautiful.
   d Sally baked a cake in the shape of Spider-Man, which it was inspired by the superhero.

3 **Combine the two sentences in a–g with *that*, *who*, or *whose*.**
   a Nicki Minaj and Mariah Carey are judges. Their fights on camera were popular on Twitter.
   b Catherine is the girl. She won the diamond engagement ring.
   c The location is usually far away from civilization. The organizers choose it.
   d Simon Cowell is a reality TV producer. His shows include *American Idol* and *The X Factor*.
   e Kim's the woman. She won after the other 14 contestants left the island.
   f He's chosen a song. The song is close to his heart.
   g The dances can be difficult. The professionals teach them the dances.

4 ▶ 6.3 **Cross out four relative pronouns that are not necessary. Listen to check and repeat.**

HELP US IMPROVE YOUR TV
Please take a moment to complete our survey.
1 How often is the team that you cheer for on TV?
2 Are there any TV hosts that / who you can't stand? Who?
3 Would you like to see more shows that have "real" people?
4 Do you prefer movies that make you laugh or cry?
5 Are there any theme songs that you like to sing? Which one(s)?
6 Do you like news anchors who make jokes?
7 Are there any shows that you'd like to prohibit? Which one(s)?

5 **Correct the mistakes with relative pronouns in three of the responses below. Then match the responses to the questions in 4.**
   a No, not really. I think it's a job where they should be serious.
   b Every week. Botafogo, that are the best team in Brazil, play in the top league.
   c Definitely. I hate all the actors are fake.
   d I don't think shows have violence should be on in the daytime.
   e Movies which make me laugh are more enjoyable than the ones that make me cry.
   f Well, I like the one at the start of the news. Strange, I know!
   g I hate the one who is on every Sunday. He's really annoying!

6 **Make it personal** Think of your own answers to the questions in 4. Share them with a classmate. Any surprises?

6.3 What was the last movie you saw?

1 Read and match 1–6 to a–g to make sentences. There is one extra.

1 The Marvel Cinematic Universe ...
2 *The Avengers* has made ...
3 *Star Wars* is popular ...
4 The movies have made billions for ...
5 *Harry Potter* is popular with ...
6 The Harry Potter franchise ...

a George Lucas over more than four decades.
b has made 20 movies in just 10 years.
c will probably have many more movies in the future.
d more money than any of their other movies.
e was filmed in the UK.
f all over the world.
g young and old movie fans.

2 ▶ 6.4 Read the online article and complete the bold phrases with *that*, *which*, *who*, or *whose*. Insert commas where necessary. Listen to check.

3 Find the relative clauses in each description, and mark them restrictive (R) or non-restrictive (N).

Movies in three sentences!

Spider-Man, who was originally a Marvel superhero, has had six movies. The fourth one premiered in 2017 with a cast that included a new Spider-Man played by Tom Holland. Mary Jane Parker, who was the love interest between 2002 and 2007, was cut from the 2012 and 2014 movies.

Author Suzanne Collins, whose novels inspired four movies, must be pretty pleased with the amazing success of *The Hunger Games* saga. These exciting movies, which have captivated young adults worldwide, tell the story of a compulsory death match. It's a televised match that the contestants must win in order to survive.

4 ▶ 6.5 Insert two speech pauses (/) in four of sentences a–e. Listen to check and repeat with pauses and intonation. Which sentence doesn't have speech pauses? Why?
   a *The Dark Knight* which is my favorite Batman movie won four Oscars.
   b Heath Ledger who played the scariest Joker ever seen won an Academy Award after he died.
   c Christian Bale who played Batman wasn't nominated for an Oscar for his part.
   d Johnny Depp is the actor that has made Jack Sparrow so unforgettable.
   e *Pirates of the Caribbean* which was inspired by Disneyworld's attraction has made over five billion dollars so far.

5 **Make it personal** What are your top three movies of all time? Why do you like them so much? Make a list then share it with a classmate.

6.4 Where do you usually watch movies?

1 **Complete the sentences with the words in the box in the correct form.**

   cast   clip   prequel   script   shoot   trilogy   view

   a Although it was released over 20 years later, *Star Wars: Episode 1* was actually a _____ to the earlier movies.
   b Look! My new YouTube _____ has over a thousand _____ already!
   c *The Lord of the Rings* is considered to be one of the most well-known _____ of all time.
   d The new *X-Men* movie has an all-star _____.
   e There are rumours that Steven Spielberg is going to _____ a new movie in Iceland, with a _____ he wrote himself.

2 ▶6.6 **Listen to this joke warning and answer a–g.**
   a What's the name of the virus?
   b Is it safe to touch?
   c What can it destroy?
   d What's the antidote?
   e What are three places it can be found?
   f Who should you send the message to?
   g And if you can't do that, what does it mean?

3 ▶6.7 **Order words in a–e to make more advice for sufferers. Listen to check and repeat.**
   a on / you / go / time / sure / make / home / .
   b about / somewhere / a / think / vacation / taking / .
   c enough / to / always / water / have / drink / .
   d do / try / you / more / can / to / never / than / .
   e take / more / you / efficient / you'll / if / breaks, / be / regular / .

4 **Rearrange the words in B's responses to make expressions of surprise.**
   1 A: Did you know Angela has six dogs?
      B: kidding, / Really? / right? / You're
   2 A: Phew! I've finally finished my homework!
      B: Thank / way! / goodness! / No
   3 A: I've got 10 brothers and sisters.
      B: serious? / you / Are
   4 A: My uncle's a movie director.
      B: out / here! / What? / of / Get

5   **Make it personal** Think of some surprising information about yourself or someone you know. Tell your partner. Was she / he surprised? Now tell another classmate. Who has the most surprising information? Whose reaction was the best?

   My mom is an astronaut! She's been to the moon!

   What? You're kidding, right?! Has she been to the moon?

   Connect
   Record yourself talking about the last movie you watched. Share it with a classmate. Have they seen it, too?

6.5 Who are the wildest celebrities you know?

1 Read the article. True (T) or False (F)?
   a All celebrities are famous for their talents.
   b If you don't look the same as others, people might think you're a celebrity.
   c After some time, you will become a dish such as soup or salad.
   d Your friends' sense of fashion is equally as important as your own.
   e If your father dresses like a chauffeur, everybody will think you are a star.

CHEAT'S GUIDE TO LIVING LIKE A STAR

We see them on TV and read about them in magazines. Today there is no escape from the celebrity lifestyle, and there is a growing number of celebrities who are famous for … er, well … being famous. But why go to the trouble of learning to sing, auditioning for a film, or embarrassing yourself on a reality TV show? Follow our tips and you could live the life of a celebrity, sort of.

1. **Get noticed.** This really is the most important part. If you look different and stand out from the crowd, people will want to know what your secret is (whatever you tell them, don't tell the truth!). Now, of course, we don't recommend that you instantly follow Katy Perry's example and be boiled in a pot with carrots before being presented as a meal. Start small and work up to becoming soup (or salad if that's what you prefer). Try a new hairstyle and maybe some accessories.

2. **Accessories.** Think of accessories as more than just clothes. Accessorizing is a lifestyle! From the phone you use to the friends you hang out with—everything has to make YOU look good. OK … it might be that your current friends don't have the "right" sense of fashion and style to show you at your best. It's time to get serious. Drop those friends and find new ones that match your new glamorous lifestyle a little better. And if you can't find any new friends, get a dog.

3. **Followers.** Every celebrity needs followers. You know, those people who go around with them hoping to become famous as well. Of course, there are the professional followers, too—think security guards, drivers, photographers. You won't be able to afford all of these people just yet, but that shouldn't be a problem. Try asking your dad to wear a suit and sunglasses when he drives you to the mall; everybody will think he is your personal driver.

2 ▶ 6.8 Listen and choose the best summary.
The girls are talking about:
   a what stars demand in their dressing rooms.
   b what female stars expect in their dressing rooms.

3 ▶ 6.8 Listen again and circle the correct answers in a–f. Check in ▶ 6.8 on page 59.
   a They say Beyoncé requires **baked** / **fried** chicken.
   b Katy Perry insists her room be **painted** / **furnished** in a **specific** / **colorful** way.
   c Lynn can't believe that Katy wants a **series** / **pair** of **French lamps** / **lights**.
   d Britney often requested a **picture of** / **photo that belonged to** Lady Diana.
   e Rihanna has a **long** / **short** list of things she likes to **eat** / **drink**.
   f If you get in free to **a Rihanna** / **an Adele** show, **you must** / **she will** give money to charity.

4 ▶ 6.9 Follow the model.

> I heard Adele wants chicken salad sandwiches in her dressing room. / No way!

> She wants chicken salad sandwiches? No way!

5 **Make it personal** Find a picture of a celebrity you like when they were younger. Share it with a friend and see if they can guess who it is.

Can you remember…
- 14 TV genres? SB→p. 72
- 2 ways of watching shows in other languages? SB→p. 73
- how to use restrictive relative clauses? SB→p. 75
- how to use non-restrictive relative clauses? SB→p. 76
- 5 expressions to show surprise? SB→p. 81

7 7.1 Does technology rule your life?

1 Read the article about designing your own app. What do you need to do when it's ready?

So you want to make your own app?

Want to make an app and sell it but have no idea where to begin? Well, first things first, ¹_____ down and don't worry! There are plenty of ways to ²_____ out what you need to know. You can ³_____ out a book from the library, read about it on the Internet, or you can even download an app to learn how to make apps! The list ⁴_____ on. Whatever method you choose, you'll soon find that you ⁵_____ up what you need to know quite easily.

But learning how to design your app and making it is just the first step. Once it's ready, you'll need a strategy to reach your clients. Essentially, you're ⁶_____ up a business. It's a very difficult market to ⁷_____ into as there are literally millions of apps out there. You'll need to be active in promoting it. So ⁸_____ down on relaxation time and get out there!

2 Complete the article in **1** with the verbs in the box in the correct form.

| break | calm | cut | find |
| go | pick | set | take |

3 ▶7.1 Match the words to make phrases related to technology. Listen and check and underline the stress.
   a distance   conferencing
   b movie streaming   app
   c video   time
   d screen   learning
   e online selling   theft
   f identity   platform

4 Which of the phrases in **3** can you see on the screens?

5 🎧 **Make it personal** Have you ever had to call tech support or solve a tech problem? What was the problem? Did they / you resolve it? Tell a classmate.

7.2 What was the last little lie you told?

1 Read and complete the blog entry with *say* or *tell*.

Five little lies we tell our kids.

There are many lies we parents ¹_____ our children. We don't want to hurt or deceive them but to prevent potential problems from happening. Oh, and to make our lives easier, of course.
Here are five of the most common little lies.

1 "We're nearly there."
On any journey, of any length, whether it's a road trip or a short walk to the shops, we hear, every two minutes, "Are we nearly there yet?" The only possible answer to this is to ²_____, "Yes, nearly there." Never, ever ³_____ the truth. Even if you've still got three hours to go.

2 "Your picture is brilliant!"
In reality, the people have no bodies and the sky is underground, but we want them to feel good about it, so we ⁴_____ a little lie. If it really is good (for them), we'll ⁵_____ them so and stick it to the refrigerator.

3 "Sorry, there's no more ice cream left."
Well, at least until you go to bed. Then it's going to be an ice cream party down here! This is a good little lie to ⁶_____ for anything similar: candy, cake, cookies, whatever you want to eat. It's much easier to ⁷_____ this than to try and explain the importance of healthy eating. Especially when you're the one eating ice cream!

4 "We're leaving without you."
You're trying to leave the house, and they're taking forever to find their shoes, put them on, turn the TV off, etc. You ⁸_____ them you're in a hurry but it doesn't work. Finally, with no patience left, you ⁹_____ this and start to walk out the door. As if by magic, they're suddenly behind you fully dressed and ready to leave.

5 "We'll come back and buy it next time."
You know you definitely won't, but you ¹⁰_____ this because you know that they'll forget the next time you come. And you make sure you won't return for a long, long time.

2 Reread and answer a–e. Which lie 1–5 …

a is really a bit selfish because you want the same thing as your kids want?
b is one you tell when you hope they won't remember something?
c is one you should always tell when you're traveling somewhere?
d do you tell to scare them to do something more quickly?
e is one you tell to make them feel good?

3 ▶ 7.2 Diana's parents told her the five lies from **1**. Change the underlined pronouns and verbs in lies 1–5, and complete her complaints. Listen to check.

They lied to me!

1 They said _____
But it was another three hours!

2 They said _____
But the people looked like cows!

3 They said _____
But I heard them eating it after I'd gone to bed!

4 They said _____
But I knew they wouldn't!

5 They said _____
But we haven't been back there for six months!

4 ▶ 7.3 Listen and report lies a–f with the correct pronouns (P) and verbs (V).

a He said the check ₍ᵥ₎_____ in the mail.
b He said ₍ₚ₎_____ ₍ᵥ₎_____ pay next time.
c She said ₍ₚ₎_____ ₍ᵥ₎_____ still be good friends.
d He told Carol ₍ₚ₎_____ ₍ᵥ₎_____ great.
e She told Tina ₍ₚ₎_____ ₍ᵥ₎_____ him for his money.
f He said it ₍ᵥ₎_____ never happened to ₍ₚ₎_____ before.

5 Use *told* to report Anna and Mark's dialogue, if possible. If not, use *said*. Change pronouns and verbs as necessary. Follow the model.

Mark: I'll marry you, Anna!
Anna: I've never been interested in marriage.
Mark: I know you love me, Anna!
Anna: I can't marry you, Mark! I'm in love with someone else.

Mark told Anna he would marry her.

I once told a friend / my mother that …

6 🎤 **Make it personal** What's the worst lie someone told you? Tell a classmate.

35

7.3 How much of your day is screen time?

1 ▶7.4 Listen to Mr. Keller's call. Who's he getting help from?

  a A help desk agent.
  b A friend who's good with computers.
  c His wife of 20 years.

2 ▶7.4 Which five questions a–g did you hear? Listen again to check.
  a What kind of tablet do you have? ☐
  b Have you installed iTunes on your computer? ☐
  c What are you talking about? ☐
  d Are you familiar with the different icons? ☐
  e Do you have a Mac or a PC? ☐
  f When did you buy it? ☐
  g How can I upload music to my tablet? ☐

3 ▶7.5 These indirect question phrases are in phonetics. Can you decipher them? Listen to check and repeat.
  a /kən juː tel miː/
  b /aɪ wʌndə(r) ɪf/
  c /aɪ hæv noʊ aɪdɪə ɪf/
  d /aɪ niːd tə nəoʊ ɪf/
  e /də juː nəoʊ ɪf/
  f /də juː hæv eniː aɪdɪə/
  g /kəd juː tel miː/

4 Change a–g in **2** to indirect questions. Use the phrases from **3**.
  a *Can you tell me what kind of tablet you have?*
  b *I wonder if* _____.
  c _____
  d _____
  e _____
  f _____
  g _____

5 ▶7.6 Listen to the random question generator and change the questions into indirect questions.

  RANDOM QUESTION GENERATOR
  THEY WANT TO KNOW . . .
  A *how old I am.*
  B _____
  C _____
  D _____
  E _____
  F _____

6 ▶7.7 Write the words with **bold** letters in the correct sound column. Listen and repeat a–e to check.
  a Never p**u**ll the pl**u**g out by the power cable.
  b Please p**u**sh the green b**u**tton to c**u**t off the power.
  c P**u**t this c**u**shion **u**nder you to get more c**o**mfortable.
  d If you can't sh**u**t the browser window, it might be a b**u**g.
  e Don't let your noteb**oo**k inbox get too f**u**ll.

  ʊ   ʌ

7 🟢 **Make it personal** Share your answers to **5** with a classmate.

7.4 Are machines with personality a good idea?

1 Thais is telling her sister about the questions in her oral test yesterday.
Read what she said and complete the original questions.
   a First they asked how old I was. "How old _are you_?"
   b They asked what I did last weekend. "_____ last weekend?"
   c They asked if I liked studying. "_____ studying?"
   d They asked when I would finish school. "When _____ school?"
   e They asked if I was going to have a party. "_____ going to have a party?"
   f They asked how much my English had improved. "How much _____ English _____?"

2 Correct the mistakes in sentences a–e.
   a Sue asked me to not call her tonight.
   b I asked her where was she going.
   c She asked me why did I want to know.
   d I told her to not be rude to me.
   e She said me to leave her alone.

3 A traveler is going through customs with a new phone. Are a–h requests (R) or real questions (Q)?
   a Did you buy that phone in this country, madam?
   b Can you let me see it, please?
   c Do I have to pay duty on it?
   d How am I supposed to do that?
   e Could you hold on while I ask my supervisor?
   f Which carrier are you using?
   g Can you get a signal here?
   h Would you fill out this form, please?

4 ▶7.8 Match a–g to the gaps in the blog. Listen to Andy talking to a friend to check.

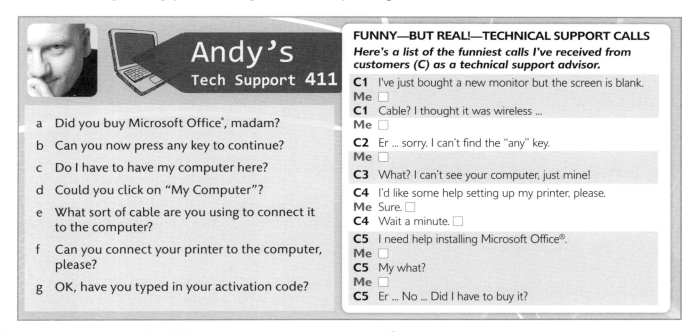

Andy's Tech Support 411

a Did you buy Microsoft Office®, madam?
b Can you now press any key to continue?
c Do I have to have my computer here?
d Could you click on "My Computer"?
e What sort of cable are you using to connect it to the computer?
f Can you connect your printer to the computer, please?
g OK, have you typed in your activation code?

FUNNY—BUT REAL!—TECHNICAL SUPPORT CALLS
Here's a list of the funniest calls I've received from customers (C) as a technical support advisor.
C1 I've just bought a new monitor but the screen is blank.
Me ☐
C1 Cable? I thought it was wireless …
Me ☐
C2 Er … sorry. I can't find the "any" key.
Me ☐
C3 What? I can't see your computer, just mine!
C4 I'd like some help setting up my printer, please.
Me Sure. ☐
C4 Wait a minute. ☐
C5 I need help installing Microsoft Office®.
Me ☐
C5 My what?
Me ☐
C5 Er … No … Did I have to buy it?

5 Reread. True (T) or False (F)?
   a C1 can't use his monitor because he has the wrong type of cable.
   b C2 thinks "any key" is a specific key on the keyboard.
   c C3 doesn't understand what "My Computer" is.
   d C4 can't set up his printer because he hasn't got his computer.
   e C5 can't install MS Office® because she has the wrong activation code.

6 ▶7.9 Report the requests or commands to help an elderly lady at the doctor's. Tell her what the doctor said. Follow the model.
Doctor: Sit down.
He asked you to sit down.

Doctor: Could you please open your mouth?
He asked you to open your mouth.

7 **Make it personal** What are your answers to 1? Share with a classmate.

37

7.5 How often do you use a pen?

1 Match a–f to 1–6 to make activities.
   a social   1 reading
   b visiting   2 online movies
   c studying for   3 video games
   d leisure   4 museums
   e playing   5 networking
   f watching   6 class

2 **Make it personal** Make a–d true using activities from **1**.
   a I consider _____ much more interesting than _____.
   b _____ is one of the most boring activities ever!
   c I spend more time _____ than _____.
   d I really should spend less time _____.

3 Match three of a–f to the student's notes, then abbreviate the other three.
   a "The author states that the Internet is actually responsible for keeping people apart."
   b "These days, more people send texts than call."
   c "Fathers and mothers seem to find less time to spend with their children."
   d "Libraries have fewer customers now."
   e "The book said four out of ten students cannot read when they finish primary school."
   f "Playing games is the most common use of smart phones for the under-15 age group."

Notes
   ○ 40% sts can't read when finish prim. sch.
   ○ net keeps ppl apart
   ○ parents spend less time w/ children

4 Rearrange the words to complete the conversations.
   1 A: *that / We / deny / can't* robots will do all our jobs in the future.
      B: *disagree / I / totally.* There are some jobs only humans can do.
   2 A: That guy on the TV is speaking nonsense.
      B: Well, *agree / disagree / may / you / or,* but *points / he / valid / some / makes.*
   3 A: No, they don't think …
      B: *second. / finish / a / on / me / let / Hold.*
   4 A: Translation technology nowadays is excellent.
      B: Yeah, *more / couldn't / I / agree.*
   5 A: I think teens spend too much time on the Internet.
      B: *true / be / That / may,* but *think / you / don't* there are some benefits to it?
   6 A: Well, *mean / depends / it / what / by / on / you* "advantages", exactly.
      B: *exactly / point / My!*

5 Order the words to make "discussion" phrases. There's one extra word in each.
   a by / of / what / depends / you / on / mean / it / …
   b let / hold / on / finish / me / in / a / second / .
   c that / can't / deny / to / we / …
   d true, / that / be / is / may / but / …
   e be / more / agree / I / couldn't / .
   f totally / am / disagree / I / .

6 ▶ 7.10 Listen to six extracts from pp. 94–95 in the SB, and number expressions a–f in **5** as you hear them.

7 **Make it personal** How much time have you spent on social media in the last seven days? Compare with a classmate. Any surprises?

Can you remember …
▸ 8 phrasal verbs? SB → p. 87
▸ 5 verbs for using a computer? SB → p. 90
▸ 1 verb to report a command? SB → p. 93
▸ 1 verb to report a request? SB → p. 93
▸ 6 phrases for expressing your views? SB → p. 95

8.1 How important are looks?

1 ▶ 8.1 Listen to the podcast. Which photo shows Lily, and which shows Kate?

1

2

2 ▶ 8.1 Listen again. True (T) or False (F)?
 a Lily doesn't like her natural looks.
 b Whenever she takes a selfie, something goes wrong.
 c Lily thinks it's fine to use filters and change photos before posting them.
 d Kate posts selfies every day.
 e She sometimes gets a friend to help her.
 f She doesn't care if people don't like her selfies.

3 Complete the extracts from the podcast with photography words.
 a No, you see I'm really camera- …, I hate it when people take my photo.
 b I never get the right angle, or it comes out with …-eye.
 c Or even worse, I get … by a bird or something!
 d I love all the apps you can get to … selfies.
 e Nobody can tell they've been …!
 f Then I use a couple of different apps to … the image.

4 Read the article quickly and choose the correct summary.
 a The writer thinks fake videos are a good thing.
 b The author thinks fake videos are a bad thing.
 c The author thinks there are both good and bad things about fake videos.

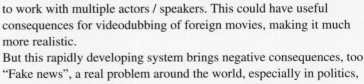

Can we trust what we see?

It's common knowledge that most of the human images we see in magazines and on social media have been retouched or perfected, but the same is now fast becoming true for videos, with extraordinary consequences.

The idea of fake videos has been around for ages, from YouTube pranks to funny "bad lipreading" videos, but recently, researchers at the University of Washington shocked the world by producing an entirely false video of Barack Obama giving a speech. What they did was take different audio extracts from talks, interviews, and speeches he's given, then use AI to create a video of him giving those talks. The technology was originally designed to improve video conferencing, as the audio is usually good on calls, but the video, taking up more bandwidth, often stops or isn't very good quality. Researchers hoped video calls could keep the audio true, but use AI to create much higher quality videos.

At the moment, this technology can only be used for one person speaking, and they can only produce a headshot. But that is changing fast, with new developments using a source actor to create gestures and facial expressions to apply to a different face. The system is also beginning to work with multiple actors / speakers. This could have useful consequences for videodubbing of foreign movies, making it much more realistic.

But this rapidly developing system brings negative consequences, too. "Fake news", a real problem around the world, especially in politics, could become an even bigger worry, as people are able to create entirely fake videos of national leaders and other important politicians. Whilst solutions are being developed to try to prevent this, nobody knows what lies ahead for video technology.

5 Reread. True (T) or False (F)?
 a Fake videos are a new thing.
 b Researchers created a fake video from real audio.
 c They wanted to improve video conferencing.
 d At the moment the fake videos show a person's whole body.
 e Fake videos could cause problems in the future.

6 **Make it personal** Do you think fake video technology is a good or bad thing? Why? Discuss with a classmate.

8.2 Do you like watching illusions?

1 **Match statements 1–5 to the responses.**

1 What was that loud bang? Was it a gun?
2 Hank and Sue are late again.
3 Kate still hasn't finished that report.
4 Enzo didn't pass the exam.
5 I arrived at the office at 4:30 p.m., but there was nobody there.

a Oh, she will. She can't have forgotten.
b They must have gone home early.
c They must have got lost again. They never take their GPS.
d No. It might have been a car or motorbike engine.
e Well, he can't have studied very hard.

2 ▶8.2 **Complete a–e with *must have*, *might have*, or *can't have* + the verbs below. Listen to check.**

| be | come | oversleep | see | win |

a The thief _____ in through that window. Look—it's still open.
b **A:** A woman answered the phone. I guess it was his wife.
  B: It _____ his wife. She died last year.
c The players look so happy. They _____ the match.
d Janet is late today. She _____.
e You _____ my sister last week. She was working in China.

3 **Look at the photo of a "floating man." How do you think he does this illusion?**

4 ▶8.3 **Listen to Josh and Alicia discussing the "floating man". Do they mention any of your ideas?**

5 ▶8.3 **Complete the extracts with the modal perfect and the verbs in parentheses. Then listen again and check.**

a He _____ (**be**) actually floating!
b He _____ (**have**) wires connected to his back.
c I think he _____ (**have**) a special frame under his body.
d It _____ (**be**) a very strong frame.
e … which he _____ (**hide**) under that rug on the ground.

6 ▶8.4 **Listen and rephrase with *must've*, *might've*, or *can't 've*. Follow the model.**

> Maybe he ate something bad.

> He might've eaten something bad.

7 🅰 **Make it personal** What's the best street performance you've ever seen? Tell a classmate.

8.3 Have you ever cut your own hair?

1 Read Sam's email and order these items as she mentions them, 1–3. Match each one to her feeling about it.

 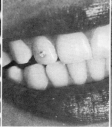 

☐ too expensive   ☐ not available where she lives   ☐ did it but regrets it

Hi Ada,
Hope everything's OK with you.
Listen, I need your help! Can you call me when you get this, please? Only you can understand what I'm going through now. You know Jason and I have been planning our wedding for ever. Ever since we got engaged last month I've been thinking about what to do to mark the date. Remember that eyeball jewel implant we saw in Amsterdam? I decided to have that, but I found out you can't get it done here. Can you believe it? Anyway, Jason gave me this gorgeous ring, so I decided to have a little diamond put in my front tooth to match it. But, wow, when I talked to the dentist, I realized I couldn't afford that, no way.
Well, to cut a long story short, last week I decided to get a tattoo on my arm—it's a red heart, with "Jason" in the center. I was surprised it didn't hurt more to be honest. But then, you'll never guess what happened on Saturday. Jason broke up with me. Really. Just like that! I think he's found somebody else, but he says he hasn't. We'll see. Anyway, now I just have to lose this tattoo. You're having yours removed with a laser, right? Should I do it now or wait a while? Please call me a.s.a.p.
xoxo,
Sam

2 ▶8.5 Write four sentences to summarize the information in the email in **1**. Listen and compare.

She wanted to speak to Ada but sent her an email instead.
 a She wanted to get a jewel …
 b She thought of getting …
 c She got …
 d Now she …

3 Reread. True (T), False (F), or don't know (D)?
 a Ada must be Sam's best friend.
 b Sam and Jason had been engaged for a long time.
 c Sam threw away Jason's ring.
 d The tattoo took ages to do.
 e Sam was expecting to split up with Jason.
 f Jason might have a new girlfriend.
 g Ada and Sam both have tattoos and want to laser them off.

4 ▶8.6 Listen and rephrase the sentences. Follow the model.

Model: *I have my hair cut at the hair salon. Yesterday.*
You: *I had my hair cut at the hair salon yesterday.*

5 Answer the questions in the ID Task Manager to find what you should do with tasks a–g, and add three more of your own.
 a clean / room
 b cut / hair
 c clean / something (what?)
 d redecorate / something (what?)
 e make dinner
 f manage your social network
 g fix / something (what?)

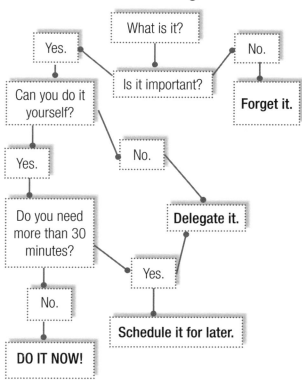

ID Task Manager

6 **Make it personal** For each item in **5** you delegate, make a statement like this:

I'm going to get my (teeth cleaned). I'll ask (my dentist) to do it.

7 **Connect**

Go to draw.io and make a flowchart to help you make a decision about something. Send it to a friend and ask them if it helped them make a decision

8.4 Do you have a lot of furniture in your room?

1 Use the clues to complete the crossword.

Across
1 Put a glass of water on me and your alarm clock.
3 Put your books in me.
5 Sit on me.
7 Look at me and see yourself.
8 Rest your head on me.
10 Sleep on me.

Down
2 Fold and put your clothes in me.
4 Sleep under me.
5 Hang your clothes in me.
6 Switch me on to see.
9 Put me on the floor.

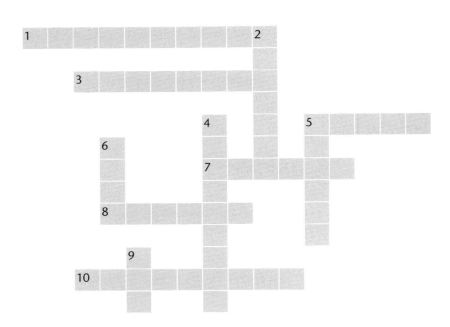

2 Read the first paragraph of the article, and circle the correct alternative in a–c.
  a More / Fewer people are living in cities.
  b Apartments in a few / many cities are getting smaller.
  c Designers are / aren't adapting to the changes.

Modern Home **DESIGN**

The world is urbanizing, and, with more and more people living in a small space, we are seeing changes in the houses and apartments we live in. One of the biggest, or should I say smallest, changes is in the size of our living space. Modern apartments, from New York to Tokyo and London to Rio, are getting increasingly smaller, and therefore, we are having to find interesting new ways to make everything fit. Here is our favorite space-saving design of the week.

The BedUp
At night it looks like any other ¹_____, but when you wake up in the morning you can lift the ²_____ up so that it is suspended from the ³_____. Imagine the space you can save—3 square meters to be exact. Under the ⁴_____ is a ⁵_____ so that you can work during the day. Small ⁶_____ in the bottom of the ⁷_____ give plenty of light so you can see what you are doing. At night you clear the top of your ⁸_____ and the ⁹_____ drops back to the ¹⁰_____, ready for you to climb in and go to sleep. Genius!

Come back next week for more top designs!

3 Read the second paragraph and complete 1–10 with these words. You can use each word more than once.

  bed   ceiling   desk   floor   lamps

4 ◯8.7 Complete a–g with tag questions. Listen to check and repeat. Pay attention to the intonation and mark the tags ↗ or ↘.

Random Question Generator

a You're not American, _____?
b It's hot today, _____?
c You like soccer, _____?
d You had an English class yesterday, _____?
e The teacher won't give a test this week, _____?
f You'll finish your homework soon, _____?
g You'd like a coffee now, _____?

5 **Make it personal** Record a description of your house or apartment for a partner, then share it with them. Use all the words in the puzzle in **1**.

8.5 What's the hardest part of language learning?

1 Read the article and match the headings to paragraphs a–d. There are two extra.

- Mix your methods
- Read a lot
- Don't be afraid!
- Open your ears
- More than the language
- Guessing is good

Four language learning hints

Learning a new foreign language is hard work—but there are things you can do to make it quicker and easier. Read on to find out.

a
We spend most of our "communication time" listening, so this is obviously an essential skill to develop. But how? Living abroad is expensive and language classes don't always focus on listening. Well luckily for you, sound is all around you—from songs to streamed TV shows to podcasts. All you need to do is find the time to put your headphones on. A little every day is best.

b
How you feel about the language is the key to progression. If you learn about the culture behind the language, you will understand more about the language itself and feel more comfortable speaking with fluent speakers.

c
Sometimes we don't know exactly what a word means, even in our own language, and that is fine. In a foreign language this obviously happens more often, so learn to relax about it. Now, dictionaries are great and every language student should have one, but don't pick it up for every word you don't know. Instead, learn to focus on the words you know and trust your guesses for the ones you don't.

d
This is the most important tip of all. It doesn't matter how many conjugations you know or how much vocabulary you've studied. If you are paralyzed with fear when you have to produce it, it is all a wasted effort. Everybody will be pleased that you are trying; the more you try, the better you'll feel, and the better you feel, the more you'll want to learn. So forget your insecurity. Hold your nose and jump in! Mistakes are learning opportunities. The more you speak, the quicker you will improve. So go for it!

2 **Reread and underline:**
   a three things to listen to.
   b a problem with studying in another country.
   c a way to feel better when talking to fluent speakers.
   d advice for looking up words.
   e two things that happen when you make an effort to speak.

3 ▶8.8 Add a suffix (*-ion*, *-ive*, *-ly*, *-ial*, *-able*, *-ity*) to form a word from the text, making the necessary changes. Mark the new stress and listen to check.

a com•fort_____
b commu•nicate_____
c •essence_____
d ex•pense_____
e inse•cure_____
f •obvious_____

4 ▶8.9 Complete comments a–e with one word, and correct one mistake in each. Listen to check.

a I agree! Speaking is more important then reading and writing. But they are _____ important, too. *Posted by NYAL*

b I'm much _____ at reading than listening and I want improve. Thanks for the tips! ☺ *Posted by EdBoy*

c I watched two episodes of a TV show online, but I couldn't understanding _____ of them. ☹ *Posted by Cori*

d I love listening! But I prefer American accents _____ British ones. They are more easier to understand. *Posted by Kweli*

e @Kweli, do you think? I can't understand _____ of them. I more prefer non-native accents like Japanese or German. *Posted by GlobalGirl*

5 🎤 **Make it personal** Write a comment about your listening skills. Use the comments in 4 to help you. Share it with a friend. Do you agree?

Can you remember …
- 7 phrasal verbs about photography? SB→p. 99
- the difference between *must have*, *might have*, and *can't have*? SB→p. 100
- how to use the causative with *have* and *get*? SB→p. 103
- 11 furniture words? SB→p. 104
- rules for tag questions in ⊕ and ⊖ statements? SB→p. 105
- how intonation changes the function of tag questions? SB→p. 105
- 3 ways to predict information when listening? SB→p. 106

9.1 Does crime worry you?

1 ▶9.1 Circle the word with the different underlined sound. Listen to check.

a	a br<u>i</u>be	the pol<u>i</u>ce	a sp<u>ee</u>ding fine
b	a cr<u>i</u>me	to k<u>i</u>dnap	v<u>i</u>olence
c	organi<u>z</u>ed	pira<u>c</u>y	to go to pri<u>s</u>on
d	a cre<u>d</u>it card	to s<u>t</u>eal	sta<u>t</u>istics

2 ▶9.2 Listen to extracts 1–4. How many times do you hear the sounds in the pictures?

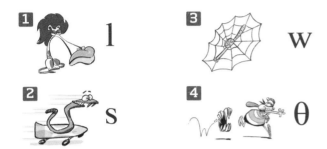

3 ▶9.2 Listen again and write the extracts.

4 Complete the table. Mark the stress on the words you write.

5 Change the underlined words to rewrite a–f.

a In the movie *Psycho*, Norman Bates <u>murders</u> travelers.
   In *Psycho*, the character Norman Bates is a _murderer_.
b A recent report says the number of <u>bribes</u> paid to politicians round the world tripled between 2015 and 2018.
   _____ in politics tripled over three years round the world according to a recent report.
c <u>Kidnappers</u> have taken a local businessman and are demanding money.
   Criminals _____ a businessman and are holding him until they receive cash.
d The Mafia is an international <u>criminal organization</u>.
   The Mafia is an international group that specializes in _____ .
e Three men <u>robbed</u> the bank yesterday and got away with over $5,000.
   There was a _____ at the bank yesterday.
f The police are looking for a female suspect after the <u>theft</u> of a painting from a museum.
   The police are searching for a woman after she _____ a painting from a museum.

6 ▶9.3 Listen to a tour guide and answer a–d.

a Who is the man in the photo?
b Where did he live?
c Who was Herbert Hoover?
d Why did the man in the photo finally go to prison?

7 ▶9.4 Complete extracts a–d with the verbs in parentheses in the simple, continuous, perfect, or perfect continuous tense. Listen to check.

a You _____ at the site of one of the most famous Chicago legends. (**look**)
b _____ you _____ who lived at the Lexington Hotel? (**know**)
c Oh yeah! I _____ about him. (**hear**)
d They arrested him because he _____ tax for many years on his illegal money. (**not pay**)

8 🗣 **Make it personal** What famous crimes have there been in your country? Discuss with a partner.

44

9.2 How could your city be improved?

1 ▶9.5 Put the words in a–d in order to make sentences. Cross out one extra word in each. Listen to check.
 a named / of / innovative / the / was / most / Medellín / world's / recently / city / .
 b was / different / were / eight / judged / by / it / criteria / .
 c and / created / communities / was / public / government / reached / spaces / were / programs / these / .
 d neighborhood / by / a / considered / dangerous / once / this / was / slum / .

2 Read the web comments and mark them ⊕ positive or ⊖ negative.

What makes you proud of your city?

Isabel: My favorite singer, Shakira, ¹_____ born here. *9 months ago*

Jed: Help! I ²_____ surrounded by idiots all the time. I need to get out of here! *11 months ago*

Caitlin: Well, I just love the Statue of Liberty. It ³_____ given by the French. *11 months ago*

Jose: We have a beautiful park that ⁴_____ filled with trees and birds. It's very peaceful. *1 year ago*

Donna: Er, let's see. There ⁵_____ the place ... oh no, wait. How about all the ... hang on. We have a great ... nope, nothing. *1 year ago*

Simon: We have the world's first subway system. It started in 1863—but it ⁶_____ updated a lot since then! *18 months ago*

3 Complete the comments in 2 with the verb *be*. Which one is not the passive voice?

4 Read the article and match the headings 1–4 to paragraphs a–c. There's one extra heading.
 1 Global success
 2 Birth of a system
 3 Quality not quantity
 4 How it works

URBAN MOBILITY

BRT system in Curitiba

a When the city of Curitiba, Brazil, hit one million inhabitants in the 1970s, it couldn't afford a $300-million subway system. So <u>somebody developed an alternative system</u>, the Bus Rapid Transit (BRT). Today, <u>people consider it</u> a success because it combines the speed of trains with the low cost of buses.

b <u>People often compare Curitiba's bus system</u> to a subway system: exclusive lanes, pre-paid ticket counters, good quality stations, and sensors that communicate with smart traffic lights. Today, <u>Curitiba's 2.3 million residents use its buses</u> to commute to work quickly and efficiently.

c <u>People have adopted the BRT system</u> in 83 cities worldwide, including Guangzhou, one of China's fastest-growing cities, and <u>the Canadian government will soon implement it</u> in parts of Saskatoon.

5 Transform the underlined phrases in 4 to the passive voice. Only use *by* + **agent** if necessary.

6 ▶9.6 Transform what you hear into the passive voice. Follow the model.

We have made a lot of progress.

A lot of progress has been made.

7 **Make it personal** What makes you proud of your city? Think of the top three things, then share with a classmate. Any surprises?

9.3 Have you ever been to court?

1 ▶9.7 Listen to two friends discussing a news story. Check the correct headline.

> 19-year-old arrested for illegal downloads: 13 GB found on hard drive
> NY teen arrested for selling movie before official release date

2 ▶9.7 Listen again. True (T) or False (F)?
   a All of Peter's downloads were illegal.
   b He was sentenced to five years in prison.
   c He shared a download link for *Toy Story 4* on the Internet.
   d He made a lot of money selling the movie.

3 ▶9.8 Listen to the rest of the dialogue. Are these the opinions of the man (M), woman (W), or neither (N)?
   He should:
   ☐ be acquitted
   ☐ do community service
   ☐ pay a fine
   ☐ be sentenced to life
   ☐ be sentenced to one year in prison

4 Match the start of criminal biographies 1–2 to two of endings a–c.

1. Adam Worth (1844-1902) was the original master criminal. At 17, he joined the American Union Army but was soon registered as "killed in action", giving him the opportunity to begin his criminal career. In 1869, when detectives were tracking him after a bank robbery in Boston, he decided to move to Europe. From there, he organized crimes such as illegal gambling in Paris, diamond thefts in South Africa, art thefts in England, and bank robberies in Belgium.

2. Today he is known as Frank W. Abagnale, but this is just one of nine identities he has used. Frank started by writing false paychecks for his various bank accounts. Then at 16, he decided to travel the world so he created an employee ID and pilot's licence and then phoned Pan Am airways claiming to be a pilot who had lost his uniform. With the right clothes, he flew around the world staying in five-star hotels and using fake checks, a life that inspired the movie *Catch Me If You Can*.

…

a. French police eventually caught him, but 12 other countries also wanted to charge him with fraud. After a year in prison in France, he spent six months in a Swedish jail. Next he was returned to the U.S., where he was sentenced to 12 years. After just five, the FBI approached him to work as a security consultant, a job that he still has today.

b. He moved first to Australia and then to Brazil. Four years later, the police discovered where he was hiding, but by that time he'd had a son and could not be extradited. He stayed in Brazil for 31 years before returning voluntarily to the UK to face the rest of his 30-year sentence. He spent eight years in prison, but was released just before his 80th birthday.

c. He earned the nickname "the Napoleon of Crime" for his various criminal activities and was also the inspiration for the character Moriarty: Sherlock Holmes' criminal adversary. He was eventually caught for a robbery in Belgium and sentenced to seven years in prison, although he was released after four for good behavior.

5 Reread and answer whether a–f are true of Adam Worth (A), Frank W. Abagnale (F), or both (B).
   a started committing crimes at a young age.
   b is no longer alive
   c was an international criminal
   d was released early
   e used his criminal experience legally
   f had a movie made about his life

6 ▶9.9 Listen and repeat the underlined extracts from 4. Notice the connections, schwas, and silent letters.

7 **Make it personal** Circle the correct preposition in a–e. Note your answers then share them with a classmate.
   a How much stress are you **under / with** at the moment?
   b Do you stop for a coffee **in / on** your way to work or school?
   c What is **in / on** the street corner near your house?
   d Have you ever waited more than an hour **for / to** a bus?
   e How many **from / of** your friends are the same age as you?

46

9.4 Where will you be living ten years from now?

1 ▶9.10 Listen and number the phrases, 1–10, as you hear them.

- [2] Want to go?
- [ ] Do you think he'll have stopped smoking?
- [ ] We'll be working tomorrow.
- [ ] We love beans cooked by your mother.
- [ ] It will spread across the park.
- [1] One, two, go!
- [ ] Do you think he loved hot smoking?
- [ ] It will be working tomorrow.
- [ ] It will have been cooked by your mother.
- [ ] Wheels, spread across the park.

2 Read the article and cross out the three unnecessary sentences.

Stay safe online

The boom in technology means that laptops, smart phones, and tablets are everywhere. Unfortunately, so are the criminals who are trying to get inside them. Read our security tips to learn how to protect yourself from cybercrime.

Tip 1: Make sure your anti-virus software is **up-to-date**. Let it expire before you renew it. Hackers are creating new viruses all the time and only the very latest software can truly protect you.

Tip 2: Get a **tracking** app. Tablets and smart phones are the perfect **target** for thieves. Download a tracking app so the police can follow your device and find it.

Tip 3: Use strong **passwords**. Combinations of numbers and letters are a good idea. Add capital letters, too, if you can. Try using your name and birthday—nobody will guess that! And don't use the same password for multiple accounts.

Tip 4: Click carefully. Don't **click** on links in emails and social networks, especially if you don't know where they came from.

Tip 5: Turn Wi-Fi off. If you can use your device as a Wi-Fi **hotspot**, protect it with a password and turn off the hotspot when you're not using it. Don't use the Internet at home. This will prevent other people signing in to your network.

3 Match the **bold** words in **2** to their definitions and examples a–f.

a _____ noun (C) an area with a lot of activity. A popular area. Usually two words but one when referring to the Internet. E.g. *This area was a crime _____ a few years ago, but it's safe now.*

b _____ verb (-ing, -ed) to follow evidence. E.g. *The hunters _____ the tiger through the forest.*

c _____ adj. very modern. E.g. *The surgeons used _____ techniques.*

d _____ noun (C) a thing you want to get, attack, or achieve. E.g. *Our sales _____ is 500 units per month.*

e _____ noun (C) a word or phrase that lets you enter. E.g. *You can't come in until you give me the _____.*

f _____ verb (-ing, -ed) select something on a computer screen by pressing a button. E.g. *Use the mouse to _____ on the icon.*

4 Rewrite a–e using **by**.

a You can make your computer more secure if you use virus protection software.
b The last guests arrived just before 10:00 p.m.
c Some hackers uploaded the malware.
d Midnight is the latest I'll be home. I may get home before that.
e Tony improved a lot because he worked hard.

5 ▶9.11 Listen to two colleagues. True (T) or False (F)? Is Sam A or B in the photo?

a Both men are looking forward to the weekend.
b Sam has to give his boss the report first thing on Monday.
c Sam is going to watch sport at the weekend.
d Sam likes the Lakers.

6 ▶9.11 Complete extracts a–d with three words in each. Listen again to check, and repeat.

a I think I _____ all the way through.
b He just gave it to me and he _____ Monday.
c Hopefully _____ finished in time to watch the game.
d If the Lakers win, my prayers _____ answered.

7 Write ➕ or ➖ future sentences in 1–3 about Sam and Phil. Use the verbs given.

1 Sam _____ (**have fun**) this weekend.
2 Sam _____ (**finish the report**) Saturday evening.
3 Phil _____ (**see his children**) this weekend.

8 🔵 **Make it personal** What do you do to stay safe on social media? Discuss with a classmate.

9.5 Do you watch TV crime dramas?

1 Read the headline and choose the best definition for the crime.

Man Charged with Arson After Cigars Catch Fire

a **arson**: *noun*. Smoking in public places.
b **arson**: *verb*. To play with fire.
c **arson**: *noun*. Burning something deliberately.

2 ▶9.12 Read and order the rest of the story, 1–5. Listen to check.

○ The insurance company refuses to pay the lawyer and he takes them to court. The judge decides that because the insurance company hadn't specified what kind of fire was unacceptable, they would have to pay.

○ The insurance company pays the lawyer but then … they have him arrested for arson, saying that he had deliberately burned his own property to claim the insurance money!

○ So, have you heard the story about the lawyer and the cigars? Here's how it goes.

○ About a month later he contacts the insurance company to ask for his money because his cigars have disappeared in "a series of very small fires".

○ A lawyer buys a box of very rare, expensive cigars. To protect them, he takes out an insurance policy so that if they are damaged he can receive some money.

3 ▶9.13 Listen to three dialogues. Match three of excuses a–e you hear to photos 1–3.
a Just hear me out.
b It's not what it looks like!
c It's not what you're thinking.
d It's not what it seems.
e I can explain.

4 ▶9.13 Listen again. True (T) or False (F)?
a Brad's computer had a problem and crashed.
b Brad's sorry for upsetting Yvette.
c Terry accepts responsibility for the kitchen.
d Terry's mother believes him.
e Leony's ex-boyfriend has sent her a text.
f Leony's sorry that Mark is upset.

5 ▶9.14 Look back and match lesson titles 9.1–9.5 to answers a–f. Listen to check and write the follow-up question each time.
a ☐ Er … I don't know. I guess I'll still be living in this city somewhere.
b ☐ No, of course I haven't!
c ☐ It doesn't really worry me too much. I live in a safe neighborhood and I've never been a target.
d ☐ Not really, no. They're not my favorite sort of program.
e ☐ I guess it would be better if there was more public transportation at night.

6  **Make it personal** Discuss your answer to the question in lesson title 9.1 with a classmate. Any surprises?

Can you remember …
▶ 10 crimes? SB→p.112
▶ 4 verb aspects? SB→p.113
▶ how to form the passive voice? SB→p.115
▶ 6 punishments for crimes? SB→p.116
▶ 2 verb tenses to talk about the future? SB→p.119
▶ 5 phrases for giving excuses? SB→p.121

10.1 What drives you crazy?

1 Match a–e to 1–5 to make quotes about anger. Which one suggests anger is positive?

a "Anger is never without reason,
b "When angry, count to four;
c "People won't have time for you
d "Don't make me angry.
e "When people are sad, they don't do anything.

1 You wouldn't like me when I'm angry." David Banner
2 They just cry. But when they get angry, they **bring about** a change." Malcom X
3 but **seldom** with a good one." Benjamin Franklin
4 when very angry, swear." Mark Twain
5 if you are always angry or **complaining**." Stephen Hawking

2 Match the **bold** words in **1** to their definitions.

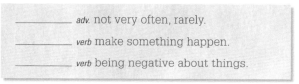

_____ adv. not very often, rarely.
_____ verb make something happen.
_____ verb being negative about things.

3 ▶10.1 Match dialogues 1–3 to what has angered each person. There are two extra.
☐ bad drivers ☐ insincerity ☐ school ☐ weather ☐ work

4 ▶10.1 Listen again. True (T) or False (F)?

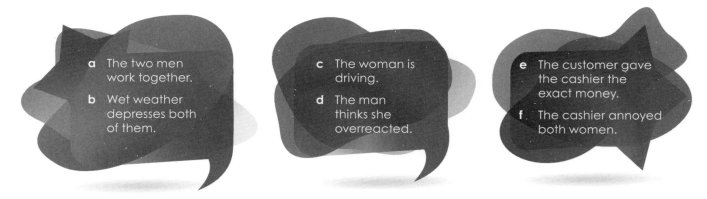

a The two men work together.
b Wet weather depresses both of them.
c The woman is driving.
d The man thinks she overreacted.
e The customer gave the cashier the exact money.
f The cashier annoyed both women.

5 ▶10.2 Listen and repeat a–e making the connections. Notice the silent letters.
a ups_and_downs
b little by little
c sick_and_tired_ of_it
d peace_and quiet
e again_and_again

6 ▶10.3 Listen to dialogues 1–5. At the beep, write the missing phrase, a–e, from **5**.

7 🗣 Make it personal Share your favorite love, hate, or anger quote from **1** with a classmate.

10.2 What do you love to hate?

1 Read the article about pet hates and add these headings. There is one extra.

> Car modifications   Chewing gum
> Eating on public transportation   Music in stores

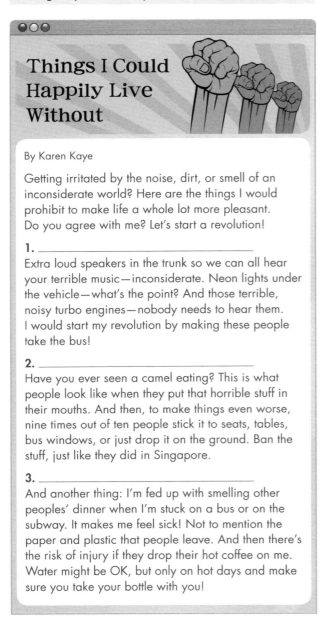

Things I Could Happily Live Without

By Karen Kaye

Getting irritated by the noise, dirt, or smell of an inconsiderate world? Here are the things I would prohibit to make life a whole lot more pleasant. Do you agree with me? Let's start a revolution!

1. _____
Extra loud speakers in the trunk so we can all hear your terrible music—inconsiderate. Neon lights under the vehicle—what's the point? And those terrible, noisy turbo engines—nobody needs to hear them. I would start my revolution by making these people take the bus!

2. _____
Have you ever seen a camel eating? This is what people look like when they put that horrible stuff in their mouths. And then, to make things even worse, nine times out of ten people stick it to seats, tables, bus windows, or just drop it on the ground. Ban the stuff, just like they did in Singapore.

3. _____
And another thing: I'm fed up with smelling other peoples' dinner when I'm stuck on a bus or on the subway. It makes me feel sick! Not to mention the paper and plastic that people leave. And then there's the risk of injury if they drop their hot coffee on me. Water might be OK, but only on hot days and make sure you take your bottle with you!

2 Reread the article and answer a–e.
   a Which problem does Karen feel is dangerous?
   b Which item is illegal in another country?
   c Which problem does not cause litter?
   d Which problem does Karen suggest a punishment for?
   e Which problem causes Karen to have a physical reaction?

3 ▶10.4 Complete the comments on the article with these verbs. Add a preposition if necessary. Listen to check and notice the /ŋ/ sounds.

> complain   listen   make   meet   stop   throw

a 💬 **Len** 1 hour ago
If people showed a little more consideration, this city would be much nicer. We're all responsible _____ things better. Let's get out there and do it. No more gum! Viva the revolution!

b 💬 **Lady1** 2 days ago
Don't you think there are bigger things to worry about? Poverty, crime, violence. _____ these problems should be the priority.

c 💬 **Crazyboy** 2 days ago
Why don't you just stay at home and avoid _____ other people? Problem solved.

d 💬 **SamSame** 3 days ago
Not _____ your trash in the trash can is just laziness, there's no other excuse for it. It makes the city look really bad.

e 💬 **Kimbo7** 3 days ago
Hey! I enjoy _____ to my music when I'm driving. It's better than hearing people like you complain all the time.

f 💬 **Fifi88** 3 days ago
Instead _____ about people on the Internet, why don't you learn to be a little more tolerant?

4 Do the posts agree (A) or disagree (D) with the writer?

5 ▶10.5 Listen to five more comments. Write five words in each of a–e.

a @ **Crazyboy**
You _____. She's allowed to have her opinion.

b @ **Lady1**
Sure, nice idea. But who's _____? What can we do?

c @ **SamSame**
Honestly, I'm _____ that.
When did a few pieces of paper hurt anybody?

d @ **Kimbo7**
Come on, you've got to admit it.
She does _____.

e @ **Len**
_____ improving the city, sure, but banning chewing gum? Don't you think that's a little extreme?

6 🗣 **Make it personal** Add your own "pet hate" to the article in **1**. Share it with a classmate. Are they annoyed by the same thing?

50

10.3 How assertive are you?

1. Take our unit 10 preposition quiz. Complete the phrases in **bold** with a preposition.

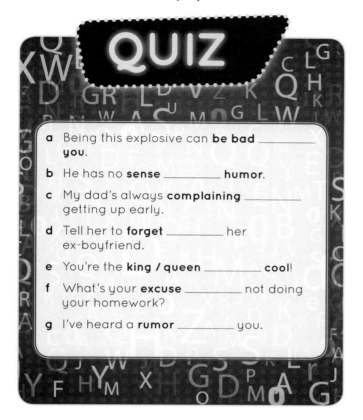

a. Being this explosive can **be bad** _____ you.
b. He has no **sense** _____ humor.
c. My dad's always **complaining** _____ getting up early.
d. Tell her to **forget** _____ her ex-boyfriend.
e. You're the **king / queen** _____ cool!
f. What's your **excuse** _____ not doing your homework?
g. I've heard a **rumor** _____ you.

2. Complete sentences a–d with an infinitive and a gerund phrase using the given words.
   a. stop / ask for / directions
   After driving for half an hour we realized we were lost, so we _____.
   After we bought our new GPS we _____.
   b. try / open / the door
   My hotel room was so hot because the a/c was broken. I _____ and windows, but it made no difference.
   The other day I locked my keys inside the car! I _____ with a paperclip, like in the movies, but it didn't work.
   c. remember / visit / grandparents
   I must _____ this weekend. It's their 50th wedding anniversary.
   Do you _____ when you were a child? What did you do together?
   d. stop / buy / milk
   After work I _____ because I had run out at breakfast.
   My wife and I _____ after the health scares. They said on the news that it was dangerous.

3. *Tense review.* Complete the movie review with the best form of the verbs in parentheses.

Red, who _____ (**play**) by Jason Sudeikis, is a flightless bird who _____ (**live**) on an island with other flightless birds. Red has trouble controlling his temper, and one day he _____ (**order**) to take an anger management class, because he _____ (**break**) an egg when he _____ (**lose**) his temper. Soon the island _____ (**visit**) by a group of "friendly" pigs who are welcomed by the birds. Red becomes suspicious but nobody listens to him. One day, they wake up and find the pigs _____ (**destroy**) the island. Everyone is sorry they _____ (**not believe**) Red when he tried to warn them. Now the angry birds must attack Piggy Island to try and get their eggs back. Can they do it?

4. ▶10.6 Listen to five situations and respond after the beep using a–e with an infinitive or gerund.
   a. Why don't we stop (**have**) a break?
   b. I don't remember (**put**) them there.
   c. Have you tried (**drink**) some water?
   d. Could you please stop (**do**) that?
   e. Please, try (**remember**).

5. **Make it personal** What other movies do you know about an angry person? Share with a classmate.

6. **Connect**
   Go to brainyquote.com and find an interesting quote on hate or anger. Send it to a classmate and see what they think.

51

10.4 How similar are you to your friends?

1 Complete the brochure with *yourself*, *themselves*, or *myself*. Do you do any of these things?

Guide to Emotional Well-being

a ➡ Every day, repeat the phrase "I like _____, I like _____. I love _____!"

b ➡ See _____ as others see you. You'll be surprised how positive the impression is.

c ➡ Understand that if someone is treating you badly, they probably don't like _____ either.

d ➡ Do _____ a favor. Learn to be independent. Get out and do things on your own.

e ➡ Accept that everybody doubts _____ sometimes. It's natural, but you can learn to beat it.

2 Study these sentences. Match phrasal verbs 1–8 to definitions a–h.

1 Watching the news always <u>brings me down</u>.
2 I never read the instructions for a new gadget, I just use it and try to <u>figure it out</u>.
3 My older sister used to <u>boss me around</u> all the time when we were young.
4 I <u>get along well with</u> my parents.
5 You look like you're <u>coming down with</u> a cold.
6 My wife always <u>lifts me up</u> when I'm feeling sad.
7 I hate it when I <u>fall out with</u> my family.
8 Once you've decided what to do, you should <u>stick to</u> it.

a tell somebody what to do
b become sick with something
c make somebody feel sad
d have an argument with somebody
e continue, not change your mind
f have a good relationship with somebody
g find the answer, understand
h make somebody feel happier

3 ▶10.7 *Intuitive quiz!* Match 1–8 to the responses. Then complete with phrasal verbs from **2** and the correct object (or no object). Listen to check. How good were your guesses?

1 What's wrong? Are you sick?
2 I just don't know how to use this software.
3 Wow, you look great!
4 Oh, no, I failed my driving test!
5 Clara always tells me what to do.
6 I really wanted to stay in last night, but then John called and …
7 Why aren't you speaking to Lisa?
8 Do you like your brother?

a Don't let it _____. You can always take it again.
b Oh, we _____ last weekend and had a fight.
c Ugh, I think I'm _____ the flu.
d Oh, yes, I _____ him.
e Let me see. I'm sure we can _____ together.
f You shouldn't let her _____ like that.
g Aw thanks! You always know how to _____.
h No, really? Don't let him change your mind! Decide what you want and _____!

4 ▶10.8 Listen again and say the correct response after the beep.

5 **Make it personal** Choose three of the questions or sentences in **3** and write your own responses. Read them to a classmate. Can they guess which questions or sentences they respond to?

10.5 What do you find hardest about English?

1 Match a–f to 1–6 to make quotes. Check your favorite.

- **a** Learn from the mistakes of others. You …
- **b** Don't be afraid of making mistakes. Be …
- **c** Everyone makes mistakes. The wise are not …
- **d** Anyone who has never made a …
- **e** The greatest mistake you can make in …
- **f** Nothing that is worth …

- **1** those who never make mistakes, but those who forgive themselves and learn from their mistakes. *Ajahn Brahm*
- **2** mistake has never tried anything new. *Albert Einstein*
- **3** can't live long enough to make them all yourself. *Eleanor Roosevelt*
- **4** learning can be taught. *Oscar Wilde*
- **5** afraid of not learning from them. *Anonymous*
- **6** life is to be continually fearing you will make one. *Elbert Hubbard*

2 ▶10.9 Proofread and correct students' sentences a–j. Four have no mistakes; the others have two mistakes each. Listen to a teacher giving the class feedback to check. How many did you get right?

- a I told to her it is difficult and asked her to help me.
- b A lot new hotels are building in my city.
- c It started raining soon after we left the house.
- d My dad complains to get up early in the morning.
- e I can't remember where is the my car.
- f Where did you get your eyes checked?
- g Can you tell me who wrote this song?
- h How long are you living this city?
- i He was awarded an Oscar for his role in the movie.
- j She works like a secretary for a company who specializes in import / export.

3 Circle the correct alternatives in the poster.

Our strengths and weaknesses in English

1 I **think** / **find** it easy **to read** / **read** in English but a little boring.
2 I'm not so good **to remember** / **at remembering** new words.
3 I have a lot of **difficulty** / **difficult** pronouncing "sh" and "ch."
4 **To listen** / **Listening** is very hard.
5 **It's** / **Is** difficult to speak without pausing a lot.

4 ▶10.10 Give the advice below to students 1–5 in **3**. Put the <u>verbs</u> in the correct form. Listen to five student-teacher dialogues to check.

- a A good way of <u>improve</u> your pronunciation <u>be</u> <u>record</u> yourself.
- b Try <u>focus</u> on the stressed words.
- c How about <u>learn</u> some common phrases like "I mean" or "you know"?
- d You should <u>consider</u> <u>read</u> things you <u>be</u> interested in.
- e Have you <u>think</u> about <u>keep</u> a notebook for new words?

5 Look back through Student's Book units 6–10 and choose:

Page number:	Reason you chose this one?
The most interesting reading text.	
The best song line.	
The most difficult grammar point.	
The funniest cartoon in the Grammar section (p. 138–157).	
The most enjoyable listening / video.	

6 **Make it personal** Share your answers to **5** with a classmate. Do they agree?

Can you remember …

- 8 mood words? SB→p. 124
- 6 binomial phrases? SB→p. 125
- 4 verbs followed by a gerund? SB→p. 126
- 4 words / phrases followed by *for*? SB→p. 127
- 4 words / phrases followed by *of*? SB→p. 127
- 3 verbs with a different meaning when followed by an infinitive or a gerund? SB→p. 128
- 6 phrasal verbs? SB→p. 132
- 4 phrases to describe strengths and weaknesses? SB→p. 132
- 6 phrases for making recommendations? SB→p. 133

Audioscript

Unit 6

6.2
M = man   W = woman

1. M It's the first thing I look at in the morning and the last thing I check at night. I have to know what's happening in the world.
   W Well, I try to limit how much time I spend on it. There is so much information on there that it can take over your life.
2. W Yep, same time every day. I love it. All that drama, the hair and the heavy make-up. Some are very good, too. Great acting, great screenplays, and beautiful locations.
   M Great acting? You must be joking! No way! I have no patience for soaps. The TV networks show them instead of my team, it really annoys me. I love watching my team play.
3. M I'm voting for Jamal, he's pretty awesome on the stage.
   W Totally. Yeah, great voice, but the judges are giving him a hard time.
4. M Love them all, you know? Old episodes of *House*, *Grey's Anatomy*, you name it.
   W Yep, me, too. Weird, though. We're not even doctors.
5. W Can't stand Letterman. Don't like the acid humor. I love Ellen, though … Ellen DeGeneres?
   M Nope. Never watched Ellen, but come on, Letterman's hilarious.

6.6
Warning!
There is a dangerous virus going around. It's called WORK.
If you receive WORK from your colleagues, boss, or anyone else, via email or any other means, DON'T TOUCH IT UNDER ANY CIRCUMSTANCES!
This virus will destroy your private life completely. If you come into contact with WORK, put on your jacket, take two good friends and get out.
The only antidote is known as EN-TER-TAIN-MENT. You can find it in bars, clubs and movie theaters. Take the antidote repeatedly until WORK has been completely eliminated from your system.
Forward this warning immediately to at least five friends. If you realize that you do not have five friends, this means that you are already infected and that WORK already controls your life.
Remember! It is a deadly virus!

6.7
a Make sure you go home on time.
b Think about taking a vacation somewhere.
c Always have enough water to drink.
d Never try to do more than you can.
e If you take regular breaks, you'll be more efficient.

6.8
L = Lynn   D = Djamilla

L Hi, Djamilla. Hey, I've just been reading a list of things artists want in their dressing rooms, you know, when they perform. They are crazy!
D Yeah! Any good ones?
L Loads. Guess what Beyoncé wants?
D No idea. Flowers? Diet Coke? A huge bathtub?
L No, Bey wants really juicy baked chicken, with fresh garlic, salt, black pepper, and cayenne pepper, you know?
D No way! Like really hot chicken? Maybe it's good for her voice.
L Yeah. Hot babe Bey eats real hot chicken in the dressing room.
D Well, I heard Katy Perry wants a really specific list of crazy stuff.
L Oooohhh! What does California girl want in her dressing room?
D She wants, like … a modern, glass top dressing room table and uh … a pair of really ornate French orange floor lamps.
L You're kidding, right? A couple of ornate French lamps!!!
D I know, how crazy is that?
L Shhhhhhh. Listen. I heard Britney Spears used to demand a framed picture of Lady Diana … mphhhhhh.
D What? You can't be serious. A picture of Lady Diana?
L I swear it's true. Well, at least that's what I heard. Bizarre, right? But not everybody is that crazy. I mean, RiRi only wants Oreo cookies, nothing fancy.
D RiRi? Who's that?
L What! You don't know? That's Rihanna— girlfriend!
D Oh, right! RiRi, cool! So, she only wants cookies? That's sweet.
L I know, right. I guess she can't live without them!
D "It takes me all the way. I want you to staaaay!"
L Woo! Go girl! And you know Adele? She insists that anyone who gets free tickets for her shows has to make a donation to a charity.
D Wow. Free tickets. I wish! Girl, I'd love to see Adele. She's awesome.
L Yeah … That would be just great.

Unit 7

7.3
a The check is in the mail.
b You pay this one, I'll pay next time.
c We can still be good friends.
d You look great, Carol!
e Please believe me, Tina, I didn't marry him for his money.
f This has never happened to me before.

7.4
G = Greg   J = Janet

J … Sure! How can I help you?
G Well, I need to know how to upload music from my computer to my tablet.
J OK. Let's see if I can help you. Uh … First of all, can you tell me what kind of tablet you have?
G Yes. It's an iPad.
J OK. I wonder if you've installed iTunes on your computer?
G I what? I have no idea what you're talking about, Janet … I'm not really familiar with software names.
J Oh, dear. Never mind … Uh … Do you at least know if you have a Mac or a PC?
G Yes, that I can tell you. I have a MacBook.
J Good, Greg! So you do have iTunes after all! Phew!
G Whatever. Maybe you could now tell me how I can upload music to my tablet?
J Yes, of course, you just …

7.5
a Can you tell me …
b I wonder if …
c I have no idea if …
d I need to know if …
e Do you know if …
f Do you have any idea …
g Could you tell me …

7.6
a How old are you?
b Where do you live?
c Do you have a fast car?
d When did you start learning English?
e Can you dance well?
f Who would you take to a desert island?

7.10
Extract 1
The book's called *The Dumbest Generation* and basically it says that the Internet is making young people stupid.
Well, he has a point.
Seriously Tom?

59

Audioscript

Yeah, I mean we can't deny that teens are buying fewer books ...

Extract 2
We're not reading as much as people in their 30s or 40s, you know. I mean, book stores like Borders are going out of business week after week. I find that ...
Well, it depends on what you mean by reading. It's ... it's not that teens are reading less.

Extract 3
I don't know, but you see, the point is, reading has been on the decline for ...
Barbara, but don't you think ...
Hold on a second, let me finish. Listen, people have been reading less for at least 30 years, long before the Internet ever existed.

Extract 4
The book says teens are getting dumber. I totally disagree. If anything, people's IQs have gone up, not down, over the past 90 years or so.

Extract 5
That may be true, but don't you think there's something wrong here?

Extract 6
Young people are starting to avoid face to face contact because of the Internet.
Yeah, I couldn't agree more.

Unit 8

8.1

K = Kate   L = Lily

K So Lily, let's talk about selfies. Do you post them?
L Ha, oh no, no, no. Never.
K What? Never?
L No, you see I'm really camera-shy, I hate it when people take my photo. The problem is, I just never look good in photos.
K Oh, but you're beautiful!
L Ha thanks, no it's not that I don't like the way I look, I just have bad luck with selfies. I never get the right angle, or it comes out with red-eye. Or even worse, I get photobombed by a bird or something! Nope, nope, nope. Not for me.
K You know what I think your problem is?
L What's that?
K You never use filters or anything! I love all the apps you can get to retouch selfies. They're almost all free and they're really good. Nobody can tell they've been photoshopped!
L But that's cheating!
K It's not cheating, it's being creative!
L So I'm guessing you post selfies on social media then, Kate?
K At least twice a day, without fail. It's a bit of a process. First I take lots – and I mean LOTS – of selfies, then swipe through and choose the best one. Sometimes if I can't decide I send a few to my friend to choose the best.
L Wow, really?
K Yes, of course! Then I use a couple of different apps to doctor the image. You know, hide my spots, make my skin smoother, that kind of thing.
L OK ...
K Then finally I post it – the timing is very important. First thing in the morning is best, because people are waking up and look at their phones first thing, so you get more likes.
L Ha, you surprise me Kate! Definitely not for me, though.

8.3

J = Josh   A = Alicia

K Ah, that was a good day out today, wasn't it?
A Yes, I had a great time. I'm still confused about how that street performer was floating in air, though.
J Ha, well one thing's for sure, he can't have been actually floating!
A Yes, I know, but how did he do it?
J I don't know. He may have had wires connected to his back, holding him up?
A Yes, but connected to what? There was nothing above him. I think he might have had a special frame under his body, hidden by his clothes.
J You think so? It must have been a very strong frame if so.
A Yes, but perhaps it was connected to a heavy base, which he might have hidden under that rug on the ground.
J Ah, yes I see. I think you're right. It must have been that!

8.5

a She wanted to get a jewel implant in her eye, but they didn't do it.
   She wanted to get a jewel implant in her eye, but she couldn't get it done there.
b She thought of getting a diamond put in her tooth.
c She got a tattoo, but then she broke up with Jason.
d Now she wants to get the tattoo removed as soon as possible.

8.7

a You're not American, are you?
b It's hot today, isn't it?
c You like soccer, don't you?
d You had an English class yesterday, didn't you?
e The teacher won't give a test this week, will she?
f You'll finish your homework soon, won't you?
g You'd like a coffee now, wouldn't you?

8.8

a This is a comfortable chair.
b Good communication is very important.
c Exercise is essential if you want to lose weight.
d My new jeans weren't very expensive.
e Counseling can help you deal with insecurity.
f Dude, that girl is obviously in love with you.

8.9

a I agree! Speaking is more important than reading and writing. But they are both important, too.
b I'm much better at reading than listening and I want to improve. Thanks for the tips!
c I watched two episodes of a TV show online, but I couldn't understand either of them.
d I love listening! But I prefer American accents to British ones. They are easier to understand.
e @Kweli, do you think? I can't understand either of them. I prefer non-native accents like Japanese or German.

Unit 9

9.2

1 Lots of locals told me to be extra careful.
2 Got stopped for speeding. Police officer didn't accept bribe. Stupid.
3 Theft is when someone takes something without you knowing.
4 OK. I think I can help you. Theft is when someone takes something from you.

9.3

G = guide   T = tourist

G Welcome to Chicago City Crime Bus Tour. Today, I'm taking you around the city and giving you some of the history, the dark history of this place. And here we are, first stop. OK, you're looking at the site of one of the most famous Chicago legends.

60

Audioscript

T1 But ... but these are just new apartment buildings.
G Uh, yeah, that's right. But right here, on this spot, was the famous Lexington Hotel.
T1 A hotel? But I thought this was a crime tour?
G That's right, uh ... it is. OK, let me ask you. Do you know who lived at the Lexington Hotel? Al Capone. That's right! Mr. Crime himself.
T2 Oh, yeah! I've heard about him. And you're telling me he lived in a hotel? A major criminal ...
G Well, he had to live somewhere, right? But this wasn't just any hotel. He had secret rooms in there and escape tunnels. He was prepared.
T1 So why didn't the police just go and get him?
G Oh, they tried. I mean, they wanted him for murder, for illegal alcohol, for corruption. He paid all the politicians, you know. And ...
T2 So the politicians were protecting him?
G Well ... Not all of them. The president Herbert Hoover personally asked for Capone's arrest in 1929. The police finally arrested him in 1931. And do you know what for? It wasn't because he had killed somebody, or for bribery, or because he had robbed a bank or something. No, they arrested him because he hadn't paid tax for many years on his illegal money!

9.5

a Medellín was recently named the world's most innovative city.
b It was judged by eight different criteria.
c Public spaces were created and government programs reached these communities.
d This neighborhood was once considered a dangerous slum.

9.7

M = man   W = woman

M Did you hear about the teenager that was sent to jail for piracy? Peter Jackson, that's his name, I think.
W Oh, yeah? Like what, selling or just downloading stuff for personal use?
M Well, it says here that they found tens of thousands of mostly illegal movies and songs and games on his hard drive—more than 30 GB apparently.
W Whoa! That's a lot, isn't it?
M Oh, yeah. He'll appear in court next Tuesday, and he could get up to five years.
W What? For downloading stuff? That's not fair!
M Well, but it's more than that. Apparently, he had access to an advance copy of *ToyStory 4* ... He started charging people to download it before it was commercially available and shared the link on reddit.

9.8

W = woman   M = man

W But, honestly, do you? Do you think that's fair?
M What?
W A five-year sentence.
M Well, no, but I think he's got to spend some time in prison—at least a year, maybe. Otherwise, how else is he going to learn?
W Really? Come on. That is so unfair.
M What do you mean? I mean, I'm not saying he should be sentenced to life or anything, but ...
W But he's young and he has his whole life ahead of him. And do we really want to put a boy like Peter in the middle of other dangerous criminals? I mean ...
M So what exactly are you suggesting? That he should simply be acquitted? Just like that?
W No, of course not. Maybe he should, I don't know, pay a fine—I mean, a huge one—and then do some sort of community service or something. But definitely not go to jail.

9.9

a He joined the American Union army.
b He was registered as killed in action.
c He decided to move to Europe.
d Frank started by writing false pay checks.
e He created an employee ID.
f The FBI approached him.
g He was released just before his 80th birthday.

9.10

One, two, go!
Want to go?
Do you think he loved hot smoking?
Do you think he'll have stopped smoking?
We'll be working tomorrow.
It will be working tomorrow.
It will have been cooked by your mother.
We love beans cooked by your mother.
Wheels, spread across the park.
It will spread across the park.

9.11

P = Phil   S = Sam

P Thank goodness it's Friday. So, what are you doing this weekend, Sam?
S Nothing fun, I'm afraid, Phil. I think I'll be working all the way through.
P Big project, huh?
S Yeah, it's this report for my boss. He just gave it to me and he wants it by Monday lunchtime.
P No way. That's pretty tough, dude.
S Tell me about it. But if I just stay home, hopefully I'll have finished it in time to watch the game on Sunday night.
P Oh, you watching that?
S Of course, man! I wouldn't miss it. I tell you, if the Lakers win, my prayers will have been answered.
P Huh, I didn't know you were a Lakers fan. You learn something every day. Well, I'll be thinking of you when I'm up at the lake.
S Oh yeah? So what are you doing?
P Oh, I've got the kids this weekend. We're going camping. Yep, we'll be sitting around a fire, singing and cooking on the barbecue and you'll be working hard at home. Well, have fun, big guy.
S Yeah, thanks a lot. Have a good weekend, Phil. Take it easy.

9.12

So, have you heard the story about the lawyer and the cigars? Here's how it goes. A lawyer buys a box of very rare, expensive cigars. To protect them, he takes out an insurance policy so that if they are damaged he can receive some money. About a month later he contacts the insurance company to ask for his money because his cigars have disappeared in "a series of very small fires". The insurance company refuses to pay the lawyer and he takes them to court. The judge decides that because the insurance company hadn't specified what kind of fire was unacceptable, they would have to pay. The insurance company pays the lawyer, but then ... they have him arrested for arson, saying that he had deliberately burned his own property to claim the insurance money!

9.13

1
Y = Yolanda   B = Brad

Y Dude, where were you?
B Hi, Yolanda.
Y But seriously, Brad, you knew today was the class presentation and ...

61

Audioscript

B Listen, I'm sorry, alright. Just hear me out if ...
Y Go on then. But this better be good.
B Well, you see, I was working on the presentation last night, just doing the final parts, you know ...
Y Right.
B And, so, well ... I was really tired. It was about three in the morning. And ...
Y And? What happened?
B Oh, I'm such an idiot. I just finished everything and well, I was so tired, you see, and I clicked the wrong button. I mean, I didn't save it and ...
Y Brad!
B I know. I'm such an idiot.
Y Yeah you are and why didn't you call me?
B Well, it isn't what you're thinking. I was going to come, I really was. I just kind of ... I overslept.

2
M = Mom   T = Terry
M What the ... what's happened in here?
T Err, hi Mom, I ...
M Terry, what have you been doing? The kitchen is ... it's destroyed!
T Mom, it's not what it looks like. Honestly, it wasn't me.
M Well, if it wasn't you, who was it?
T That's what I'm trying to tell you. I was upstairs, right, and I heard this loud bang and then I heard the cat and I came downstairs.
M Oh, it was the cat, was it? I see. Well, the cat will have to help me clean it up, won't he?
T But, but Mom!

3
M = Mark   L = Leanie
M Hey, Leanie. You got a text message here.
L Thanks. Could you bring my phone?
M Sure. Err, Leanie. Is this Dave, your ex? 'Hi sweetie.' Leanie, what is this?
L What? Oh, right. Honey, don't worry. It's not what it seems. This is Dave my boss, not Dave my ex. And seriously, Mark, you don't need to worry about this Dave. He's like nearly 60 and has two kids and ...
M But 'sweetie'?
L Oh come on. You're overreacting. Anyway, he calls everyone that.

▶ 9.14
a Where will you be living in five years?
   Err, I don't know. I guess I'll still be living in this city somewhere.
b Have you ever been to court?
   No, of course I haven't!
c Does crime worry you?
   It doesn't really worry me too much. I live in a safe neighborhood and I've never been a target.
d Do you watch TV crime dramas?
   Not really, no. They're not my favorite sort of program.
e How could your city be improved?
   I guess it would be better if there was more public transportation at night.

Unit 10

▶ 10.1
M = man   W = woman
1 M1 Oh, I just can't stand days like this! Can you?
  M2 What? You mean the meeting?
  M1 Well, yeah, that was a pretty long one, but no. I mean this. All this rain, the gray skies, the cold ... Winter just really depresses me. I can't wait for spring.
  M2 Yeah, but it's good for the garden. And it cleans the city a little.
  M1 Yeah, right.
  M2 Oh, come on, it's not that bad. I mean, when it's like this you can't go out anyway, so it's better to be here at work. I mean, think about it. What else could you be doing?
  M1 Yeah, I guess you've got a point. But still, I wish it would stop raining.
2 W Hey, look! This is where I went to school.
  M Oh, what? That build ... Hey! Look out!
  W Oh! Idiot! Put your lights on! Idiot!
  M Whoa! That was close.
  W What an idiot! How am I supposed to see him at night if he doesn't put his lights on? Grrrr!
  M I know. I hate it when people do that. It's so dangerous. The other day I was driving to ...
3 M OK, that's five dollars and 78 cents. Is that everything?
  W1 Uh, yes ... Yes, thank you. Uh ... Here, six.
  M That's great. And 22 for you. Have a nice day!
  W1 Thank you ... Oh, that does annoy me!
  W2 Uh ... What does?
  W1 That! "22 for you! Have a nice day!" What is that about? Really, it's just so ... So fake! I mean, I only want to buy some vegetables and some milk, it's not like we're best friends or anything. I mean, I don't know him, he doesn't know me ... It's just, grrr!
  W2 OK. I think you need to calm down a little. He's just doing his job.
  W1 Ugh, really? It's just too much, it's so ... plastic! Yuck! It's like, imagine if I meet a complete stranger and say ...

▶ 10.3
J = John   B = Bob
1 J Hey Bob. How's your new house project going?
  B Oh! Hi John. Well, we've put the walls up, as you can see. And the windows are coming next week, but it will be a while before we're living in it. But you know, we're getting there little by little.

R = radio   W = woman
2 R ... and it looks like there's heavy traffic again on the major routes downtown, no surprises there. On the interstate roads there are ...
  W Heavy traffic, huh? Don't need to tell me! Oh, this traffic is driving me crazy! I'm sick and tired of it.

M = man   S = Stewie
3 M Hey. What's up Stewie? You look pretty down.
  S Oh, you know ... It's, well, it's Harriet.
  M Oh, I see. So ... Are you guys arguing again?
  S Yeah, kind of.
  M Look man, every relationship has ups and downs.

M = mother   J = Joel
4 M Joel! Joel... Have you cleaned your room yet? Joel! I'm not going to tell you again. Go clean your room before Grandma gets here.
  J Mom! I was playing. I almost beat him that time!
  M Joel, I don't want to hear it. Now, get into your room and don't come out until it's clean. I've told you again and again.

M = mother   S = son
5 M Ah. It's so good to finally have some peace and quiet.
  S Mom! Can I go home and play video games now?
  M Ah ...

▶ 10.5
1 You should apologize for saying that.
2 But who's responsible for solving those things?
3 I'm sick and tired of hearing that.

Audioscript

4 She does have a reason for complaining.
5 There are many ways of improving the city.

10.6

a How long have we been driving now?
Err, about five hours.
Man, no wonder I feel tired.
Well, look, there's a gas station up here. Why don't [beep]. Why don't we stop to have a break?

b Hon, have you seen my keys?
Yeah, they're where you left them.
Oh yeah? Where's that?
On the bedside table.
Oh yeah. Huh, I don't [beep]. I don't remember putting them there.

c Oh, these stupid hiccups. I've been hiccupping for hours.
Oh, I'm sorry, I shouldn't laugh.
Have you [beep]. Have you tried drinking some water? That always works for me.

d Err, Jim, I'm trying to work here.
Oh, sorry dude.
Jim, seriously.
Yeah, OK, sorry.
Jim, could you [beep]. Could you please stop doing that?

e Lucy, have you seen my new shoes?
Yes Mom. You know my shoes didn't match my dress, so ...
That's OK. So where are they?
Err in your closet. I don't remember.
Lucy, please [beep]. Please try to remember, I need them now.

10.7

1 What's wrong? Are you sick?
Ugh, I think I'm coming down with the flu.
2 I just don't know how to use this software.
Let me see. I'm sure we can figure it out together.
3 Wow, you look great!
Aw thanks! You always know how to lift me up.
4 Oh no, I failed my driving test!
Don't let it bring you down. You can always take it again.
5 Clara always tells me what to do.
You shouldn't let her boss you around like that.
6 I really wanted to stay in last night, but then John called and ...
No, really? Don't let him change your mind! Decide what you want and stick to it!
7 Why aren't you speaking to Lisa?
Oh, we fell out last weekend and had a fight.
8 Do you like your brother?
Oh yes, I get along well with him.

10.9

Sentence a. Ready? I told her it was difficult and asked her to help me.
Oh yes. 'Told her.' Not 'told to her.'
Next one. A lot of new hotels are being built in my city.
Are being built? Being built? OK.
It started raining soon after we left the house.
That's OK!
My dad complains about getting up early in the morning.
Oh! About getting.
I can't remember where my car is.
Oh! Where my car is.
Where did you get your eyes checked?
Hey, that one's correct!
Can you tell me who wrote this song?
That one's correct, too!
How long have you been living in this city?
Have you been living in this city?
He was awarded an Oscar for his role in the movie.
Correct!
She works as a secretary for a company that specializes in import / export.
She works 'as' a secretary, not 'like' a secretary.

10.10

a I find it easy to read in English but a little boring.
You should consider reading things you're interested in.
b I'm not so good at remembering new words.
Have you thought about keeping a notebook for new words?
c I have a lot of difficulty pronouncing 'sh' and 'ch'.
A good way of improving your pronunciation is recording yourself.
d Listening is very hard.
Try to focus on the stressed words.
e It's difficult to speak without pausing a lot.
How about learning some common phrases like 'I mean' or 'You know'?

Answer key

Unit 6

6.1

1 What Makes Today's Series More Addictive Than Ever Before?

2 a have / using b having c has d are e told
Correct sequence according to paragraphs of the text: c, e, d, b, a.

3 a to (T)
   b of (F)
   c than (T)
   d for (F)
   e on (F)

4 a sports events
   b medical drama
   c reality TV
   d TV streaming services
   e soap opera
   f talk show
   g music program
   h social media

5 1 h 2 e/a 3 c 4 b 5 f

6.2

1 a The / in / of (F)
   b The / of (T)
   c The / in (F)
   d of (T)
   e a / of (T)
   f of / the / on (F)

2 a The contestant **who is** leaving the island this week is Fifi. / *Survivor.*
   b The women who **live** in the house want to get married. / *The Bachelor.*
   c The island **that** we chose is very beautiful. / *Survivor.*
   d Sally baked a cake in the shape of Spider-Man, **which was** inspired by the superhero. / *The Great British Baking Show*

3 a Nicki Minaj and Mariah Carey are judges whose fights on camera were popular on Twitter.
   b Catherine is the girl who / that won the diamond engagement ring.
   c The location that the organizers choose is usually far away from civilization.
   d Simon Cowell is a reality TV producer whose shows include *American Idol* and *The X Factor*.
   e Kim's the woman who / that won after the other 14 contestants left the island.
   f He's chosen a song that is close to his heart.
   g The dances that the professionals teach them can be difficult.

4 1 that
   2 who
   5 that
   7 that

5 a 6 OK
   b 1 Every week. Botafogo, which is the best team in Brazil, play in the top league.
   c 3 Definitely. I hate all the actors who / that are fake.
   d 7 I don't think shows which / that have violence should be on in the daytime.
   e 4 OK
   f 5 OK
   g 2 OK

6.3

1 b 2 d 3 f 4 a 5 g 6 c e is extra

2 ... , **whose** universe includes ... /, **which** has made ... / **that** / **which** has reached every corner of the planet / ... , **who** created and directed most of the movies / .... , **whose** novels sold millions of copies to all age groups / ... , **which** were mainly written in a cafe, / **that** / **which** she created.

3 **Spider-Man:** Spider-Man, who was originally a Marvel superhero, has had six movies. (N)
The fourth one premiered in 2017 with a cast that included a new Spider-Man played by Tom Holland. (R)
Mary Jane Parker, who was the love interest between 2002 and 2007, was cut from the 2012 and 2014 movies. (N)
The Hunger Games: Author Suzanne Collins, whose novels inspired four movies, must be pretty pleased with the amazing success of *The Hunger Games* saga. (N)
These exciting movies, which have captivated young adults worldwide, tell the story of a compulsory death match. (R)
It's a televised match that the contestants must win in order to survive. (R)

4 a *The Dark Knight* / which is my favorite Batman movie / won four Oscars.
   b Heath Ledger / who played the scariest Joker ever seen / won an Academy Award after he died.
   c Christian Bale / who played Batman / wasn't nominated for an Oscar for his part.
   d This sentence doesn't have speech pauses, because it is a restrictive relative clause.
   e *Pirates of the Caribbean* / which was inspired by Disneyworld's attraction / has made over five billion dollars so far.

6.4

1 a prequel
   b clip, views
   c trilogies
   d cast
   e shoot, script

2 a It's called work.
   b No, in any circumstances.
   c It can destroy your private life completely.
   d It's entertainment.
   e Bars, clubs, and movie theaters.
   f At least five friends.
   g It means you're already infected and work already controls your life.

3 a Make sure you go home on time.
   b Think about having a vacation somewhere.
   c Always have enough water to drink.
   d Never try to do more than you can.
   e If you take regular breaks, you'll be more efficient.

4 1 Really? You're kidding, right?
   2 No way! Thank goodness!
   3 Are you serious?
   4 What? Get out of here!

6.5

1 a F b T c F d T e T

2 a

3 a baked
   b furnished / specific
   c pair / French lamps
   d picture of
   e short / eat
   f an Adele / you must

Unit 7

7.1

1 Be active in promoting it.

2 1 calm
   2 find
   3 take
   4 goes
   5 pick
   6 setting
   7 break
   8 cut

3 a distance learning
   b movie streaming app
   c video conferencing
   d screen time
   e online selling platform
   f identity theft

4 1 b 2 a 3 e 4 c

7.2

1 1 tell 2 say 3 tell 4 tell 5 tell 6 tell
   7 say 8 tell 9 say 10 say

2 a 3 b 5 c 1 d 4 e 2

3 1 we were nearly there
   2 my picture was brilliant
   3 there was no more ice cream left
   4 they were leaving without me
   5 we'd come back and buy it next time

4 a was
   b he would
   c we could
   d she looked
   e she didn't marry / she hadn't married
   f had, him

5 Mark told Anna he would marry her. / Mark said he would marry Anna. Anna said / told Mark (that) she had never been interested in marriage. Mark told Anna he knew she loved him. / Mark said he knew (that) Anna loved him.
Anna told Mark that she couldn't marry him. Anna told Mark she was in love with someone else.

66

Answer key

7.3

1 b

2 a, b, c, e, g

3 a Can you tell me ...
   b I wonder if ...
   c I have no idea if ...
   d I need to know if ...
   e Do you know if ...
   f Do you have any idea ...
   g Could you tell me ...

4 b you have installed iTunes on your computer.
   c I have no idea what you're talking about.
   d I need to know if you're familiar with the different icons.
   e Do you know if you have a Mac or a PC?
   f Do you have any idea when you bought it?
   g Could you tell me how I can upload music to my tablet?

5 b where I live.
   c if I have a fast car.
   d when I started learning English.
   e if I can dance well.
   f who I would take to a desert island.

6 /ʊ/ pull, push, put, cushion, notebook, full
   /ʌ/ plug, button, cut, under, comfortable, shut, bug

7.4

1 b What did you do
   c Do you like
   d will you finish
   e Are you
   f has your / improved

2 a Sue asked me **not to** call her tonight.
   b I asked her where **she was** going.
   c She asked me why **I wanted** to know.
   d I told her **not to** be rude to me.
   e She **told** me to leave her alone.

3 a Q b R c Q d Q e R f Q g Q h R

4 e, b, d, f, c, g, a

5 a F b T c T d T e F

7.5

1 a social networking
   b visiting museums
   c studying for class
   d leisure reading
   e playing video games
   f watching online movies

2 Personal answers.

3 e, a, c
   (suggested answers)
   b + ppl text than call
   d Libraries – customers now
   f games + common smartphone use < 15 yrs

4 1 A: We can't deny that robots will do all our jobs in the future.
   B: I totally disagree. There are some jobs only humans can do.
   2 A: That guy on the TV is speaking nonsense.
   B: Well, you may agree or disagree, but he makes some valid points.

   3 A: No, they don't think ...
   B: Hold on a second, let me finish.
   4 A: Translation technology nowadays is excellent.
   B: Yeah, I couldn't agree more.
   5 A: I think teens spend too much time on the Internet.
   B: That may be true, but don't you think there are some benefits to it?
   6 A: Well, it depends what you mean by "advantages".
   B: My point exactly!

5 a It depends on what you mean by... / of
   b Hold on a second, let me finish. / in
   c We can't deny that... / to
   d That may be true, but... / is
   e I couldn't agree more. / be
   f I totally disagree. / am

6 1 c 2 a 3 b 4 f 5 d 6 e

Unit 8

8.1

1 photo 1 Lily photo 2 Kate

2 a F b T c F d T e T f T

3 a shy b red c photobombed
   d retouch e photoshopped f doctor

4 c

5 a F b T c T d F e F
Personal answer.

8.2

1 1 d 2 c 3 a 4 e 5 b

2 a must have come
   b can't have been
   c must have won
   d might have overslept
   e can't have seen

3 Personal answer.

4 Personal answer.

5 a can't have been
   b may have had
   c might have had
   d must have been
   e might have hidden

8.3

1 3, 2, 1
too expensive = teeth; not available where she lives = eye; did it but regrets it = tattoo

2 a implant in her eye, but they didn't do it / she couldn't get it done there.
   b a diamond put in her tooth, but she couldn't afford it.
   c a tattoo, but then she broke up with Jason.
   d wants to get the tattoo removed as soon as possible.

3 a D b F c D d D e F f T g T

5 Personal answers.

6 Personal answers.

8.4

1 **Across**
   1 nightstand 3 bookcase 5 chair
   7 mirror 8 pillow 10 double bed
   Down
   2 dresser 4 comforter 5 closet 6 lamp
   9 rug

2 a More
   b many
   c are

3 1 bed 2 bed 3 ceiling 4 floor 5 desk
   6 lamps 7 desk 8 desk 9 bed 10 floor

4 a are you? ↘ b isn't it? ↘ c don't you? ↘
   d didn't you? ↗ e will he / she? ↗
   f won't you? ↗ g wouldn't you? ↘

8.5

1 a Open your ears
   b More than the language
   c Guessing is good
   d Don't be afraid!

2 a Songs, streamed TV shows, podcasts.
   b Living abroad is expensive.
   c ... learn about the culture behind the language.
   d ... learn to focus on the words you know and trust your guesses for the ones you don't
   e Any two of: Everybody will be pleased that you are trying / the better you'll feel / the more you'll want to learn / the quicker you will improve

3 a com•fortable
   b communi•cation
   c es•sential
   d ex•pensive
   e in•security
   f ob•viously

4 a both / ... more important **than** reading and writing.
   b better / ... and I want **to** improve.
   c either / ... but I couldn't **understand** either of them.
   d to / They are **easier** to understand.
   e either / ... ... I **prefer** non-native accents ...

Unit 9

9.1

1 a a bribe
   b to kidnap
   c to go to prison
   d to steal

2 1 5
   2 6
   3 4
   4 3

3 1 Lots of locals told me to be extra careful.
   2 Got stopped for speeding. Police officer didn't accept bribe. Stupid.
   3 Theft is when someone takes something without you knowing.

67

Answer Key

4 OK, I think I can help you. Theft is when someone takes something from you.

4

Crime	Criminal	Verb
bribery		to bribe (sb)
burglary	a burglar	to break into (a house)
drug dealing	a drug dealer	to deal drugs
kidnapping	a kidnapper	to kidnap (sb)
murder	a murderer	to murder / kill (sb)
robbery	a robber	to rob (person / place)
theft	a thief	to steal (sth)

5 b Bribery
  c have kidnapped
  d organized crime
  e robbery
  f stole

6 a He's Al Capone.
  b He lived in a hotel.
  c The president of the U.S. at the time.
  d He was arrested because he hadn't paid tax for many years on his illegal money.

7 a are looking
  b Do / know
  c 've heard
  d hadn't paid

9.2

1 a Medellín was recently named the world's most innovative city. / of
  b It was judged by eight different criteria. / were
  c Public spaces were created and government program reached these communities. / was
  d This neighborhood was once considered a dangerous slum. / by

2 1 ⊕ 2 ⊖ 3 ⊕ 4 ⊕ 5 ⊖ 6 ⊕

3 1 was 2 am 3 was 4 is 5 is 6 has been
  5 is not passive voice.

4 a 2 b 4 c 1

5 a An alternative system **was developed**. It's **considered** a success.
  b Curitiba's bus system **is often compared** to an underground railway, Curitiba's buses **are used** by its 2.3 million residents.
  c The BRT system **has been adopted** in / by 83 cities worldwide. **It will soon be implemented** by the Canadian government.

9.3

1 NY teen arrested for selling movie before official release date

2 a F b F c T d T

3 be acquitted (N)
  do community service (W)
  pay a fine (W)
  be sentenced to life (N)
  be sentenced to one year in prison (M)

4 1 c 2 a

5 a B b A c B d B e F f F

7 a under b on c on d for e of

9.4

1 2   1
   4   3
   5   6
   8   7
   10 9

2 Let it expire before you renew it., Try using your name and birthday—nobody will guess that!, Don't use the Internet at home.

3 a Hotspot / hotspot
  b Track / track (any verb form)
  c Up-to-date / up-to-date
  d Target / target
  e Password / password
  f Click / click

4 a You can make your computer more secure **by** using virus protection software.
  b The last guests had arrived **by** 10:00 p.m.
  c The malware was uploaded **by** some hackers.
  d I'll be home **by** midnight.
  e Tony improved a lot **by** working hard.

5 a F b F c T d T   Sam is man A.

6 a 'll be working
  b wants it by
  c I'll have
  d will have been

7 a won't have / won't be having fun
  b won't have finished the report by / won't finish the report on
  c will see / is seeing / is going to see / will be seeing his children

9.5

1 c

2 4   1
   5   3
       2

3 1a, 2d, 3b

4 a F b T c F d F e F f F

5 a 9.4 Where will you be living in five years' time?
  b 9.3 Have you ever been to court?
  c 9.1 Does crime worry you?
  d 9.5 Do you watch TV crime dramas?
  e 9.2 How could your city be improved?

Unit 10

10.1

1 a 3 b 4 c 5 d 1 e 2
  The Malcolm X quote sees anger as a positive emotion.

2 seldom, bring about, complaining

3 1 weather   2 bad drivers   3 insincerity

4 a T b F c T d F e F f F

6 1 b 2 c 3 a 4 e 5 d

10.2

1 1 Car modifications
  2 Chewing gum
  3 Eating on public transportation

2 a 3 b 2 c 1 d 1 e 3

3 a for making
  b Stopping
  c meeting
  d throwing
  e listening
  f of complaining

4 a A b D c D d A e D c D

5 a should apologize for saying that,
  b responsible for solving those things
  c sick and tired of hearing
  d have a reason for complaining
  e There are many ways of

10.3

1 a for b of c about d about e of f for
  g about

2 a stopped to ask for directions / stopped asking for directions
  b tried opening the door / tried to open the door
  c remember to visit my grandparents / remember visiting your grandparents
  d stopped to buy milk / stopping buying milk

3 is played, lives, is ordered, broke, lost, is visited, have destroyed, didn't believe

4 a Why don't we stop to have a break?
  b I don't remember putting them there.
  c Have you tried drinking some water?
  d Could you please stop doing that?
  e Please, try to remember.

10.4

1 a myself b myself c myself d yourself
  e themselves f yourself g themselves

2 1 c 2 g 3 a 4 f 5 b 6 h 7 d 8 e

3 1 c coming down with
  2 e figure it out
  3 g lift me up
  4 a bring you down
  5 f boss you around
  6 h stick to it
  7 b fell out
  8 d get along well with

10.5

1 a 3 b 5 c 1 d 2 e 6 f 4

2 a I told **her** it **was** difficult and asked her to help me.
  b A lot **of** new hotels are **being built** in my city.
  c OK
  d My dad complains **about getting** up early in the morning.
  e I can't remember where **my car is**.
  f OK
  g OK
  h How long **have you been living in** this city?
  i OK
  j She works **as** a secretary for a company **that** specializes in import / export.

68

Answer Key

3 1 find / to read
2 at remembering
3 difficulty
4 Listening
5 It's

4 1 d You should **consider reading** things you're interested in.
2 e Have you **thought** about **keeping** a notebook for new words?
3 a A good way of **improving** your pronunciation **is recording** yourself.
4 b Try **to focus** on the stressed words.
5 c How about **learning** some common phrases like "I mean" or "you know"?

5 Personal answers.

Phrase Bank

This Phrase Bank is organized by topics.
▶ The audio is on the 🆔 Richmond Learning Platform.

TV

Unit 6
I don't watch a lot of TV, but I sometimes watch …
That's not me at all. I'm really into …
People can watch TV outside the house now.
Yes, and my parents didn't use to have a remote control to change channels.
Well, these days you can subscribe to lots of different services, so we have a lot more options.
True, but there are too many options sometimes.
I sometimes watch English language programs with subtitles to practice my English.

Describing people

Unit 6
She's not really my thing.
She's an American TV host who interviews famous people.
I've seen Joaquin Phoenix in a few interviews. He's really rude, which is embarrassing for the talk-show host.

Giving opinions

Unit 6
I was totally addicted to *How I Met Your Mother* a few years ago.
I loved the first episode of *Mad Men*. It was so stylish!
I didn't use to like them to be honest. I thought they were weird.
"Despacito" is a very catchy song.
The music in that movie is great.
I've seen lots of "Harlem Shake" videos. My class made one and uploaded it.
Really? I didn't like them to be honest. I thought they were weird.

Unit 7
I think they're becoming less and less interested in foreign affairs.
I think the weakest arguments are the ones about Tom's son. I mean, who cares?
I think it's awful to say young people are ignorant. Of course we're not!
I know! We have access to so much information. How can we be ignorant?
I'd never read that book. I mean, life's too short.
Don't trust anyone under 30? Come on!
We can't deny that …
Hold on a second, let me finish.
Well, it depends on what you mean by reading.
That may be true, but don't you think …?
Well, you may agree or disagree, but he makes some valid points.
Yeah, I couldn't agree more.
My point exactly! I totally disagree.

Unit 9
I think all of them were pretty stupid, but the guy who showed his ID was the worst.

That's why I really think songs, books and music should be completely free.

Making deductions

Unit 7
I think the first one could be a piano.
Maybe. Or a cell phone. That would make sense.
It seems to me that our teenagers are a bit different.

Unit 8
Maybe there was a metal pole in his jacket.
I don't think so. Maybe he was attached to wires.
The driver might've put his wallet on the car roof when he was opening the door.
And then he must have forgotten about it and started driving. What do you think?
I imagine the first one probably belongs to a woman because …

Unit 9
First one … Well, let's see. Maybe he left his driver's license at the store and went back to get it?
I think the burglar is going to say he entered the wrong house.
Maybe they're … waiting to meet …

Expressing surprise

Unit 6
What? Get out of here!
Really? You're kidding, right?
No way! You mean your sister actually met Emma Stone?
My goodness!
Are you serious?
That can't be true. I don't believe you.

Unit 7
Oh, yeah? How come?

Talking about technology

Unit 7
No, I guess I'm just lucky when I buy things.
I heard something about a virus that made private social media information become public.
I guess it'll say we can check anything on our phones. And to be careful about fake news!
There are too many choices now. It was easier to focus before.
Effortless? No way! It takes ages to learn to use technology well!
Yes, and people had better memories. You don't have to remember anything anymore. Your phone knows everything.
Do you know any good apps that can help you pick up a language?
Yes, there are lots! Duolingo is a good one.
I love Evernote Scannable! You just zoom into the document or card or whatever, and the app converts it into a

Phrase Bank

scan. Then you can just scroll through all of your saved documents.
I'm not sure. It could be a vacuum cleaner.
Stephen Hawking used a cheek-controlled communication system.
And this meant he could speak through a computer.
I use it a lot. I can tell it who to call.
I only use it to choose songs to play.
My GPS is voice-activated, but it's kind of stupid.
Oh, yes, you can mount it on the wall yourself.
It works just as well as the famous brand, but it's half the price.
You'll be able to use it in any country, don't worry.
Some of the keys are different, but it's basically the same thing.

Unit 9
I try to create really difficult passwords.

Indirect questions

Unit 7
Excuse me, could you tell me where the station is?
Do you know where he went?
Could you tell me whether it could work in any car?
Do you know if people with disabilities would be able to use it?

Reporting

Unit 7
The salesman said some of the keys were different.
He said that it worked just as well as the famous brand.
The delivery guy told me I could mount it on the wall myself.
On the site it said I'd be able to use it in any country.
The store manager said it had just arrived.

Photography and photographs

Unit 8
I use Photoshop to remove unncessary objects from my photos – like trash cans!
I've never used it. I like my photos to show reality.
Well, I guess it depends how you use it. If you work in the advertising industry, then it has had a positive influence.
Look at this one. It looks like the giraffe is photobombing them!
The caption could be, "I'm much better looking than him!"
She disappears when someone tries to take a photo. She's incredibly camera-shy.
Retouching your vacation photos to make the weather look better is really easy!
This flash should reduce red-eye.
The court discovered that the prosecution had doctored the image.
The photographer managed to get a candid picture of the princess laughing.
The picture on the front cover had been photoshopped to make him look muscular.

Did you see that great photo from the Oscars a few years ago? Even celebrities are into this photobombing craze.

Speculating about the past

Unit 8
The tickets must have been very expensive.
He can't have known my date of birth.
I don't know how he did that trick. He must have had the ring in a secret pocket.
He can't have levitated.
He might have practiced enough.
It can't have been comfortable in that block of ice.

Unit 9
Hmm … I don't know. It might've been a mistake.

Actions / services other people do for you

Unit 8
We still need to have the cake made.
We're going to have a new suit made.
I got my nails done, too.
Did you have it dyed?
Really? I don't know how to. I'd have to get it fixed.
I can't stand my living room The paint is a horrible color. I'm going to have it repainted one of these days.

Expressing preferences

Unit 8
I prefer Ray-Ban. Their designs are cooler.
I love this class. It's really interesting.
Which one do you like better?
Both are OK, I guess.
I think I like the old one better than the new one.
I don't really like either of them.
I actually prefer the second one to the first.

Tag questions

Unit 8
You really like baseball, don't you?
You haven't done anything crazy, have you?
It's great, isn't it?
He'll love it, won't he?
You didn't do it all yourself, did you?
That rug wasn't there before, was it?
You know he's going to be over the moon, don't you?

Crime and punishment

Unit 9
To me, credit-card fraud is the least serious crime.
Well, it depends on the amount of money you steal, doesn't it?
Most students, four out of five actually, think credit-card fraud has increased.
The crime everybody I asked would eliminate forever is …
I think the bank robber should be sentenced to at least five years.
No, that's not fair. I mean, what if she dies in prison?

Phrase Bank

Talking about the future

Unit 9
By 2025, cyber attacks will have become the world's top threat.
He'll be telling us if we should take these warnings seriously.
Cybercriminals will be carrying out attacks wirelessly, and we won't be protected.
They will have developed the ability to spread viruses across multiple devices very, very easily.
Cybercriminals will have targeted 20 percent of all the world's smart phones …
I won't be working in ten years, I'll have retired.
It's possible we'll all be driving electric cars by 2030.
Really? I doubt that very much. I think lots of people will have stopped driving completely.

Giving excuses

Unit 9
This is not what it looks like!
Just hear me out!
It's not what you're thinking.
It's not what it seems.
Hold on! I can explain.

Moods

Unit 10
I'm not convinced it's all true. I don't think that "nothing can upset me"!
You mean you're never grumpy? What's your secret?
Life is short, and I'm just happy to be alive!
Carlos reminds me of my brother. A bit grumpy!
I definitely have my ups and downs, but I'm usually in a better mood in winter, when it's cooler.
Not me. I'm much more emotional than that.
No, I don't have pet peeves. I'm cool as a cucumber!
Yes! When someone talks during a film and then asks, "Who's he?" "What happened?" etc.
People who change the TV channel without asking.
Yeah, and taxi drivers who know keep talking about themselves!
I'm sick and tired of …

Learning English

Unit 10
Let's see … First one … I agree. I think I'm good at grammar.
I'm not. I'm good at listening, but I'm really bad at grammar.
I'm OK with grammar—especially verb tenses. But I find pronunciation hard, like the "th" sound.

Making recommendations

Unit 10
To practice listening, watch TV first without subtitles, then again with subtitles to check.
Try to focus on expressing your ideas fluently.
A good way of practicing is watching Internet videos.

You should consider giving pronunciation a little more attention.
Try to avoid reading slowly all the time.
How about learning "make an effort" instead of "effort"?
Have you thought about using a pronunciation book with audio to practice? Or finding some pronunciation videos on YouTube?

Other useful expressions

Unit 6
Well, I guess it's important to get permission to film in some places.
Yes, she offered to share her cab from the airport.
I think she asked Sia why she wears a wig like that.
Well, I'd like to ask her where she gets her inspiration from.
I love James Corden's Carpool Karaoke, where he sings with musicians. Have you see any of them? He actually did a great one with Sia!

Unit 7
OK, so he said "cat," but he meant "car." I guess "blood" could be …
They might say a color looks great on you when it really doesn't!

Unit 8
I'd probably fix a broken faucet myself.
I like to have a special meal out, blow out my candles, then go dancing.
I was an only child, so yeah, my mom spoiled me a lot.

Unit 9
Hey, what do you think you're doing?

Unit 10
Mario, welcome to the group. What brings you here?
Yeah, I think so. A friend of mine took a course like this once.

Word List

This is a reference list. ▶ The audio is on the 🆔 Richmond Learning Platform.

Unit 6

TV genres and expressions
cartoons
cooking programs
documentaries
dubbed
game shows
medical drama
music programs
news programs
reality TV
reviews
season
sitcoms
soap operas
sports events
stand-up comedy
subtitles
talk shows
to be addicted to
to subscribe to
trailer
wildlife programs

Movies and videos
best-selling
blockbuster
cast
clips
prequel
role
script
sequel
to be nominated
to be set in
to shoot
to star
trilogy

Other words
accent
composer
renowned
views

Unit 7

Phrasal verbs
break into
calm down
cut down on
find out
go on
pick up
set up
take out

Using touch screens
to double tap
to drag and drop
to scroll
to swipe
to zoom

Other words
break down
bugs
carrier
launch
warranty

Unit 8

Photoshop
camera-shy
candid photo
red-eye
to doctor images
to photobomb
to photoshop

Furniture
bedside table
bookcase
chair
closet
comforter
double bed
dresser
blanket
lamp
mirror
pillow
rug
wall
window

Opinion essays
Although / Even though / Though
Consequently
Despite / In spite of
For instance
In addition to that
It is usually said that
On the one hand
On the other hand
To sum up

Unit 9

Crime and punishment
acquit
be arrested
bribery
burglary
charge with
convict
credit card fraud
domestic abuse
drug dealing
fine
kidnapping
murder
(music) piracy
release
robbery
send to jail
sentence (to)
take to court
tax evasion
theft

Careers for the future
3D printing engineers
book-to-app converters
nano-medics
privacy manager
turbine specialist

Other words
captive
carry out
gang
shoot
spread
targeted
taxpayer
threat
warnings

Unit 10

Moods
cool as a cucumber
grumpy
moody
pet peeves
short-tempered
to be in a good mood
to bite your nails
to get fed up with
to swear
to yell at

Binomials
again and again
little by little
peace and quiet
sick and tired
sooner or later
ups and downs

Phrasal verbs
to boss sb around
to bring sb down
to come down with sth
to cut down on
to figure sth out
to lift sb up
to look for sth
to put off sth
to stick to sth

Other words
can't stand
critical
emotional support
payback plan
tough

Richmond

58 St Aldates
Oxford
OX1 1ST
United Kingdom

Third reprint: September 2020
ISBN: 978-84-668-3253-3
CP: 105632

© Richmond / Santillana Global S.L. 2019
All rights reserved. No part of this book may be reproduced, stored in a retrieval system or transmitted in any form by any means, electronic, mechanical, photocopying, recording or otherwise, without the prior permission in writing of the Publisher.

Publishing Director: Deborah Tricker
Publisher: Luke Baxter
Media Publisher: Luke Baxter
Content Developers: Paul Seligson, Deborah Goldblatt, Damian Williams
Managing Editor: Laura Miranda
Editors: Shona Rodger, Helen Wendholt
Proofreaders: Lily Khambata, Diyan Leake, Rachael Williamson, Daniel Deacon
Design Manager: Lorna Heaslip
Cover Design: Lorna Heaslip
Design & Layout: emc Design Ltd
Photo Researcher: Magdalena Mayo, Helen Reilly
Audio Production: John Marshall Media Inc.
ID Café Production: Mannic Media

We would like to thank all those who have given their kind permission to reproduce material for this book:

SB Illustrators: Bill Brown, Alexandre Matos, Beach-o-matic, Laurent Cardon, Guillaume Gennet, Phil Hackett, Alvaro Nuñez, Leonardo Teixeira, Rico

WB Illustrators: Alexandre Matos, Rico

SB Photos:
123RF/mopic, Getty Images Sales Spain; A. G. E. FOTOSTOCK/ Lubitz + Dorner; ALAMY/Everett Collection Inc, David Cattanach, Jim Newberry, Maciej Bledowski, Eddie Gerald, TP, Marmaduke St. John, PJF Military Collection, age fotostock, Marek Poplawski, Jemastock, Andrea Raffin, Jim O Donnell, Ian Allenden, WENN UK, runsilent, Jochen Tack, Elnur Amikishiyev, aberystwyth, B Christopher, ABC/ Everett Collection Inc, Jess Kraft/Panther Media GmbH, Mim Friday, Astronaut Images, dbimages, dpa picture alliance, Cyberstock, Steve Sant, Terry Harris, ZUMA Press, Inc, Domiciano Pablo Romero Franco, Moviestore collection Ltd, Fernando Quevedo de Oliveira, Mpi04/Media Punch/Alamy Live News, Irina Fischer, Collection Christophel, Ink Drop, M4Os Photos, WENN Ltd, Panther Media GmbH; CARTOONSTOCK/Way, Roy Delgado, Ian Baker, Zuvela.O, Bucella, Mike Baldwin; GETTY IMAGES SALES SPAIN/Hero Images, Andriano_cz, Littlebloke, Soren Hald, Thinkstock, Kadmy, NikFromNis, BenLin, wwing, Bulgac, Gipi23, Jodiecoston, Champc, BartCo, Kike Calvo, Joe_Potato, Brosa, ASIFE, Vladimir Vladimirov, shootdiem, ZIG8, Fuse, ViewApart, BSIP, StockFood, Andreas Schlegel, Steve Hix, Tzogia Kappatou, Stephan Hoerold, Sirawit99, Purestock, Altrendo Images, Martin-dm, Dulezidar, comptine, Paul Zimmerman, Neustockimages, S-cphoto, RapidEye, Sally Anscombe, Jhorrocks, Daniel Schoenen, Moodboard, Lily Roadstones, ShutterOK, Kyle Lee/EyeEm, Catherine Ledner, TIMOTHY A. CLARY, Stockbyte, Monika Proc/EyeEm, Wavebreak, Weedezign, Westend61, Witthaya Pradongsin, Aiqingwang, Andy Sacks, Dave Reede, Portland Press Herald, Juanmonino, Alessandro De Carli/EyeEm, Fotog, NNehring, Peter Cade, Petrunjela, Tom Hoenig, Ktsimage, CaseyHillPhoto, Shironosov, AndreyPopov, AntonioGuillem, Austinadams, Imagno, Karwai Tang, Kondor83, Leungchopan, Hanohiki, Elena Pueyo, Phaelnogueira, Filmwork, Nick Clements, Barcroft, Monty Rakusen, Lisa Stirling, marcduf, Wrangel, Johner Images, TVP Inc, RoNeDya, Jason LaVeris, JGI/ Tom Grill, Rmnunes, MixMike, Alex Lapuerta, Llgorko, Tim Robberts, Steve Cicero, Jpa1999, South_agency, Alex Robinson, Ariel Skelley, Doug McKinlay, SergeyNivens, Humonia, Jeffrey Mayer, Joel Carillet, PeopleImages, Jupiterimages, Keith Brofsky, Klaus Vedfelt, Mike Coppola, Beinder, Marcelo Horm, Paul Bradbury, Luis Alvarez, Stuart Pearce, Studio-Annika, Wundervisuals, Andresr, KateSmirnova, Cecilie_ Arcurs, GoodLifeStudio, Johnny Louis, Manuel ROMARIS, Martin Barraud, Mischa Keijser, da-kuk, Image Source, Paulprescott72, Philipp Nemenz, FreezingRain, Silverlining56, Zero Creatives, AleksandarNakic, Rayman, David Forman, Desiree Navarro, Igor Vershinsky, Alvis Upitis, Photos.com Plus, Priscilla Gragg, Simona Flamigni, Pumba1, Yuri_Arcurs, Yagi-Studio, PIKSEL, T3 Magazine, Alexander Spatari, Corbis Historical, Fancy/Veer/Corbis, Phil Walter, laszlo_szelenczey, Andrew Bret Wallis, Michael Heim/EyeEm, Hill Street Studios, Lee Whitehead/EyeEm, Pascal Le Segretain, Richard Theis/EyeEm, Mmac72, Nancy Honey, Andrey Vodilin/EyeEm, Ben Pipe Photography, GIUGLIO Gil/Hemis.Fr, Jose Luis Pelaez Inc, Monkeybusinessimages, Jean Baptiste Lacroix, Mint Images, Gareth Cattermole/TAS18, Narin Deniz Erkan/EyeEm, PhotoAlto/Odilon Dimier, Lowryn, Kittiyut Phomphibul/EyeEm, Mark Edward Atkinson/Tracey Lee, Manuel-F-O; ISTOCKPHOTO/Getty Images Sales Spain; SHUTTERSTOCK/ Lucasfilm/Bad Robot/Walt Disney Studios/Kobal, 20th Century Fox/ Paramount/Kobal, Red Umbrella and Donkey, Patrimonio designs Ltd, KA Photography/KEVM111, Ultimate Prods./Kobal, Lewis Tse Pui Lung, Gurgen Bakhshetyan, Moviestore Ltd, Netflix/Kobal, Moviestore collection Ltd, Intararit, Artazum, Ollyy; Tom Fishburne/Marketoonist. com; copyright Vixisystem; Penguin Random House; Arnos Design Ltd; www.govloop.com; copyright PLeIQ; www.italki.com; Faber & Faber; SPLASH NEWS; telfie.com; player.me; Starbucks; copyright Kengaru; geobeats; iTunes; IUCN; Gap; ARCHIVO SANTILLANA

WB Photos:
ALAMY/Zoonar GmbH, PictureLux / The Hollywood Archive, imageBROKER / Alamy Stock Photo, Jeffrey Blackler; GETTY IMAGES SALES SPAIN/Kati1313, Pidjoe, Bmcent1, Tim Hawley, Sam Edwards, LordRunar, Maskot, Ridofranz, Wavebreak, Westend61, RobHoglund, RugliG, Popperfoto, SensorSpot, Jacobs Stock Photography Ltd, Graiki, LittleBee80, 10'000 Hours, Giuilio Fornasar, Paul Quayle, Aldo Murillo, Ethan Miller, Luis Alvarez, Caspar Benson, Klaus Vedfelt, Siri Stafford, Wavebreakmedia, Yuricazac, William Perugini, Betsie Van der Meer, Jose Luiz Pelaez Inc, Monkey Business Images, High Street Studios LLC, Maria Taglienti-Molinari, Portra, Tetra Images - Jessica Peterson, JohnnyGreig; SHUTTERSTOCK/ Rovio/Columbia/Sony Animation/ Village Roadshow/Kobal/Shutterstock, ZQFotography, Preto Perola, Levent Konuk, A SDF_MEDIA, gorbelabda, iQuoncept, Poznyakov, Gravicapa, file404; ARCHIVO SANTILLANA

Podcast / Video: My Damn Channel; Geobeats

The Publisher has made every effort to trace the owner of copyright material; however, the Publisher will correct any involuntary omission at the earliest opportunity.

Printed in Brazil